PRINCIPLES OF THE LAW

The American Law Institute

AGGREGATE LITIGATION

As Adopted and Promulgated

BY

THE AMERICAN LAW INSTITUTE

AT WASHINGTON, D.C.

May 20, 2009

ST. PAUL, MN

AMERICAN LAW INSTITUTE PUBLISHERS

2010

Mat #40853269

ISBN: 978-0-314-92735-4

American Law Institute Publishers has no responsibility for the persistence or accuracy of URLs for external or third-party internet websites referred to in this publication, and does not guarantee that any content on such websites is, or will remain, accurate or appropriate.

The American Law Institute

OFFICERS[†]

Michael Traynor, *Chair of the Council and President Emeritus*
Roberta Cooper Ramo, *President*
Allen D. Black, *1st Vice President*
Douglas Laycock, *2nd Vice President*
Bennett Boskey, *Treasurer*
Susan Frelich Appleton, *Secretary*
Lance Liebman, *Director*
Elena A. Cappella, *Deputy Director*

COUNCIL[†]

[†] *As of March 4, 2010*
* *Director Emeritus*

COUNCIL

PRINCIPLES OF THE LAW OF AGGREGATE LITIGATION

REPORTER

SAMUEL ISSACHAROFF, New York University School of Law, New York, NY

ASSOCIATE REPORTERS

ROBERT H. KLONOFF, Lewis and Clark Law School, Portland, OR
RICHARD A. NAGAREDA, Vanderbilt University Law School, Nashville, TN
CHARLES SILVER, University of Texas School of Law, Austin, TX

ADVISERS

SARAH EVANS BARKER, U.S. District Court, Southern District of Indiana, Indianapolis, IN
JOHN H. BEISNER, Skadden, Arps, Slate, Meagher & Flom, Washington, DC
DAVID M. BERNICK, Kirkland & Ellis, Chicago, IL
SHEILA L. BIRNBAUM, Skadden, Arps, Slate, Meagher & Flom, New York, NY
DAVID JOHN BURMAN, Perkins Coie, Seattle, WA
ELIZABETH J. CABRASER, Lieff Cabraser Heimann & Bernstein, San Francisco, CA
SHEILA CARMODY, Snell & Wilmer, Phoenix, AZ
EDWARD H. COOPER, University of Michigan Law School, Ann Arbor, MI
MARINA CORODEMUS, Corodemus & Corodemus, Iselin, NJ
HOWARD M. ERICHSON, Fordham University School of Law, New York, NY
KENNETH R. FEINBERG, Feinberg Rozen, Washington, DC
GEOFFREY C. HAZARD, JR., University of California, Hastings College of the Law, San Francisco, CA; University of Pennsylvania Law School, Philadelphia, PA
DEBORAH R. HENSLER, Stanford Law School, Stanford, CA
SUSAN YVONNE ILLSTON, U.S. District Court, Northern District of California, San Francisco, CA
MARY KAY KANE, University of California, Hastings College of the Law, San Francisco, CA
CAROLYN B. KUHL, Superior Court of California, County of Los Angeles, Los Angeles, CA
DAVID F. LEVI, Duke University School of Law, Durham, NC
ARTHUR R. MILLER, New York University School of Law, New York, NY
GEOFFREY P. MILLER, New York University School of Law, New York, NY
DIANNE M. NAST, Roda & Nast, Lancaster, PA
JOHN PAYTON, President and Director–Counsel, NAACP Legal Defense and Educational Fund, Inc., New York, NY
SAM C. POINTER, JR., Lightfoot, Franklin & White, Birmingham, AL [Deceased 2008]
JUDITH RESNIK, Yale Law School, New Haven, CT
JOSEPH F. RICE, Motley Rice, Mt. Pleasant, SC
A. JAMES ROBERTSON, II, Superior Court of California, City and County of San Francisco, San Francisco, CA
LEE H. ROSENTHAL, U.S. District Court, Southern District of Texas, Houston, TX
WILLIAM B. RUBENSTEIN, Harvard Law School, Cambridge, MA

MEMBERS CONSULTATIVE GROUP

PRINCIPLES OF THE LAW OF AGGREGATE LITIGATION

(as of May 20, 2009)

VII

MEMBERS CONSULTATIVE GROUP

MEMBERS CONSULTATIVE GROUP

DIRECTOR'S FOREWORD

Aggregate Litigation, including class actions, is a significant part of the American legal system. Important social values require aggregate litigation for their achievement. Some legitimate interests cannot be protected and certain wrongdoers cannot be deterred through individual lawsuits. Yet aggregate litigation challenges procedural norms that have evolved over many centuries of common law adjudication of disputes between two individuals.

Half a dozen years ago, a small group of distinguished judges, academics, and lawyers, all experienced in class action litigation, happened to be present at an ALI meeting. After some discussion, they unanimously told me that the Institute could contribute significantly by promulgating Principles of the Law of Aggregate Litigation. They also told me that Professor Samuel Issacharoff of New York University was the best person in the country to lead the effort. I, no expert on this subject, accepted this advice, although I was worried that the project might engender unproductive dissonance between those who represent class action plaintiffs and those who speak for defendants.

Now, with the project completed, I know that I received excellent advice. Sam Issacharoff accepted this challenge. He recruited three outstanding helpers, Dean Robert Klonoff and Professors Richard Nagareda and Charles Silver. First-class groups of Advisers and ALI members reviewed multiple drafts and provided helpful comments, as well as criticism that was almost always constructive. As we proudly publish this work, it is already clear that American courts are citing the recommended Principles and that law-reformers in Europe and Asia are finding the Principles useful as their countries consider procedural changes that would increase the use of collective lawsuits.

This project has progressed more quickly than most of ALI's work, yet with no compromise of the Institute's traditional procedures for full debate and discussion. The efficiency of the work is largely the result of the intense commitment of the four Reporters. We are immensely grateful to them and to all who have advised them. We also thank LexisNexis Group for its generous financial support to this important project.

LANCE LIEBMAN
DIRECTOR
THE AMERICAN LAW INSTITUTE

February 16, 2010

REPORTERS' PREFACE

This has been a long and difficult undertaking for us. We came to this project familiar with the high-profile cases that dominate the field and with the academic debates that inform further analysis. Five years later, we conclude the project with a far greater appreciation for the difficulties of reconciling the demands of mass society with the rights and procedures generated by a long legal tradition in what were often far simpler times.

We are deeply grateful to the many, many people who have participated in this project both formally and informally, not only within the processes of The American Law Institute but also outside—in academic conferences, international gatherings, and other settings where the Principles put forward here were scrutinized, criticized, and tested. Through it all, it has been a tremendous learning experience for the Reporters and, we hope, for the participants in this undertaking.

First and foremost, we wish to thank the ALI, its Council, and its leadership for launching us on this venture and then having the resolution to see this project through to the end. Many of the issues covered herein are controversial, and much rides, both legally and economically, on getting them right. This project would have been inconceivable without the efforts of the ALI's Director Lance Liebman, who decided to undertake this work and recruited the team that put it together. We were also fortunate to have the support of the two ALI Presidents who oversaw our efforts and offered unflagging enthusiasm, Michael Traynor and Roberta Ramo.

Thanks as well to the many staff members at The American Law Institute for their efforts, not just in organizing all the meetings and productions, but in their cheery determination to make sure that this was as polished a product as the limitations of the Reporters would allow. The people we should single out for help in this endeavor are Judy Cole, Todd Feldman, Sandrine Forgeron, Nancy Shearer, and Marianne Walker. And we owe a special thanks to Elena Cappella, the Deputy Director of the Institute, who is stepping down just as our project draws to a close and whose support and substantive input have been invaluable through this process.

One of the difficulties in attempting to state the Principles of this area of law is the reality of the practice and the stakes in the underlying disputes. The bar is split between those on the plaintiff side and those on the defense side. The size of the cases and the difficulty of the law have created a relatively concentrated bar of extraordinarily skilled attorneys, a group of deeply involved judges, and some truly knowledgeable academics. From the beginning, the ALI sought to draw important representatives of all of these groups into this project as Advisers. Over the past five years, the participation and support of this group have been key to our being able even to get this project off the ground. In addition, we had the good fortune to benefit from the well-attended, well-informed, and lively meetings of the Members Consultative Group.

The ALI process is demanding for Reporters and participants alike. One cannot help but be taken by the institutional commitment to "getting it right" and to assisting in the development and refinement of important legal principles. In retrospect, the undertaking seems even more daunting than it did initially. But, for all of us, it was a rewarding experience and we are deeply appreciative of having had this opportunity.

SAMUEL ISSACHAROFF
ROBERT H. KLONOFF
RICHARD A. NAGAREDA
CHARLES SILVER

SUMMARY OF CONTENTS

TABLE OF CONTENTS

TABLE OF CONTENTS

CHAPTER 2

AGGREGATE ADJUDICATION

TOPIC 1

INTRODUCTORY PROVISIONS

TABLE OF CONTENTS

TABLE OF CONTENTS

TABLE OF CONTENTS

TABLE OF CONTENTS

TABLE OF CONTENTS

TOPIC 3

NON–CLASS AGGREGATE SETTLEMENTS

TABLE OF CONTENTS

PRINCIPLES OF THE LAW

———

THE AMERICAN LAW INSTITUTE

———

AGGREGATE LITIGATION

INTRODUCTION

All aggregate proceedings encompass the interests of multiple persons, but some are much larger than others. A typical automobile-accident case in which an injured driver and passenger sue as coplaintiffs is a multiparty lawsuit, but the number of persons is small and existing procedures handle this type of case well. Other aggregate proceedings are massive. Lawsuits alleging product defects, securities fraud, or other wrongs may include tens, hundreds, thousands, or even millions of claimants, and may involve many respondents as well. These large cases, which present significant management problems, entail significant costs, and pose serious risks of underrepresentation, are the focus of this project. Although many techniques have evolved to help handle these cases, experience with them has been mixed and serious challenges remain.

Notice procedures in damages class actions provide a convenient example. It must be clear to everyone that notice has little chance of converting class members with small interests into active participants in class actions. Sending these claimants notices wastes money and time. Even so, the practice continues, reflecting a well-intentioned belief that the apparent potential for individual participation lends greater legitimacy to the aggregate proceeding. Notice is a mainstay of due process in conventional lawsuits, where parties have sizeable stakes and can protect themselves only by acting. The practice of distributing notices to class members with small claims evinces the belief that they are entitled to due process too. But good intentions produce bad results when policymakers misunderstand litigants' incentives. When absent class members have small claims and may be best served by following the lead of named plaintiffs, notice-based efforts to convert them into active litigants are doomed.

Aggregate proceedings require procedures designed with their distinctive features in mind. Often, litigants can build these procedures themselves. For example, when bargaining is practicable and the benefits of cooperation can be limited to parties who sign on, plaintiffs and defendants can form voluntary litigation groups. In these settings, "bottom up" contracting can reduce the need for "top down" regulation. External rules may even harm litigants by limiting their freedom to meet their needs as they wish. However, in many contexts, including class actions, persons involved in litigation cannot bargain face-to-face and regulations must carry enormous weight.

This articulation of Principles seeks to identify good procedures for handling aggregate lawsuits. In particular, it seeks to identify

1

techniques that promote the efficiency and efficacy of aggregate lawsuits as tools for enforcing valid laws. Often, this means avoiding under-enforcement stemming from deficient incentives, but it may also mean avoiding over-enforcement brought on by aggregating remedies. The decision to allow aggregation may bear crucially on the future of a lawsuit. Without aggregation, justice under law may be unaffordable. With it, the stakes of litigation may change significantly. This project aims to help judges, legislators, and others make the aggregation decision correctly. It also aims to improve the management of cases in which aggregation is allowed. While this project does not aim to provide a comprehensive code governing all aspects of aggregate litigation, the aim is nonetheless to provide the framework for recommended law reform and to provide some language suitable for inclusion in statutes or rules. The audience for this project includes judges, legislators, other rule-makers (such as state bar associations and their advisory committees), researchers, and others with control of or interests in civil litigation. Because class actions and other aggregative devices are being developed outside the United States as well, the audience may also include foreign judges, lawmakers, and academics.

Chapter 1

DEFINITIONS AND GENERAL PRINCIPLES

---

§ 1.01 Parties, Represented Persons, Claimants, and Respondents

(a) A party is a person named as such in a legal proceeding.

(b) In appropriate circumstances, a party may represent a nonparty in litigation, so that a final judicial order binds the nonparty as well as the party. A represented person includes, but is not limited to, a nonparty who:

(1) authorized a party to provide representation in an action;

(2) is represented by an official or agency invested by law with authority to represent the person's interests; or

(3) belongs to a class of persons similarly situated, designated as such with the approval of the court and led by a party.

(c) When a claim exists outside of litigation, the person asserting it is a nonparty claimant and the person opposing it is a nonparty respondent.

(d) The labels "claimant" and "respondent" refer, respectively, to persons asserting and responding to claims, without regard to whether a lawsuit has been filed.

Comment:

a. Parties. The distinction between parties and nonparties is traditional and fundamental. Parties have many rights and responsibilities that set them apart from nonparties. Ordinarily, a person becomes a party by being named as a plaintiff or a defendant in a

3

complaint and becoming subject to a court's jurisdiction. One may also become a party in other ways, such as by intervening.

In this document, the word "party" refers to persons who have traditionally been afforded this status under longstanding procedural rules. Parties are also described as "plaintiffs" and "defendants," as appropriate. The black letter omits the jurisdictional requirement mentioned above because it is technically correct to describe as a party a defendant or other person who contests a court's jurisdiction after being joined to a complaint.

Illustrations:

    1. Husband, a victim of mesothelioma, sued Defendant, a manufacturer of products containing asbestos. Wife joined Husband's complaint as a coplaintiff, claiming loss of consortium and support. Husband, Wife, and Defendant are parties.

    2. Husband, a victim of mesothelioma, sued Defendant, a manufacturer of products containing asbestos. Wife did not join Husband's complaint. Husband and Defendant are parties, but Wife is not.

    b. Parties bound. Ordinarily, final judgments and other orders entered in lawsuits bind parties, and only them. This rule applies in aggregate lawsuits, with the result that all persons joined as plaintiffs or defendants are bound by final judgments, and all unjoined persons are not, absent an exception relating to represented persons.

Illustrations:

    3. Five former employees at a shipbuilding plant sued their employer, claiming asbestos-related injuries. All five claims are tried in a single trial against the common defendant. The final judgment binds all five plaintiffs. Other employees who did not sue are not bound even if their work histories and injuries are similar.

    4. Plaintiff sued 10 defendants in federal court, charging all with participating in an anticompetitive conspiracy, in violation of the antitrust laws. The final judgment binds Plaintiff and all 10 defendants, all of whom are parties. Other persons who may have participated in the conspiracy or been injured by it are not bound, assuming they are not otherwise brought into the suit.

c. Represented persons. The category of represented persons is also traditional. It includes nonparties who participate in relationships with parties of diverse types. These relationships include, but are not limited to, agreement to be represented by another, succession to an interest in property, control of the defense of a claim in which one has a financial stake, and other forms of privity. Generally speaking, a represented nonparty is bound only when adequately represented. See § 1.05.

Like conventional lawsuits, aggregate proceedings may also bind represented nonparties. These nonparties are referred to as "represented persons," as "absent class members," or by similar terms. Although unnamed or absent class members are not parties in the full general sense of the term, some authorities refer to them as "absent plaintiffs," "absent parties," or "passive parties." Usually, these labels are harmless, and absent class members' true status is understood. However, the labels can mislead, for example, by suggesting that absent class members have rights or responsibilities normally reserved for parties. These labels are therefore avoided.

The conditions under which a party may stand in judgment for another as a class representative are set out in Chapter 2. Many other representative proceedings also exist, including actions by an association that may bind its members, suits in which one property owner sues on behalf of others with future interests therein, actions by taxpayers brought to enforce a public obligation, and parens patriae suits.

Illustrations:

5. Plaintiff brought a class action against 10 defendants in federal court, charging all with participating in an anticompetitive conspiracy, in violation of the antitrust laws. The class encompassed all claimants who were similarly situated to Plaintiff during a defined period. Assuming the class is properly certified, the final judgment binds Plaintiff and all 10 defendants as named parties, and all nonparty claimants falling within the class definition as represented persons.

6. A, an employee of B, brings an action, on behalf of himself and all other employees of B, to recover sums deducted by B from employee wages and paid over to C and to enjoin B from making any such deductions in the future. The court permits the action to be maintained as a class suit. A is a party. Other employees of B are represented persons. Whether judgment is given for A, but only for an injunction restraining future deduc-

tions, or against A, it is binding on A and the other employees of B. The judgment would likewise be binding if B had brought the action against A as representative of B's employees, assuming the court permitted it to be so maintained.

7. A, the Attorney General, sues B, a charitable organization, to restrain it from engaging in activities alleged to be beyond its legal powers, it being recognized that a taxpayer may bring an action for the same purpose. A judgment against A precludes an action for the same purpose by C, a taxpayer, if C has statutory authority to bring such actions.

8. An agency of government sues B, an employer, to compel B to modify its employment practices insofar as they have racially discriminatory effects. A judgment in favor of the agency does not preclude C, an employee of B who has been adversely affected by B's employment practices, from obtaining other specific relief for himself, if the agency's power to pursue corrective remedies is not preemptive.

9. The members of the council of an Indian tribe bring an action to determine the boundary line between the lands of that tribe and another. The judgment is binding on A, a member of the tribe, with respect to ownership and occupancy rights he may have in the land as a member of the tribe.

10. Following the criminal conviction of X Corporation and two of its officers on charges of tax evasion, Shareholder A filed a derivative action against X Corporation and its management, alleging a breach of fiduciary duties. The trial court dismissed the suit as being time-barred. The ruling was not appealed. Other shareholders received no notice of the proceeding or the result. Subsequently, Shareholder B filed a derivative action containing the same allegation and naming substantially the same defendants. If Shareholder A represented all shareholders adequately, Shareholder B's lawsuit is precluded.

d. Nonparty claimants and nonparty respondents. Lawsuits are unusual. Persons normally raise and resolve claims without them. Aggregate proceedings may resolve claims that have not ripened into lawsuits and that are held by persons who are not represented persons. For example, a settlement proposal extended to persons with unfiled claims may accomplish this result. Alternative-dispute-resolution mechanisms, such as mediation, may also reach persons who have not filed lawsuits.

The term "nonparty claimant" identifies a person holding an unfiled claim. The term "nonparty respondent" applies to a person facing an unfiled claim. Nonparty claimants and respondents may be natural persons or entities.

    e. Claimants and respondents. Aggregate proceedings can involve parties (plaintiffs and defendants), represented persons, nonparty claimants, and nonparty respondents. For convenience, the words "claimants" and "respondents" are used in this document to refer to persons in any of these categories. More specific labels are employed when a person's status is important.

REPORTERS' NOTES

Comment a. The definition of "party" derives from the Restatement Second of Judgments § 34(1) ("A person who is named as a party to an action and subjected to the jurisdiction of the court is a party to the action."). See also Fed. R. Civ. P. Rule 10(a) ("The title of the complaint must name all the parties."); 5A Charles Alan Wright & Arthur R. Miller, *Federal Practice and Procedure* § 1321, 380 n.3 (3d ed. 2005) ("This portion of Rule 10(a) is derived from Equity Rule 25, which required that the full name of all the parties be given when known."). The definition of represented persons is drawn from the Restatement Second of Judgments § 41, which also identifies categories of persons, such as beneficiaries of trusts, not expressly included here.

Usually, legal proceedings bind only parties. Restatement Second, Judgments § 34(2)–(3) ("A party is bound by and entitled to the benefits of the rules of res judicata with respect to determinations made while he was a party.... A person who is not a party to an action is not bound by or entitled to the benefits of the rules of res judicata...."). 18A Charles Alan Wright, Arthur R. Miller & Edward H. Cooper, *Federal*

Practice and Procedure § 4449, 330 (3d ed. 2005) ("The basic premise of preclusion is that parties to a prior action are bound and nonparties are not bound."). This principle "is of constitutional dimension." Restatement Second, Judgments § 34, Reporter's Note to Comment *a* (citing authorities).

In many aggregate lawsuits, all persons bound are named parties. "Unlike absent class members, each plaintiff in a non-class action [i.e., a mass lawsuit,] has chosen to participate in the suit and is named individually in the pleadings. This is equally true whether the non-class litigation is an individual lawsuit or a massive aggregation through party joinder, consolidation, federal multi-district litigation transfer, or state-wide centralization." Howard M. Erichson, *Beyond the Class Action: Lawyer Loyalty and Client Autonomy in Non-Class Collective Representation*, 2003 U. Chi. Legal F. 519, 523.

Comment b. Legal proceedings bind persons who receive notice and an opportunity to be heard. "This principle is limited, however, by rules recognizing that a non-party may be bound, for example, where he is represented by a party or where his interests are derivative from those of a person who was a party." Restatement Second, Judgments § 34, Reporter's Note to Comment *a*. When deciding whether a person is bound by a prior legal proceeding, it is therefore important to determine whether the person was a party and, if not, whether the person fell within an exception to the rule against binding nonparties. The definition of represented person in this Section is intended to capture all participants in aggregate proceedings who are not named parties yet who, under the right circumstances, are bound by judgments and settlements in these cases.

Comment c. Absent class members are represented nonparties, not parties properly so-called. See Diane Wood Hutchinson, *Class Actions: Joinder or Representational Device?*, 1983 Sup. Ct. Rev. 459 (1984) (arguing that it is more appropriate to think of a class action as a suit in which one party represents others than as a suit to which many parties, all of whom stand on an equal footing, are joined). Generally speaking, parties' rights and duties in lawsuits are extensive, while nonparties' rights and duties are few. Applying party-like labels to absent class members can therefore cause confusion. In particular, it can cause one to miss the need to consider the merits of allowing or requiring class members to act like parties, when the class members at issue have not become parties by intervening. See, e.g., In re Paine-Webber Inc. Ltd. Partnerships Litig., 94 F.3d 49, 53 (2d Cir. 1996) (referring to class members whose motion to intervene was denied as "passive parties," stating that class members "are for some purposes parties," and

holding that denial of motion to intervene was not a final order because class members could appeal the district-court judge's refusal to order creation of a subclass after entry of a final judgment). See also Devlin v. Scardelletti, 536 U.S. 1 (2002) (holding that an unnamed class member, although not a party, was entitled to file an appeal).

A class action can bind a group of represented persons when a named party provides adequate representation. See, e.g., Hansberry v. Lee, 311 U.S. 32, 42–43 (1940) ("It is familiar doctrine of the federal courts that members of a class not present as parties to the litigation may be bound by the judgment where they are in fact adequately represented by parties who are present. . . ."); Report of the IBA Task Force on International Procedures and Protocols for Collective Redress, *Guidelines for Recognizing and Enforcing Foreign Judgments for Collective Redress* (October 16, 2008) § 1.02(ii) (requiring adequate representation as a condition for applying preclusive effect of class-action judgment or settlement against absent claimants). This requirement and tools for ensuring adequate representation are addressed in § 1.05, infra.

Illustrations 6–9 are adapted from the Restatement Second of Judgments § 41. On types of representational proceeding that are not class actions, see 18A Wright, Miller & Cooper, *Federal Practice and Procedure* §§ 4456–4461. On attorney-general standing in the charitable-trust context, see Joshua B. Nix, *The Things People Do When No One Is Looking: An Argument for the Expansion of Standing in the Charitable Sector*, 14 U. Miami Bus. L. Rev. 147, 176 (2005) ("In every state, state attorneys general are entrusted with the responsibility of safeguarding the public's interest in charity either by statute or by common law."). Illustration 10 is based on Nathan v. Rowan, 651 F.2d 1223 (6th Cir. 1981).

Actions in rem resemble aggregate proceedings. 18A Wright, Miller & Cooper, *Federal Practice and Procedure* § 4449 at 335 ("Judgments grounded on one of the several species of property jurisdiction may have effect without personal jurisdiction and at times may bind 'the whole world,' although the effects are limited by the nature of the jurisdiction. . . ."). See also Restatement Second, Judgments § 30, Comment *a* ("In certain actions based on jurisdiction over tangible or intangible property—such as actions to register the title to land in the name of the plaintiff, actions by the government to forfeit a thing used in violation of the revenue or other laws, proceedings to escheat a bank deposit, or admiralty proceedings to enforce a maritime lien on a vessel by sale—a court may enter a final judgment purporting to bind all persons in the world with respect to interests in the property (traditionally described as a judgment 'in rem').")). Actions in rem receive little attention here. Property rarely forms the basis of jurisdiction in mass actions, class actions, or similar lawsuits. Aggregate dispositions of property may also be achieved through bankruptcy, interpleader, and concursus, statutory forms of aggregate proceedings designed for special situations that are also not treated in depth here. Some lessons from bankruptcy proceedings are drawn in § 3.17.

Relationships having forms other than representation may provide a sufficient basis for binding a nonparty to a final judgment. For example, a policyholder who is a defendant in a lawsuit covered by a standard liability policy does not represent the insurer, which is not ordinarily a codefendant. The insurer may be bound by the determination of issues necessarily and actually litigated in the tort lawsuit, however, if it controls the defense of the case. See Restatement Second, Judgments § 39 ("A person who is not a party to an action but who controls or substantially participates in the control of the presentation on behalf of a party is bound by the determination of issues decided as though he were a party."). A person aligned with a plaintiff may also be bound as a result of controlling the prosecution of a lawsuit behind the scenes. Montana v. U.S., 440 U.S. 147 (1979). By enumerating certain bases for binding nonparties, this Section does not attempt to exclude other bases.

The U.S. Supreme Court recently addressed the limits on preclusion against nonparties in Taylor v. Sturgell, 128 S.Ct. 2161 (2008) (refusing to recognize a general theory of "virtual representation" and enumerating six exceptions to the usual rule that judgments bind only parties properly named and served, which exceptions include consent, preexisting legal relationship, identity of interests, and assumption of control); see also Complex Litigation: Statutory Recommendations and Analysis § 5.05, Comment *b*, 282 (discussing similar exceptions described in Martin v. Wilks, 490 U.S. 755 (1989)).

Comment d. Most claims are resolved not only without trial, but without any formal litigation even being initiated. See Alfred F. Conard et al., *Automobile Accident Costs and Payments: Studies in the Economics of Injury Reparation* 3 (1964) (studying automobile-accident victims in Michigan and finding "[t]he impressive fact ... that a substantial majority of 'serious' cases, and the great mass of all cases, were terminated without court intervention"); H. Laurence Ross, *Settled Out of Court: The Social Process of Insurance Claims Adjustment* 24 (2d ed. 1980) ("The [automobile-accident] claims ... are formally grounded in law.... However, in the majority of such claims, neither the claimant nor the defendant (realistically, the insurance company) has recourse to legal professionals. Most claims are processed and terminated between the adjuster and the unrepresented claimant."). A need thus exists to label persons asserting claims or facing claims outside of litigation. Technically, it is incorrect to describe persons who face unfiled claims as defendants, as Ross does in the quoted excerpt, but no widely accepted label exists. The labels "nonparty claimant" and "nonparty respondent" are meant to fill this gap.

§ 1.02 Types of Aggregate Proceedings

(a) **An aggregate lawsuit is a single lawsuit that encompasses claims or defenses held by multiple parties or represented persons.**

(b) **An administrative aggregation is a collection of related lawsuits, which may or may not be aggregate lawsuits, proceeding under common judicial supervision or control.**

(c) **A private aggregation is an informal collection of the claims or defenses of multiple parties, represented persons, claimants, or respondents proceeding under common nonjudicial supervision or control.**

Comment:

a. Aggregate proceedings: in general. All aggregate proceedings combine claims or defenses held by many persons for unified resolution, which may be trial or settlement. Private aggregations involving unfiled claims can have only settlement or other nonjudicial forms of resolution (such as mediation or arbitration) as ends, at least insofar as the unfiled claims are concerned. Examples of aggregate proceedings include mass-tort actions, class actions, derivative lawsuits, actions naming multiple conspirators, and inventory settlements. Bankruptcy proceedings also meet this definition and provide helpful examples and lessons, but this project does not set out principles designed to govern these proceedings, which are regulated by the Federal Rules of Bankruptcy Procedure.

b. Aggregate proceedings: types. Diverse types of aggregate proceedings exist, and new variations often arise. This Section divides these proceedings into categories along functional lines. The three categories defined in this Section—aggregate lawsuits, administrative aggregations, and private aggregations—have different structures and present different problems, as explained below. The form of proceeding is one factor affecting the extent to which aggregation separates ownership of claims from control of litigation. See § 1.05.

(1) Aggregate lawsuits. Aggregate lawsuits can be joinder actions or representative actions.

(A) Joinder actions. Aggregate lawsuits proceeding as joinder actions (1) involve multiple plaintiffs or defendants, and (2) bind only parties.

Illustration:

    1. Ten employees sued their common employer, claiming to have been denied promotions as a result of unlawful discrimination. Following discovery, the plaintiffs lost on summary judgment. Months later, a second group of five employees sued the same employer, asserting similar claims and citing similar facts. The first action having been a joinder action, the summary judgment binds only the 10 employees who were named plaintiffs. The second lawsuit is not precluded.

(B) Representative actions. Aggregate lawsuits proceeding as representative actions (1) involve at least one plaintiff and one defendant, and (2) have the potential to bind other represented persons. The class action is the best-known form of representative action, but other representative lawsuits exist and may be numerically more common. Examples include actions by agents, trustees, or other persons authorized to manage affairs on behalf of represented persons or affecting their interests; parens patriae actions by governmental entities or public officials; actions by associations on behalf of their members; and actions deemed to provide virtual representation for nonparties. For simplicity, aggregate lawsuits that combine the features of joinder actions and representative actions are referred to as representative actions, despite being hybrids.

Representative proceedings of all types bind represented persons only when certain conditions are met. The conditions may depend on the nature of the proceeding, such as whether a lawsuit is a class action led by a private party or a parens patriae lawsuit led by a public official. In general, the named party and the represented person must have a common interest. The named party must have an interest in prosecuting the claim or defense zealously, and must do so in fact. The representative proceeding must produce a final order or decree. Other requirements, such as actual authority or class certification, apply to specific kinds of representative proceedings.

Illustrations:

2.   A municipality sued cellular-telephone companies to prevent construction of towers that would spoil residents' views. The municipality and defendants subsequently entered into a consent judgment allowing towers to be built. Thereafter, certain citizens sought to enjoin construction of the towers, claiming adverse impact on their views. If the municipality genuinely sought to prevent the construction and prosecuted its lawsuit zealously, the citizens' lawsuit is precluded because the municipality acted parens patriae.

3.   The members of the council of an Indian tribe brought an action to determine the boundary line between the lands of that tribe and another. A final judgment was entered resolving the dispute. Subsequently, A, a member of the tribe, sues to establish ownership and occupancy rights in land that was the subject of the first suit. The final judgment in the first lawsuit binds A because the land dispute fell within the scope of matters the tribal government had statutory authority to handle.

4.   State sued mine operator, alleging violations of federal law in connection with disposal of toxic wastes. The parties later entered into a consent decree requiring extensive clean-up activities and a payment to the State intended to cover natural-resources damages, response costs, and monitoring costs. Local residents and businesses then sued operator on behalf of a class, alleging that actions taken pursuant to the consent decree damaged their properties and economic livelihoods. Because the federal claim at issue in the first suit did not allow recovery of damages or cover damage to private property, the first suit did not preclude the second even if, in the first suit, the State sued in parens patriae. However, the consent decree did cover damages to publicly held natural resources, and plaintiffs' claims were barred to the extent their damages derived from that source.

5.   Six plaintiffs filed a class action against a state-created entity alleging unlawful housing discrimination against the poor. The lawsuit was resolved by a consent decree that certified the class and provided $100 million in housing-related benefits. Subsequently, a second group of plaintiffs, some of whom appeared as named parties in the first action, filed another class suit against

the same entity, alleging unfair housing practices that harmed certain minority students, who in turn may or may not have fallen into the prior category of the poor. The first class action was a representative proceeding, and depending on the degree of overlap between the claims, the second suit may be precluded.

(2) Administrative aggregations. This category includes all procedures that enable judges to coordinate separate lawsuits for efficient processing. Usually, cases encompassed by an administrative aggregation have separate docket numbers, but practices may vary and this is not required. Examples are intradistrict consolidations, multidistrict consolidations, and bellwether trials. Administrative aggregations are authorized by procedural rules, statutes, and case law. The requirements and limitations of each form vary with the source of authorization. Generally, all such procedures require that cases be factually or legally related, because only then is coordinated processing likely to be efficient. Informal administrative aggregation occurs when judges handling related cases in different courts or jurisdictions achieve coordination by working together outside the ambit of specific rules or statutes, as with federal–state court coordination in mass-tort cases. As used here, "coordination" refers to the pretrial packaging of similar cases for purposes of efficient pretrial proceedings, which may include discovery precedent to dispositive motions, whereas "consolidation" refers to the combination of disparate claims into a single case that will proceed together through trial.

The importance and difficulty of proper judicial management of administrative aggregations increase with the number of parties or represented persons. Existing procedures usually handle small intradistrict coordinations and consolidations well. Large multidistrict coordinations or consolidations can present significant management difficulties and require special procedures.

Illustrations:

    6. A fire at a hotel owned by Entertainment Corp. killed or injured many guests and destroyed their property. Many of these persons (or their survivors) hired the same attorneys to file suit in the city where the hotel is located. The attorneys then filed multiple lawsuits against Entertainment Corp. in the same court, whose jurisdiction is uncontested. The court may consolidate the cases for all purposes and try common issues such as causation in a single trial. But the court must manage discovery and structure

the trial process in a manner calculated to allow each plaintiff to prove damages and Entertainment Corp. to challenge each such presentation.

7. Plaintiffs A and B both used a drug manufactured by Company D. Both claim the drug is defective, but each used the drug for a different period of time and each claims a different illness. D files a motion to consolidate the cases filed in the same court for pretrial purposes, arguing that both are subject to the same defense of preemption. Consolidation is unlikely to reduce the cost of discovery significantly, and the cost of deciding the preemption motion twice can be minimized by coordinating the cases' schedules informally. The trial court has discretion to deny D's motion.

8. Plaintiffs A and B filed identical but separate class actions in a federal court and a state court, respectively. The judges presiding over these cases may communicate with each other and order A and B's lawyers to select a lead case, which will proceed while the remaining case is stayed. If the lawyers are unable to agree, the judges may confer and decide which case to stay.

9. Same situation as in Illustration 8, except the judges want both cases to proceed. The judges may confer and enter orders in both cases establishing a document repository, coordinating discovery, and implementing other measures designed to save resources.

(3) Private aggregations. Private aggregations, also called informal aggregations, involve related claims (filed or unfiled) or defenses that proceed in a coordinated manner, though under the direction or control of private persons rather than judges. Usually, the claims or defenses share a factual connection and are managed by attorneys who work cooperatively on behalf of all claimants or respondents. For example, all claimants may assert injuries stemming from the same product, and their attorneys may jointly attempt to negotiate a settlement of all claims with the manufacturer. Defendants may match or counter plaintiffs' attorneys' efforts to create litigation campaigns by cooperating with each other and by creating networks or hierarchies of defense lawyers who provide coordinated responses to claims that are formally separate. A defendant facing a large number of related claims enjoys naturally occurring economies of scale in legal proceedings; the claimants (more realistically, their attorneys) must cooperate to achieve this advantage.

Neither the presence nor the active participation of multiple attorneys employed at different firms is crucial. Mass-solicitation efforts, referral networks, and specialization may concentrate large numbers of clients with related claims in the hands of a few attorneys or even a single firm. Multiple defendants or respondents may also reduce the number of lawyers who work actively on their behalf by entering into joint defense arrangements or creating settlement consortia. The central features of private aggregations are (1) the existence of multiple and related claims or defenses, and (2) common management of the claims or defenses by private persons, typically attorneys.

REPORTERS' NOTES

Comment a. The literature on aggregate proceedings is enormous. Much of it pays little heed to the formal mechanisms of aggregation, lumping together proceedings of different types and focusing on matters like economies of scale and opportunistic behavior that are common to all. By identifying structural features of aggregate proceedings that transcend procedural lines, academics, especially those schooled in law and economics, have added greatly to procedure scholarship. See, e.g., John C. Coffee, Jr., *The Regulation of Entrepreneurial Litigation: Balancing Fairness and Efficiency in the Large Class Action*, 54 U. Chi. L. Rev. 877, 877, 885 (1987) (arguing that procedure scholars have "been reluctant to engage explicitly in incentive-based reasoning," that the problem of market failure afflicts all "entrepreneurial litigation"—a transprocedural category—and drawing upon aggregate proceedings of many types for examples). For a broader history of aggregate proceedings and complex litigation generally, see Complex Litigation: Statutory Recommendations and Analysis, 9.

Fewer writings focus on the forms of aggregation and carefully distinguish among proceedings of different types. Most that do address class actions. Consolidations and joinder actions have received considerably less scholarly attention. Private or informal aggregations have received almost none. See Judith Resnik, *From "Cases" to "Litigation,"* 54 Law & Contemp. Probs. 5, 39 (1991) (pointing out that informal litigation conduct is "less visible to the academy" than the formal variety). An important exception is Howard M. Erichson, *Informal Aggregation: Procedural and Ethical Implications of Coordination Among Counsel in Related Lawsuits*, 50 Duke L.J. 381 (2000) (discussing informal aggregations extensively). Other examples include Charles Silver, *Comparing Class Actions and Consolidations*, 10 Rev. Litig. 495 (1991); Samuel Issacharoff & John Fabian Witt, *The Inevitability of Aggregate Settlement: An Institutional Account of American Tort Law*, 57 Vand. L. Rev. 1571 (2004); Edgar C. Gentle III, *Administration of the 2003 Tolbert PCB Settlement in Anniston, Alabama, U.S.A.: An Attempted Collaborative and Holistic Remedy*, 60 Ala. L. Rev. 1249 (2009); Charles Silver & Geoffrey P. Miller, *The Quasi–Class Ac-*

tion Method of Managing Multi–District Litigations: Problems and a Proposal, 63 Vand. L. Rev. 107 (2010).

Comment b. The descriptions offered in this Section are intentionally succinct, the objective being to identify the forms of aggregate proceedings, not to analyze the forms in detail. The descriptions ignore many hybrid forms of aggregation, such as consolidated class actions. Finally, the descriptions have no normative component. Although the forms reference means of creating aggregate proceedings (such as consolidation or referral) that are governed by rules or requirements, this Section endorses neither the methods nor the relevant rules or requirements.

Comment b(1)(A). The most common way to bring a person into a lawsuit as a plaintiff or a defendant is by joining that person as a party. See § 1.01, Reporters' Notes. Sometimes, all persons who are jointly affected by a tort or are otherwise interested in the same litigation are required to join a complaint as coplaintiffs, meaning that a lawsuit will not proceed if any are absent. See 59 Am. Jur. 2d Parties § 142 ("[J]oint tenants or tenants in common are usually required to join in tort actions against third persons, such as actions for trespasses upon the common land, for injury to or conversion of the common personalty, and the like."); Fed. R. Civ. P. 19 (setting out criteria for identifying persons to be joined, if feasible).

More often, the rules of procedure are permissive, allowing persons with related claims to join as coparties but not requiring them to. See, e.g., Fed. R. Civ. P. 20(a) and (b) ("Persons *may* join in one action as plaintiffs if . . . they assert any right to relief jointly, severally, or in the alternative with respect to or arising out of the same transaction, occurrence, or series of transactions or occurrences; and . . . any question of law or fact common to all plaintiffs will arise in the action.") (emphasis added). For a discussion of joinder through Rules 19 and 20 as a primitive method of bringing numerous parties into the same lawsuit, see Complex Litigation: Statutory Recommendations and Analysis, 24–26.

The main reason for allowing joinder of plaintiffs with related claims is convenience. Permissive joinder helps parties and courts "avoid[] the unnecessary loss of time and money . . . that the duplicate presentation of evidence relating to facts common to more than one demand for relief would entail." 7 Charles Alan Wright, Arthur R. Miller, & Mary Kay Kane, *Federal Practice and Procedure* § 1652, 397 (3d ed. 2005). Given this objective, it makes sense that a court "has discretion to deny [permissive] joinder [to multiple coplaintiffs] if it determines that the addition of the party under Rule 20 . . . will result in prejudice, expense or delay." Id.

The rules that permit joinder of coplaintiffs with related claims also allow a plaintiff to join as codefendants as many persons as against whom the plaintiff asserts related claims. Fed. R. Civ. P. 20(a)(2): "Persons . . . may be joined in one action as defendants if any right to relief is asserted against them jointly, severally, or in the alternative with respect to or arising out of the same transaction, occurrence, or series of transactions or occurrences; and any question of law or fact common to all defendants will arise in the action."

Usually, the number of persons eligible to be joined is small. This would be true, for example, when an automobile accident involves only two cars both of which were occupied by only one driver. The possibility for an enormous joinder action requires a mass incident of some sort. Industrial accidents, explosions, toxic releases, and widely marketed products can generate tens, hundreds, or thousands of related claims. By soliciting clients aggressively, attorneys have enlisted tens, hundreds, thousands, and even millions of clients in these situations. For examples, see John C. Coffee, Jr., *The Regulation of Entrepreneurial Litigation: Balancing Fairness and Efficiency in the Large Class Action*, 54 U. Chi. L. Rev. 877, 886 (1987) (discussing solicitation of clients in the wake of the chemical release in Bhopal, India, of clients who used the Dalkon Shield intrauterine device, and of clients exposed to asbestos in the workplace).

Even when claimants number in the hundreds or thousands, enormous joinders may not occur. A mountain of individual lawsuits may be filed instead. See, e.g., Spera v. Fleming, Hovenkamp & Grayson, P.C., 25 S.W.3d 863 (Tex. Ct. App. 2000) (law firm with over 30,000 signed clients who suffered property damage as a result of plumbing systems made from polybutylene pipes filed each client's case separately). States that once permitted massive joinders, such as Mississippi, have also recently restricted them. See John H. Beisner, Jessica Davidson Miller, and Matthew M. Shors, *One Small Step for a County Court ... One Giant Calamity for the National Legal System* (2003), http://www.manhattan-institute.org/html/cjr_7.htm (last visited Jan. 19, 2010) (discussing massive joinders in Mississippi); and Victor E. Schwartz, Sherman Joyce, and Cary Silverman, *West Virginia as a Judicial Hellhole: Why Businesses Fear Litigating in State Courts*, 111 W. Va. L. Rev. 757 (2009) (chronicling cases and rule reforms limiting size of joinders in Mississippi). Massive joinders are more likely to be permitted when a single incident or accident generates a large number of claims than when claims stem from related events, such as use of the same pharmaceutical or medical device, that occur diachronically.

Permissive-joinder actions involving large numbers of codefendants are less common than those of the coplaintiff variety, but they exist. In many of these cases, plaintiffs allege conspiracies. A lawsuit brought to clean up a toxic-waste site may name all persons or entities thought to have deposited pollutants illegally as defendants. Under the Comprehensive Environmental Response, Compensation, and Liability Act, 42 USC § 9610, a potentially responsible defendant may seek reimbursement of clean-up costs from all others thought to have used a waste site. See Manual for Complex Litigation (Fourth) § 34.11 (2004). In both scenarios, the number of sued parties may be large even if, before the lawsuit, they had no direct contact with each other. A patentee may also name a large number of defendants as patent infringers. See, e.g., Standard Oil Co. v. Montedison, S.p.A., 540 F.2d 611, 614 (3d Cir. 1976); see also Colleen V. Chien, *Of Trolls, Davids, Goliaths, and Kings: Narratives and Evidence in the Litigation of High-Tech Patents*, 87 N.C. L. Rev. 1571 (2009) (discussing statistics on high-tech patent litigation).

Because the basic joinder rules are generally permissive, joinder's potential to reach all potential plaintiffs and defendants is inherently limited.

First, potential coplaintiffs or code-fendants may be left out of a suit. Second, when they are, other parties may be unable to bring the missing persons in. Third, other doctrines and statutes, such as those governing a court's personal and subject-matter jurisdiction or its venue, also limit the potential of a permissive-joinder action to encompass all interested persons. In theory, intervention could provide an important supplement, but it, too, is voluntary and faces significant jurisdictional limits. See also Richards v. Jefferson County, Ala., 517 U.S. 793, 800 n.5 (1996) ("The general rule is that '[t]he law does not impose upon any person absolutely entitled to a hearing the burden of voluntary intervention in a suit to which he is a stranger.'") (quoting Chase Nat'l Bank v. Norwalk, 291 U.S. 431, 441 (1934)).

In keeping with the procedural nature of permissive-joinder rules, "rights that are separate and distinct under the governing law are not transformed into joint rights" merely because plaintiffs assert them in a single complaint. 7 Wright, Miller, & Kane, *Federal Practice and Procedure* § 1652 at 399. That said, the decision to sue has important procedural implications. For example, "[w]hen there is permissive joinder, . . . final judgments may be entered for or against fewer than all the parties only in accordance with Rule 54(b)." Id. at 400.

Comment b(1)(B). Illustration 2 is based on Lucas v. Planning Bd. of LaGrange, 7 F.Supp.2d 310, 328–329 (S.D.N.Y. 1998). Illustration 3 is taken from the Restatement Second of Judgments § 41, Illustration 2, and is based on United States v. Kabinto, 456 F.2d 1087 (9th Cir. 1972). Illustration 4 is based on Satsky v. Para-mount Commc'ns, Inc., 7 F.3d 1464 (10th Cir. 1993). Illustration 5 is based loosely on NAACP v. Metropolitan Council, 125 F.3d 1171, 1175 (8th Cir. 1997), vacated, 522 U.S. 1145, reinstated on remand, 144 F.3d 1168 (8th Cir.). See also N. Cal. River Watch v. Humboldt Petroleum, Inc., 162 Fed. Appx. 760 (9th Cir. 2006) (precluding suit by a public-interest group subsequent to a parens patriae action by the state of California, even though some members of the group resided outside the state).

Representative actions come in many forms, ranging from those in which a nonparty expressly authorizes a party to provide representation, to those in which representation occurs without the represented person's knowledge or consent and possibly against that person's wishes. Agency relationships between represented persons and parties provide a paradigm of consensual representation. Actions by public officials or agencies may be paradigm cases of nonconsensual representation when they have preclusive effects. The class action falls somewhere in between. Its precise location depends primarily on the amount of notice given, and the existence and number of opt-out opportunities.

In all representative lawsuits, a party, usually but not necessarily a plaintiff, binds a represented person by obtaining a final judicial order or a judgment, which may take the form of a settlement decree. The extent to which the represented person is bound depends on the context. A represented party may suffer claim preclusion and be able to take advantage of the final judgment, should it confer a benefit. A represented party may also be bound to a lesser degree, retaining the right to litigate but suffering or benefiting from issue preclusion. The nature and extent of the preclusive effect of representative litigation depends on the facts supporting preclusion. See 18A Wright, Miller & Cooper, *Federal Practice and Procedure* §§ 4456–4462.

The preclusive power of all representational lawsuits requires a harmony of interest between the party and the precluded nonparty. Their interests need not be identical and seldom are, but they must overlap strongly. The required degree of overlap also increases as the voluntariness of the representation declines or the represented person's ability to participate in or control the lawsuit wanes. When a represented person participates in a lawsuit or controls it (despite being a nonparty), the argument for binding that person is strong, for the person has then had something approaching a day in court. Only a serious interest conflict should prevent preclusion in this situation. Lesser conflicts suffice to prevent preclusion when a represented person neither authorized a representation nor had power to control it.

Cases in which nonparties authorize parties to act on their behalf typically involve small numbers of persons and pose few difficulties. The represented persons can structure their relationships with their agents as they wish, obtaining the caliber of representation that satisfies them. The agents' ability to bind the represented persons in litigation is founded on agency law.

Cases involving trustees or persons holding similar positions are a step removed from consensual representations, but a little more troubling. Because trustees' authority derives from settlors, not beneficiaries, trustees' power to bind beneficiaries is not directly consensual. However, when litigating, a trustee acts pursuant to the same authority that covers all activities involving trust assets and is governed by the same law. Restatement Second, Judgments § 41, Comment *a* ("[T]he representative may be constituted as such through some transaction antedating the litigation wherein the representative is given authority to manage and safeguard interests of a beneficiary, for example in the appointment of an executor or administrator for an estate or the creation of a trust.... In such circumstances, the authority and responsibility to represent the beneficiary in litigation is a concomitant of the representative's general managerial authority and responsibility for the matter entrusted to him."). Consequently, the ability of trustees to resolve beneficiaries' interests in litigation is well established. See Richards v. Jefferson County, Ala., 517 U.S. 793, 798 (1996) (observing that "a judgment that is binding on a guardian or trustee may also bind the ward or the beneficiaries of a trust"). See also Restatement Second, Judgments § 41(1)(a) and (c) (recognizing the preclusive effect of a lawsuit by "[t]he trustee of an estate or interest of which the person is a beneficiary" or "[t]he executor, administrator, guardian, conservator, or similar fiduciary manager of an interest of which the person is a beneficiary").

The relationships discussed in the preceding paragraph, all of which are constituted privately or imposed by law in pressing circumstances, all of which have limited scope, and all of which involve fiduciaries, have long been thought to justify preclusion on the basis of privity. Lawsuits brought by parties whose relationships with represented persons lack one or more of these characteristics justify preclusion less easily and may require greater protection against interest conflicts. Actions by public officials or agencies, actions by voluntary membership associations, and class actions fall into this category.

Governmental actors often have authority to speak for citizens on matters of public concern. See Late Corporation of the Church of Jesus Christ of Latter–Day Saints v. United States, 136 U.S. 1, 57 (1890) (describing authority as "inherent in the supreme power of every State ... often necessary to be exercised in the interests of humanity, and for the prevention of injury to those who cannot protect themselves"). This authority may justify preclusion of private actions brought by citizens in the aftermath of governmental suits. "Where the prior action is by the public official or agency, ... the preclusive effect of the judgment appears to depend on a characterization of the interest that the public official represents. Where the interest to be protected is one held by members of the public at large, an action by a public official in behalf of that interest may be held preemptive of private remedies and preclusive effects accordingly given to a judgment in an action involving the official." Restatement Second, Judgments § 41, Reporter's Note to Comment d.

The preceding quotations tie preclusion to the pursuit of a public interest. The existence of such an interest is clearest when a government or public official sues parens patriae. Early parens patriae cases involved protection of land or other natural resources in which the state did not have a direct property interest. Missouri v. Illinois, 180 U.S. 208 (1901) (holding that Missouri was permitted to sue Illinois and a Chicago sanitation district on behalf of Missouri citizens to enjoin the discharge of sewage into the Mississippi River); Kansas v. Colorado, 206 U.S. 46 (1907) (holding that Kansas was permitted to sue as parens patriae to enjoin the diversion of water from an interstate stream); Georgia v. Tennessee Copper Co., 206 U.S. 230 (1907) (holding that Georgia was entitled to sue to enjoin fumes from a copper plant across the state border from injuring land in five Georgia counties). In later suits, the U.S. Supreme Court recognized the general power of a state to sue to protect the welfare of its citizens. See Pennsylvania v. West Virginia, 262 U.S. 553, 592 (1923) (allowing Ohio and Pennsylvania to seek to enjoin West Virginia from cutting off the flow of gas to those states, because the threatened action "seriously jeopardized" the health, comfort, and welfare of their citizens); Georgia v. Pennsylvania R.R. Co., 324 U.S. 439, 450–451 (1945) (finding parens patriae standing to seek an injunction against discriminatory freight rates); Pennsylvania v. Kleppe, 533 F.2d 668, 675 (D.C. Cir. 1976) ("It [now] appears that injury to the state's economy or the health and welfare of its citizens, if sufficiently severe and generalized, can give rise to a quasi-sovereign interest in relief as will justify a representative action by the state.").

The general power to protect citizens' welfare may not entitle a state to sue as a class representative for all forms of relief and may thereby preclude the state from binding private litigants to the outcome of the state-initiated litigation. Thus, in the statutory antitrust setting, for example, the Supreme Court has ruled that the parens patriae power does not necessarily extend to seeking direct compensation for persons injured as a result of anticompetitive behavior absent an express statutory grant of authority to recover for such harms. See Hawaii v. Standard Oil Co. of Cal., 405 U.S. 251 (1972). In some contexts, Congress has granted this authority expressly. See Hart–Scott–Rodino Antitrust Improvements Act, 90 Stat. 2484, codified at 15 U.S.C. § 15c (1976) (granting state attorneys general the authority to bring parens patriae class actions for federal antitrust violations).

The right to sue parens patriae being established statutorily, it remained to be considered whether a judgment in a parens patriae action precludes a subsequent suit by a citizen brought to vindicate the same public interest. The U.S. Supreme Court answered affirmatively. See City of Tacoma v. Taxpayers of Tacoma, 357 U.S. 320, 340–341 (1958) ("The final judgment of the Court of Appeals was effective, not only against the State, but also against its citizens, including the taxpayers of Tacoma, for they, in their common public rights as citizens of the State, were represented by the State in those proceedings, and, like it, were bound by the judgment."); Wyoming v. Colorado, 286 U.S. 494, 509 (1932) ("[W]ater claimants in Colorado, and those in Wyoming, were represented by their respective states and are bound by the decree."). Lower-court cases to like effect include Alaska Legislative Council v. Babbitt, 15 F.Supp.2d 19, 23 (D.D.C. 1998), aff'd, 181 F.3d 1333 (D.C. Cir. 1999) (holding Alaska state legislators, suing both as legislators and in their individual capacities as Alaska residents, bound by the claim-preclusive effect

of a judgment from prior action by the State of Alaska concerning implementation of the federal wildlife-management statute); Lucas, 7 F.Supp.2d 310 (consent judgment entered in suit by municipality against cellular telephone companies precluded later suit by citizens to prevent companies from building towers); and Citizens for Open Access to Sand and Tide, Inc. v. Seadrift Ass'n, 71 Cal.Rptr.2d 77 (Cal. Ct. App. 1998) (settlement of litigation between state agencies and coastal property owners precluded a citizens' association from suing to establish a public-recreation easement, despite the prior court's refusal to allow the association to intervene).

In principle, parens patriae actions can preclude large numbers of individuals from suing. In this respect, they resemble class actions with the representative function being performed by the state rather than an individual similarly situated to the represented class members. When a parens patriae action seeks to collect damages on behalf of individuals, due-process questions may arise, such as whether citizens are entitled to notice and to exclude themselves and whether a process for distributing damages to individuals must be established. Further, where the damages pertain to individual claims, the parens patriae power of the state will often need to be established either by statute or by accepted common-law principles. These Principles do not attempt to resolve these issues.

Generally, a suit by a represented person is precluded only when that person's interest and a party's interest are aligned. This requirement also exists when the prior suit was brought by a government entity or official acting parens patriae. But the overlap of interests need not be perfect. In particular, a parens patriae suit can preclude a later suit by a citizen even when it ends in a settlement or a consent decree to which the citizen objects. See *Lucas*, 7 F.Supp.2d 310; *Citizens for Open Access*, 71 Cal.Rptr.2d 77. To avoid preclusion, a citizen must demonstrate an interest conflict, a lack of motive to prosecute a lawsuit zealously, or an actual failure to prosecute. Standing alone, a resolution the citizen dislikes will not suffice. Suits by individuals are especially likely to be precluded when they seek injunctive relief for which a governmental entity has already sued.

In keeping with the distinction between general interests and other interests on which the parens patriae doctrine rests, courts have limited the preclusive effects of suits by governmental entities in many ways. In particular, a governmental action on a general interest cannot preclude a private-damages action brought to obtain compensation for a loss. Brown v. Ticor Title Ins. Co., 982 F.2d 386 (9th Cir. 1992), cert. dismissed as improvidently granted, 511 U.S. 117 (1994) (preserving private antitrust claims).

Cases in which voluntary membership associations represent their members resemble parens patriae actions. Typically, an association sues to protect an interest its members share, such as a desire for higher wages or benefits. See, e.g., Int'l Union, United Auto., Aerospace and Agric. Implement Workers of Am. v. Brock, 477 U.S. 274 (1986) (holding that union has standing to litigate eligibility for benefits on behalf of its members). Arguably, these suits are more consensual than parens patriae actions. Membership organizations are limited in scope and have standing to sue only on matters that are germane to their purpose. Members also likely have more harmonious interests than citizens in general and greater control of their fates. For cases in which organizational activities precluded suits by individual members, see, e.g., Bolden v. Pennsylvania State Police, 578 F.2d 912 (3d Cir. 1978) (involvement of fraternal order of police in litigation and design of consent decree precluded subsequent challenge to decree by nonminority police officers); Expert Elec., Inc. v. Levine, 554 F.2d 1227 (2d Cir. 1977) (members of trade association precluded from seeking to enjoin deregistration of apprentice training program by virtue of association's involvement in prior proceedings); Ellentuck v. Klein, 570 F.2d 414 (2d Cir. 1978) (estopping plaintiffs from litigating due-process issue because all were represented by a property-owners' association in prior litigation).

As in other representational lawsuits, a finding of a conflict of interests between an association and its members or of inadequate representation prevents preclusion.

The class action, governed by Rule 23 of the Federal Rules of Civil Procedure and various statutes in the federal courts, and by similar rules and statutes in the courts of most states, is the best-known form of representative proceeding. Shareholder derivative actions, which can be class actions and often are, must additionally meet the requirements of Rule 23.1 of the Federal Rules of Civil Procedure.

Unlike consensual representations, suits by voluntary membership associations, and parens patriae actions, in a class action no relationship external to the litigation need exist between a named party and a represented person. The class action therefore comes closest to the paradigm of virtual representation, in which the preclusive effect of a lawsuit depends mainly on an overlap of interests. Reflecting this, and because of concerns about inadequate representations that are critical to all representative actions, the class action is heavily regulated. Absent class members are bound only when a number of requirements are met, and typically only after they have received at least one chance to preserve the right to sue individually by excluding themselves.

Typically, a plaintiff initiates a class action by filing a pleading in which a class is preliminarily described, followed by a motion for certification. The motion, which may be revised after discovery on class-related issues, refines the class definition and requests entry of an order allowing a class action to proceed. The class may contain claimants or respondents, but plaintiff classes are by far the most common. Defendants can also request class certification, but rarely do so. See Thomas E. Willging, Laural L. Hooper & Robert J. Niemic, *Empirical Study of Class Actions in Four Federal District Courts: Final Report to the Advisory Committee on Civil Rules* (1996) (reporting that defendant classes comprise less than one percent of all certified class actions, and that named defendants rarely request certification of class actions of any type).

Following discovery on relevant issues and a hearing, a judge decides whether a class may proceed. Recognizing that a class action is a dispreferred substitute for voluntary joinder, a judge must find (1) that many persons hold claims or defenses suffi-

ciently related to support their joinder (commonality) but (2) that joinder is impracticable (numerosity). If condition (1) is lacking, a suit is warranted for only the named party. If (2) is lacking, the proper course is to join the relevant persons.

In keeping with the narrowness of the exception to the doctrine that final orders and judgments bind only parties, a party seeking to certify a class must also show (3) that a common theory supports the named party's claim or defense and those of the represented persons (typicality), and (4) that the named party will represent the absent class members adequately (adequate representation). These requirements help limit preclusion to situations like those involving other lawsuits that have historically been held to bind represented persons. In such situations, the interests of parties and represented persons overlap strongly and the party's incentive to prosecute the claim or defense is most likely strong.

Requirements (1)–(4) apply to all class suits in the federal system and are more or less the template for state-court actions as well. Class actions under modern practice rules must also meet at least one member of a set of additional criteria designed to show a compelling need to bind nonparties. These criteria are (5) a risk that an opposing party will be subject to multiple, duplicative, or inconsistent obligations; (6) a risk that absent claimants' ability to protect their interests will be impaired; (7) a common course of conduct by the party opposing the class justifying a classwide grant of declaratory or injunctive relief; and (8) the predominance of common questions of law or fact and the superiority of the class action over other available procedures. Only a class that meets one or more of conditions (5)–(8) can properly be certified.

Approximately two-thirds of all certified class actions fall into the common-question category (Requirement (8)), which is used for all manner of economic-harm cases, including securities fraud. Willging, Hooper & Niemic, *Empirical Study of Class Actions*. These cases typically involve large numbers of claimants, many or most of whom incurred small losses, and litigation of the claims asserted requires mainly evidence about the defendants' conduct, which may be referred to as the "upstream" component of the case. Samuel Issacharoff, *Class Action Conflicts*, 30 U.C. Davis L. Rev. 805 (1997); see also Chapter 2. Class actions for injunctive relief (Requirement (7)) are the second most common. Class actions of other types are rare.

The decision to certify a class triggers additional procedures, which, under existing law, vary according to class type or substantive law. For example, in common-question cases, absent plaintiffs receive notice of the lawsuit and an opportunity to request exclusion. They may also appear in the lawsuit as absent claimants or become parties by intervening. In securities class actions, absent members may compete for the role of lead plaintiff. In class actions of all types, class counsel must be chosen and class counsel's fees must be addressed.

Following certification, class actions proceed toward trial in the same manner as other lawsuits. At the trial itself, the evidence offered must prove the named plaintiff's claim. Ideally, the same evidence will also support classwide findings on all class-related substantive issues, including

damages. In most cases, some evidence is likely to bear on solely the classwide claims, such as evidence of the losses incurred by persons other than the named plaintiff.

Judges often certify classes with the consent of the named parties for the purpose of settlement alone. The most comprehensive national study, now possibly dated, found that this occurred in about 39 percent of all lawsuits where classes were certified. Thomas E. Willging, Laural L. Hooper & Robert J. Niemic, *An Empirical Analysis of Rule 23 to Address the Rulemaking Challenges*, 71 N.Y.U. L. Rev. 74, 112 (1996). More recently, the Administrative Office of the Courts of the State of California completed a study of California class actions filed between 2000 and 2006. http://www.courtinfo.ca.gov/reference/documents/class-action-lit-study.pdf (last visited Jan. 19, 2010). When certification is for settlement only, the agreement between the parties typically contains a condition requiring decertification unless the settlement becomes final, the purpose of certification (from the defendants' perspective) being to obtain global peace (or a close approximation) at an agreed price. Settlement classes can be quite large. See, e.g., In re Prudential Ins. Co. Am. Sales Practice Litig., 148 F.3d 283 (3d Cir. 1998) (resolving the claims of eight million policyholders).

A class settlement must be reviewed and approved by a judge before it can bind anyone. The review process under current practices requires two steps: preliminary approval, at which the named parties present the settlement to the court and argue in its favor; and final approval, which in cases for monetary relief occurs after the court sends settlement notice to the class, allows absent class members to opt out, and considers class members' objections (if any). When evaluating the settlement, the court must determine that it is fair, reasonable, and adequate from the perspective of the absent claimants. The processes of settlement, including a rejection of the current practice of "preliminary approval," are discussed at length in Chapter 3.

As a doctrinal matter, the class action has fallen into disfavor as a means of resolving mass-tort claims arising from personal injuries. This development reflects many factors, including concerns about the quality of the representation received by members of settlement classes, difficulties presented by choice-of-law problems, and the need for individual evidence of exposure, injury, and damages. See, e.g., Amchem Prods., Inc. v. Windsor, 521 U.S. 591 (1997) (decertifying class settlement of asbestos claims); Ortiz v. Fibreboard Corp., 527 U.S. 815 (1999) (same). Empirically, neither *Amchem* nor *Ortiz* appears to have reduced the volume of personal-injury or property class actions significantly. See Robert J. Niemic and Thomas E. Willging, *Effects of* Amchem/Ortiz *on the Filing of Federal Class Actions: Report to the Advisory Committee on Civil Rules* (September 9, 2002). Settlement classes constitute the bulk of these filings. The class-action device also continues to be used in cases involving antitrust violations, civil-rights claims, and securities violations. Its appropriateness for use in cases involving other forms of fraud may depend on whether proof of individual reliance is required. See, e.g., Sandwich Chef of Texas, Inc. v. Reliance Nat'l Indem. Ins. Co., 202 F.R.D. 484 (S.D. Tex. 2001) (certify-

ing RICO fraud class action where predicate act alleged was mail fraud); Sandwich Chef of Texas, Inc. v. Reliance Nat'l Indem. Ins. Co., 319 F.3d 205 (5th Cir. 2003) (reversing and decertifying class on ground that individualized proof of reliance was required); Bridge v. Phoenix Bond & Indem. Co., 128 S.Ct. 2131 (2008) (holding proof of reliance is not required in RICO cases where mail fraud is alleged as the predicate act). Even when individual proof of reliance is not required, individualized proof of other elements may frustrate class certification. Int'l Union of Operating Eng'rs Local No. 68 Welfare Fund v. Merck & Co., Inc., 929 A.2d 1076, 1087 (2007) (finding questions of fact surrounding defendant's knowledge of the risk of Vioxx arthritis medication would not predominate because of the significance of "evidence about [a third-party healthcare benefit payor's] separately created formularies, different types of tier systems, and individualized requirements for approval or reimbursement imposed on various plans' members and, to some extent, their prescribing physicians").

A residual category of virtual representation may be said to exist and to include cases that resemble other representational suits but fit other categories imperfectly. One type of ill-fitting case involves prior and subsequent lawsuits with groups of parties or classes that overlap imperfectly. For example, some, but not all, plaintiffs in the second suit may have participated in the first suit. Some part of the class asserted in the second suit may have been represented in the first suit as well. Judges decide these awkward cases on their facts, seeking to avoid unnecessary proliferation of lawsuits while ensuring that each distinct interest has been heard. Many of these suits are public-law cases brought to obtain injunctions or relief from consent decrees. See, e.g., NAACP v. Metropolitan Council, 125 F.3d 1171 (8th Cir. 1997), vacated, 522 U.S. 1145 (1998), reinstated on remand, 144 F.3d 1168 (8th Cir.); Tyus v. Schoemehl, 93 F.3d 449 (8th Cir. 1996); Petit v. City of Chicago, No. 90C4984, 1999 WL 66539 (N.D. Ill. Feb. 8, 1999); DeBraska v. City of Milwaukee, 11 F.Supp.2d 1020 (E.D. Wis. 1998), rev'd, 189 F.3d 650 (7th Cir. 1999).

When not certified as a class action, the shareholder derivative action is another ill-fitting variant in which preclusion appears to depend on adequate representation alone. "[I]n shareholder derivative actions arising under Fed. R. Civ. P. 23.1, parties and their privies include the corporation and all nonparty shareholders.... [The] nonparty shareholders are bound by judgments if their interests were adequately represented." Nathan v. Rowan, 651 F.2d 1223, 1226 (6th Cir. 1981) (citing Dana v. Morgan, 232 F. 85, 89 (2d Cir. 1916); Stella v. Kaiser, 218 F.2d 64 (2d Cir. 1954); Ratner v. Paramount Pictures, Inc., 6 F.R.D. 618 (S.D.N.Y. 1942)).

Finally, it is important to note the significant development of class actions and other forms of aggregation abroad. These developments, like those in the United States, are necessarily conditioned by the distinct substantive laws and procedures of each country. Nonetheless, even while our efforts are informed by judicial experience in the United States, it is impossible in this day and age not to take notice of parallel developments in other countries. For examples of rules and statutes governing the conduct of class actions outside the United States and the enforcement of class-action judgments, see, e.g., Class Proceedings Act, 1992, S.O. 1992, ch. 6 (Ontario) (last amended 2006); Chief Justice Warren Winkler et al., *Guidelines for Recognizing and Enforcing Foreign Judgments for Collective Redress: A Report of the IBA Task Force on International Procedures and Protocols for Collective Redress* (undated); Antonio Gidi, *Class Actions in Brazil—A Model for Civil Law Countries*, 51 Am. J. Comp. L. 311 (2003); John O'Hare & Kevin Browne, *Civil Litigation* 101–102 (2005) (describing Britain's "Group Litigation Order"); Willem H. van Boom, *Collective Settlement of Mass Claims in The Netherlands*, in *Auf dem Weg zu einer europäischen Sammelklage?* 171 (Reiner Schulze ed., 2009); Kapitalanleger–Musterverfahrensgesetz [Act on the Initiation of Model Case Proceedings in Respect of Investors in the Capital Markets], Aug. 16, 2005, BGBl. I at 2437 (F.R.G.), translated at http://www.bmj.bund.de/files/-/1110/KapMuG_english.pdf; see also, Christopher Hodges, *The Reform of Class and Representative Actions in European Legal Systems: A New Framework for Collective Redress in Europe*, 16–22, 37, 70–76, 76–80 (2008) (discussing the British, Dutch, and German models respectively); Fabrizio Cafaggi & Hans–W. Micklitz, eds., *New Frontiers of Consumer Protection: The Interplay Between Private and Public Enforcement* (2009); Richard A. Nagareda, *Aggregate Litigation Across the Atlantic and the Future of American Exceptionalism*, 62 Vand. L. Rev. 1 (2009); Samuel Issacharoff & Geoffrey Miller, *Will Aggregate Litigation Come to Europe?*, 62 Vand. L. Rev. 179 (2009); Deborah R. Hensler, *The Globalization of Class Actions:*

An Overview, 622 Annals Am. Acad. Pol. & Soc. Sci. 7 (2009).

Comment b(2). Illustrations 6–9 are suggested in Manual for Complex Litigation (Fourth) § 11.631 (2004). Administrative aggregation occurs when judges, often at the request of parties or with their aid, bring together or otherwise coordinate the handling of related lawsuits. At the federal level, these procedures include intradistrict consolidation and coordination, multidistrict transfer and consolidation, removal, and informal cooperation. The Manual for Complex Litigation discusses many of these techniques, identifies exemplary cases, and offers helpful suggestions concerning their use. Many states have adopted rules or statutes implementing similar techniques. See, e.g., State ex rel. Mobil Corp. v. Gaughan, 563 S.E.2d 419 (W. Va. 2002) (coordinating approximately 8000 asbestos cases for trial pursuant to West Virginia statute); Tex. R. Jud. Admin. 13, reprinted in Tex. Gov't Code Ann., tit. 2, subtit. F app. (Vernon 2003). Efficiency provides the basic justification for these procedures, all of which may require some degree of interference with one or more parties' desire to proceed in a particular forum.

Consolidation occurs when judges bring related cases together for litigation. It may occur at the trial level or on appeal. The cases remain formally separate after consolidation. They are merely processed together in hope of reducing costs by avoiding duplication and delay. Manual for Complex Litigation (Fourth) § 11.631 (2004).

The courts and the Federal Judicial Center have made important contributions to the literature on consolidations. In addition to the Manual for Complex Litigation, see Advisory Committee on Civil Rules and Working Group on Mass Torts, *Report on Mass Tort Litigation* 10 (Feb. 15, 1999), reprinted without appendices in 187 F.R.D. 293 (1999). Scholarly writings include: Deborah R. Hensler, *The Role of Multi–Districting in Mass Tort Litigation: An Empirical Investigation*, 31 Seton Hall L. Rev. 883 (2001); Joan Steinman, *The Effects of Case Consolidation on the Procedural Rights of Litigants: What They Are, What They Might Be Part 1: Justiciability and Jurisdiction (Original and Appellate)*, 42 UCLA L. Rev. 717 (1995); Joan Steinman, *The Effects of Case Consolidation on the Procedural Rights of Litigants: What They Are, What They Might Be Part 2: Non–Jurisdictional Matters*, 42 UCLA L. Rev. 967 (1995); Edward F. Sherman, *Segmenting Aggregate Litigation: Initiatives and Impediments for Reshaping the Trial Process*, 25 Rev. Litig. 692 (2006).

Technically, judges can consolidate cases pending in the same court that have any facts or legal issues in common.

Consolidation may be for trial of the entire case or only for separable common issues. Moreover, it may be appropriate even if some issues or cases are to be tried before a jury and others before the court; the same evidence must be presented only once even though the judge may consider it in some of the cases and the jury may consider it in others.

Manual for Complex Litigation (Fourth) § 11.631, at 121 (2004). As a practical matter, consolidation occurs mainly when separate lawsuits have strong overlaps, typically because all plaintiffs claim to have been injured by the same product, the same accident, or the same course of conduct. See L. S. Tellier, *Propriety of Consolidation for Trial of Actions for Personal Injuries, Death, or Property Damages Arising out of Same Accident*, 68 A.L.R.2d 1372 (1959) (reporting that "two rules stand out in determining the propriety or impropriety of consolidation for trial of actions for personal injuries, death, or property damage arising out of the same accident: (1) that in the absence of a statute affecting the situation the question rests in the sound discretion of the trial judge, and (2) that, in the interest of efficiency and convenience, there should be a consolidation of the cases for trial unless undue prejudice would thereby result to one or more of the parties"). Multidistrict consolidation, governed by 28 U.S.C. § 1407, is proper only when the Judicial Panel on Multidistrict Litigation finds that lawsuits pending in different federal district courts share common facts and that consolidating the actions in the same district will advance "the convenience of parties and witnesses and [] promote the just and efficient conduct of [the] actions." Common questions of law alone provide no basis for multidistrict consolidation.

When claims overlap strongly, the advantage of coordinating discovery and other procedures seems clear. "Whether consolidation is permissible or desirable depends largely on the amount of common evidence among the cases." Manual for Complex Litigation (Fourth) § 11.631, at 121 (2004). "Cases should not be consolidated if it would result in increased delay and other unnecessary burdens on parties, such as having to participate in discovery irrelevant to their cases." Id. § 20.11, at 218. Because

these issues depend on facts, it may be desirable to delay the consolidation decision until separate cases develop somewhat, allowing the possible benefits of coordinated processing to be gauged. Id. § 22.32.

Legal differences can also limit the gains to be had from consolidation. Legal differences may arise when the laws of multiple states govern the claims or defenses in the case. In such situations, which are especially likely when cases governed by state law are transferred across judicial districts, the court may receive briefing on the choice-of-law question before deciding a motion to consolidate. It should be noted, however, that multidistrict consolidation does not work a change in the underlying state substantive law that would have governed on the merits if a given case had remained in the federal district court in which it was originally filed. See Ferens v. John Deere Co., 494 U.S. 516 (1990) (plaintiff-initiated transfer under 28 U.S.C. § 1404 works no change in governing state law); cf. In re Korean Air Lines Disaster of September 1, 1983, 829 F.2d 1171 (D.C. Cir. 1987) (R.B. Ginsburg, J.) (holding transferee court should apply its own view of federal law, not the view of the transferor court); see also Linda Silberman, *The Role of Choice of Law in National Class Actions*, 156 U. Pa. L. Rev. 2001 (2008). The court may also facilitate litigation of different cases by grouping those that appear to be governed by the same law. Such groupings may facilitate the presentation of dispositive motions based on common legal issues. See In re School Asbestos Litig., 789 F.2d 996, 1010 (3d Cir. 1986) (acknowledging differences in four jurisdictions' law on products liability, but maintaining that class certification would not present "insuperable obstacles"). Coordinated discovery can proceed across the groups in this situation, when the factual issues continue to overlap, but each group of cases may have to be tried separately. Initial aggregation of such cases is now possible under the Class Action Fairness Act, which provides for federal subject-matter jurisdiction over class actions with specified interstate impact, and through multidistrict litigation practice under 28 U.S.C. § 1407, which permits interjurisdictional transfer of pretrial proceedings.

The nature of the underlying activity at issue in the cases may affect the desirability of consolidation, its timing, or its extent. When an accident affecting a sizeable population generates considerable litigation, "early aggregation and pretrial consolidation of all or most of the individual cases generally has proved to be feasible and efficient." Manual for Complex Litigation (Fourth) § 22.32, at 364 (2004). When mass litigation stems from incidents that are separate but related, such as independent exposures to toxic products, it may be desirable to coordinate discovery and to decide some pretrial motions, but not to hold a combined trial. Id.

Because common issues provide the basis for consolidation, a consolidated proceeding resembles a class action certified on the basis of predominating common questions. See § 1.02, Reporters' Notes. In both contexts, the object is efficiency. Yet, consolidations differ from class actions in important respects. First, consolidation reaches cases that already exist. It does not bring into court anyone who was not already there. Consolidation is not a tech-

nique for creating representational lawsuits that bind nonparties.

Second, a consolidation order does not entitle one party to represent another party. After consolidation, plaintiffs and defendants stand in judgment only for themselves. Because no party represents anyone but itself, every party must develop its own case and must technically be free to do so. For example, a class action may be consolidated with cases brought by persons who opted out of the class. "When this occurs, the judge must ensure that counsel for parties in the non-class actions have a fair opportunity to participate in the presentation of evidence and arguments at trial, particularly when their clients are primarily affected." Manual for Complex Litigation (Fourth) § 11.631, at 121 (2004).

Third, although a class action is a single lawsuit, consolidated cases start out separate and remain so. In other words, consolidation does not merge separate cases into one. See Johnson v. Manhattan Ry. Co., 289 U.S. 479, 496–497 (1933). This difference has many implications. See Steinman, *Effects of Case Consolidation, Part 1*, 42 UCLA L. Rev. 717; Steinman, *Effects of Case Consolidation, Part 2*, 42 UCLA L. Rev. 967. One small implication is that pleadings and other papers must be filed in each case separately until an order eliminates the need for this. A larger implication is that consolidated lawsuits can settle piecemeal while class actions cannot. Class settlements always resolve blocks of claims. The tendency to conflate consolidated lawsuits with single proceedings is widespread and leads to muddled thinking. Giguere v. Yellow Cab Co., 195 A. 214, 216 (R.I. 1937) ("The consolidation of cases for trial ... merely permits them to be tried together.... The causes of action remain distinct throughout such a trial, and every legal right is preserved to the respective parties as fully as if the cases had been tried separately. The distinction between such a consolidation of cases for trial only, and a complete and actual consolidation or merger of separate causes of action into only one cause ... is not always clearly kept in mind or adhered to in some of the decided cases, thereby causing apparent confusion in the law relating to this question.").

Because parties retain formal control of their individual lawsuits, consolidations lack the procedural guarantees found in class actions, where named parties litigate on behalf of others and effectively control their fates. In the representational context, the fundamental problem is that of ensuring that lead parties keep the interests of absent claimants and respondents firmly in mind and ably protect those interests. In theory, no such problem exists in consolidations because each party is individually represented by counsel and can protect itself. The need to worry about adequate representation is reduced when a person whose lawsuit is part of a consolidated proceeding can supplement a lead party's efforts to develop and present common issues and can also address any unique issues raised by the party's case. For the same reason, there is no need to permit parties whose cases are consolidated to opt out. Even those who resist consolidation can represent themselves effectively when caught up in the aggregate.

In truth, the difference between consolidations and class actions is less stark. In both proceedings, similar problems arise. For example, a class action normally operates on the basis of a single complaint, with discovery being undertaken once for all class members. In consolidations, judges often also require master complaints and unified discovery. In both kinds of proceedings, attorneys also work in teams and important tasks are divided. In both proceedings, therefore, these lawyer-teams must be created and managed. Judges usually oversee or get involved in all these matters. The possibility of collusion between plaintiffs' attorneys and defendants also arises, suggesting that judicial review of settlements in consolidations may also be warranted. See Elizabeth Chamblee Burch, *Unsettling Efficiency: When Non–Class Aggregation of Mass Torts Creates Second–Class Settlements*, 65 La. L. Rev. 157 (2004) (noting that collusion can occur in all aggregations, but that only class actions and bankruptcy proceedings provide formalized fairness protections). It seems fair to say that consolidations raise neglected due-process concerns. See also § 3.16 et seq. (discussing aggregate settlements).

In federal courts, consolidation can occur within judicial divisions, across divisions but within judicial districts, and across districts. Rule 42 of the Federal Rules of Civil Procedure and the courts' local rules govern consolidation within districts. Transfer for the purpose of accomplishing consolidation is governed by 28 U.S.C. §§ 1404 and 1407.

Statutes governing courts' subject-matter jurisdiction also affect the extent to which related cases can be consolidated. Consolidation generally becomes easier as the courts' original and removal jurisdictions expand. See, e.g., Multiparty, Multiforum Trial Jurisdiction Act of 2002, 28

U.S.C. § 1369 (2000) (giving federal district courts original jurisdiction over certain cases stemming from mass accidents subject only to minimal diversity). Restrictions on removal jurisdiction limit the ability to consolidate related cases when some are pending in state courts.

In combination, removal and transfer can be powerful tools for aggregation. For example, they enabled a single federal judge to preside over the adjudication of the claims of over 10,000 plaintiffs who claimed to be harmed by exposure to the herbicide DBCP. The plaintiffs originally filed their lawsuits in state courts located in five different Texas counties. Delgado v. Shell Oil Co., 890 F.Supp. 1324, 1335–1340 (S.D. Tex. 1995). When the number of persons involved in consolidated proceedings becomes very large, special procedures may be required. The Class Action Fairness Act recognizes the importance of numbers by limiting one branch of federal-court jurisdiction over mass actions to cases in which the monetary claims of 100 or more plaintiffs are proposed to be tried together. See 28 U.S.C. § 1332(d)(11)(B)(i) (2005).

Consolidation within judicial divisions starts with the assignment to a single judge of all related civil cases pending in the same court. Consolidation across divisions in the same district requires transfer of venue in at least one of the cases pursuant to 28 U.S.C. § 1404(a), which permits transfer of "any civil action to any other district or division where it might have been brought" for the convenience of the parties and witnesses and in the interest of justice.

Some authorities suggest that transfer across districts is less likely when plaintiffs sue in their home states, for courts are then inclined to respect plaintiffs' choice of forum even more strongly. See Pava v. Drom Int'l, Inc., 8 F.Supp.2d 1062, 1064–1065 (N.D. Ill. 1998) (holding that where an Illinois resident brought an action in his home forum, that choice "weighs heavily against transfer"); Cerasoli v. Xomed, Inc., 952 F.Supp. 152, 154–155 (W.D.N.Y. 1997) (holding that the importance of the plaintiff's choice of forum "is heightened when the plaintiff resides in his chosen forum").

Once the cases are in the same court, the presiding judge considers whether coordinating the cases is feasible and desirable, and enters an order pursuant to Rule 42 consolidating them. Thereafter, the court handles a variety of administrative matters, such as creating a master file for all the cases, deeming that all discovery is taken in all cases, and providing that documents need only be filed in the master file unless they are "uniquely applicable" to a particular case. Manual for Complex Litigation (Fourth) § 20.11, at 218 (2004).

28 U.S.C. § 1407 authorizes the Judicial Panel on Multidistrict Litigation (MDL) to transfer related civil actions from multiple districts to a single district for coordinated proceedings. Normally, the Panel's authority is invoked by motion. Parties and attorneys involved in cases handled by the Panel must notify it of any related cases of which they are aware. MDL transfer has created some enormous federal pretrial consolidations. See, e.g., In re Asbestos Prods. Liab. Litig., Nos. 875, C–92–3137–DLJ et al., 1993 WL 463301 (J.P.M.L. Nov. 2, 1993) (consolidating more than 39,000 asbestos actions). Many states also authorize transfer and consolidation of related cases.

See, e.g., W. Va. Trial Ct. R. 26.01–26.12 (establishing West Virginia's Mass Litigation Panel, charged with "develop[ing] and implement[ing] case management and trial methodologies" to manage mass litigation); 20 Okla. Stat. Ann. § 81 (2004) (permitting Oklahoma Supreme Court to establish an MDL panel of five judges with power to transfer related matters or stay actions pending resolution of common questions of law or fact); Tex. Gov't Code Ann. § 74.162 (Vernon 2003) (permitting Texas MDL panel to transfer common questions of law or fact to consolidated proceeding "for the convenience of the parties and witnesses" and to "promote the just and efficient conduct of the actions").

As with all consolidations, the object of multidistrict transfer is to reduce litigation costs by streamlining discovery and facilitating uniform rulings. The judge in the transferee court may also help matters by becoming a specialist in the litigation and by facilitating a global settlement. However, the power of this device is limited, because the authority of the transferee court extends to only pretrial matters, a restriction that cannot be circumvented by procedural maneuvering. See In re Lexecon, Inc. v. Milberg Weiss Bershad Hynes & Lerach, 523 U.S. 26 (1998) (holding that a district court may not use 28 U.S.C. § 1404(a) to transfer to itself for trial a case received pursuant to 28 U.S.C. § 1407, but must remand the case to the transferor court at the end of pretrial proceedings). The transferee court may coordinate discovery, decide dispositive motions, approve settlements, and review consent decrees. It must remand the cases to the transferor forums when the pretrial phase is complete.

Historically, remands have been few, as most cases settled or were dismissed in the transferee court. Deborah R. Hensler, *The Role of Multi-Districting in Mass Tort Litigation: An Empirical Investigation*, 31 Seton Hall L. Rev. 883 (2001).

The Manual for Complex Litigation (Fourth) § 20.132 recommends a variety of ways, each with recognized limitations, to buttress a transferee court's authority. Before remanding cases to transferor forums, the transferee court "could conduct a bellwether trial of a centralized action . . . originally filed in the transferee district." Upon remand, judges in transferor courts may encourage plaintiffs to refile their actions in the transferee district or to file amended complaints asserting venue in the transferee district or consenting to remain in the transferee district for trial. Following remand, the transferor court could transfer the action back to the transferee court pursuant to 28 U.S.C. § 1404 or § 1406. The transferee judge could seek an intercircuit or intracircuit assignment pursuant to 28 U.S.C. § 292 or § 294 and follow a remanded action, presiding over the trial of that action in that originating district.

Judges also have options for coordinating the adjudication of related cases without consolidating them. The Manual for Complex Litigation (Fourth) § 20.14 identifies these. They include: assigning all cases to a single judge designated by the chief justice or the chief circuit judge under 28 U.S.C. §§ 292–294 to sit temporarily in the district where related cases are pending (which may be within or outside of the assigned judge's own circuit); obtaining the agreement of counsel to select a "lead case," staying proceedings in other cases until the lead case is resolved, and giving the lead case presumptive, though not conclusive, effect in the other courts; convening joint telephonic conferences and entering joint orders; coordinating the appointment of experts under Fed. R. Evid. 706, special masters under Fed. R. Civ. P. 53, and lead counsel to avoid duplicate activity and inconsistencies, help resolve claims of privilege made in a number of cases on similar facts, or conduct global settlement negotiations; coordinating discovery by allowing or requiring cross-filing of deposition notices, interrogatories, and requests for production, and by making completed discovery available to litigants in the other cases (perhaps in return for sharing the cost); establishing document depositories; and staying a pending action until a related case is resolved.

The Manual for Complex Litigation also advises judges to order lawyers in cases before them to work with attorneys in cases pending in other courts, explaining that "the judge may direct counsel to coordinate with the attorneys in the other cases to reduce duplication and potential conflicts and to coordinate and share resources." Manual for Complex Litigation (Fourth) § 10.225, at 28 (2004). A judge's power to compel cooperation on the part of lawyers practicing in other courts is unclear.

Bellwether trials or test cases are often cited as possible methods of establishing settlement values for related cases and as sources of guidance on the advisability of class certification or other forms of aggregation. See In re Norplant Contraceptive Prods. Liab. Litig., 955 F.Supp. 700 (E.D. Tex. 1997) (ruling on first set of bellwether plaintiffs' complaints on behalf of recipients of

contraceptive implant). To serve these functions effectively, cases that are to serve as bellwethers must be selected with care. Ideally, the cases should be a random sample of the universe of claims sufficient to support statistically valid inferences. In practice, this is rarely possible, if only because the number of cases chosen as test cases must be too small to provide a statistically random sample, or because the entire universe of cases is too small for true statistical sampling. A second-best practice is to select a mix of cases that seems representative. An approach that allowed each side to pick all of the test cases unilaterally has been roundly criticized. See In re Chevron U.S.A., Inc., 109 F.3d 1016, 1019 (5th Cir. 1997) (noting that trial of cases selected by each side separately "is not a bellwether trial. It is simply a trial of fifteen (15) of the 'best' and fifteen (15) of the 'worst' cases contained in the universe of claims involved in this litigation").

Much of the judicial innovation in consolidation concerns informal efforts by judges to coordinate the handling of related claims pending in different courts. James G. Apple, Paula L. Hannaford & G. Thomas Munsterman, *Manual for Cooperation Between State and Federal Courts* (1997). Sometimes, communication across national borders is required. See Guidelines Applicable to Court-to-Court Communications in Cross-Border Cases, http://www.ali.org/doc/Guidelines.pdf (last visited Jan. 21, 2010), As Adopted and Promulgated by The American Law Institute in 2000, and included as Appendix B in Transnational Insolvency: Principles of Cooperation Among the NAFTA Countries (2003).

In theory, these efforts could be extended to all filed claims, but they cannot reach related unfiled claims, of which there may be many. Parties or their agents must work together to achieve efficiencies in this realm, and often do. Their efforts create private aggregations.

Comment b(3). Illustration 9 is based on Huber v. Taylor, 469 F.3d 67 (3d Cir. 2006). Illustration 10 is based on Pope v. Rice, No. 04 Civ. 4171(DLC), 2005 WL 613085 (S.D.N.Y. Mar. 14, 2005).

On the claimants' side, the rise of informal aggregation reflects several factors, including the ability of lawyers to solicit large numbers of clients with related claims and the creation of communication networks connecting attorneys. One classic context is asbestos, where lawyers working with unions have amassed thousands of clients. For other examples, see Erichson, *Informal Aggregation*, 50 Duke L.J. at 387 n.3; Charles Silver & Lynn A. Baker, *Mass Lawsuits and the Aggregate Settlement Rule*, 32 Wake Forest L. Rev. 733, 742 (1997); Byron G. Stier, *Resolving the Class Action Crisis: Mass Tort Litigation as Network*, 2005 Utah L. Rev. 863, 867 (proposing "an expansive set of litigation networks that provide much of the efficiency promised by class actions without violating state substantive law or federal constitutional law").

For claimants, private aggregation helps level the playing field. As already addressed, when it comes to economies of scale, respondents have inherent advantages. "In general, the unequal investment incentive for defendants and plaintiffs in mass tort cases translates into a much greater chance that the defendant, who aggregates all classable claims automat-

ically, will prevail on the common questions over the plaintiffs' attorney who acquires fewer than all claims." David Rosenberg, *Mass Tort Class Actions: What Defendants Have and Plaintiffs Don't*, 37 Harv. J. on Legis. 393, 401 (2000).

On the respondents' side, aggregation occurs automatically when a single respondent faces related claims. See Rosenberg, supra at 393; Bruce Hay & David Rosenberg, *"Sweetheart" and "Blackmail" Settlements in Class Actions: Reality and Remedy*, 75 Notre Dame L. Rev. 1377 (2000). To gain the efficiencies of natural aggregation, a single respondent must nonetheless expend effort. In particular, it must coordinate its response to the claims it confronts. A single respondent that develops a unified approach will internalize all the gains to be had from improving its defensive efforts and reducing costs. See Erichson, *Informal Aggregation*, 50 Duke L.J. at 384.

Coordination is harder to achieve when multiple respondents are involved, but the possibility of reducing costs by working collectively on common issues and of presenting a united front in litigation makes it advantageous. Defense lawyers understand this and often recommend joint defense arrangements to clients. See, e.g., Richard A. Deeb, *Toxic Tort Defense: Pros and Cons of Joint Defense Arrangements*, 10 No. 9 Corp. Counsellor 4, 4 (1996) ("In most toxic tort cases, issues of exposure, causation and plaintiffs' medical condition will be common to all defendants. It is often extremely beneficial for the defendants to agree to share the costs of experts and discovery on these issues.... [M]any defense groups go further. Some contemplate joint defense discovery requests, joint discovery motions, joint demurrers, joint summary judgments, joint deposition questioning, motions in limine and more."); Jeffrey T. Haley, *Strategies and Antitrust Limitations for Multiple Potential Patent Infringers*, 21 AIPLA Q.J. 327, 329 (1993) ("[A] benefit of collective efforts on defense is simply to share costs of such efforts as: (1) searches to find prior art which may render some or all of the claims invalid or may narrow the interpretation of the claims or narrow the range of equivalents for elements recited in the claims, (2) discovery from the patentee, the inventor, and related parties to establish invalidity defenses and gather evidence on interpretation of the claims, and (3) discovery from other parties to learn dates of publication of other prior art, evidence of non-experimental use, or offers for sale of the invention by the inventor or patentee more than one year before the application was filed. This discovery can be expensive and can be conducted for the benefit of all potential infringers by a single team which avoids duplication of effort. Although cases in a single district may be consolidated for purposes of discovery, avoiding duplication of effort can be accomplished without consolidation simply by sharing of gathered information among the potential infringers.").

Because informal aggregations arise spontaneously outside the formal procedural system, contracts and other understandings provide the basis for them. These contracts may take the form of referral agreements, which move clients from the attorneys they contact initially to specialists who are better able to handle their claims. Agreements to share burdens are also common (and are the only agreements one finds on the defense side, referral agreements involving respondents being unheard of).

Informal aggregations raise questions concerning the responsibilities and rights of the principals and their agents that rarely are addressed by courts. One set of questions relates to the obligations cooperating lawyers have to other lawyers' clients. Another set concerns the rights and responsibilities of cooperating lawyers inter se. Contracts obviously bear on these questions, but so do state-bar rules, rules of evidence, restrictions on the unlicensed practice, and principles of agency. See, e.g., Pope v. Rice, No. 04 Civ. 4171 (DLC), 2005 WL 613085 (S.D.N.Y. Mar. 14, 2005) (discussing attorney–client relationships in aggregate settlement); Huber v. Taylor, 469 F.3d 67 (3d Cir. 2006) (discussing attorneys' duties to clients received by referral). See generally Chapter 3.

Referrals occur mainly when lawyers represent claimants. This is easily explained. Referrals are needed when clients cannot identify lawyers who suit their needs well, typically because clients are unsophisticated or infrequent consumers of legal services. When clients and lawyers are badly matched, the predictable result is deficient representation. Referral markets correct this problem by creating incentives for lawyers to forward clients to others with whom they are better paired. Referrals are needed less often on the defense side because defendants and their insurance carriers tend to be sophisticated consumers of legal services, unlike many claimants.

A referral creates a new professional relationship between the client and the recipient lawyer to which all the usual lawyerly duties apply. See

Huber, 469 F.3d 67. Whether it also extinguishes the client's relationship with the referring lawyer depends on the parties' understanding. A referring lawyer may have more work to do. The referring lawyer may need to monitor the recipient lawyer, to facilitate communications between the recipient lawyer and the client, and to advise the client on matters like settlement. In mass-tort cases, where referring lawyers sometimes send recipient lawyers large numbers of clients, referring lawyers frequently play important roles throughout the course of litigation.

A referral is one kind of agreement between lawyers that can provide a micro-structure for aggregate litigation. Other fee- and cost-sharing arrangements also exist. In the simplest cases, these arrangements operate within firms. Firms contribute diverse resources and services to aggregate lawsuits, including client development, the time of lawyers and support personnel, and financial capital. When lawyers practicing in the same firm deliver services in a representation, they can share fees among themselves as they wish.

In other situations, lawyers at different firms join forces for the purpose of representing client groups. Frequently, these combinations bring together lawyers with clients, lawyers with money, and lawyers with technical expertise. Typically, lawyers use their retainer agreements to obtain clients' permission to associate other lawyers.

Cocounsel representations are subject to professionalism rules that permit lawyers to share fees in proportion to the services rendered or otherwise if all lawyers accept joint responsibility for the matter. Usually, fee sharing is settled by agreement when new attorneys are brought into a case.

The frequency and extent of informal aggregation make formal aggregation easier to tolerate. Critics of aggregation emphasize that each person is entitled to a day in court. Both the truth and the importance of this principle are admitted. However, individuals often have (and may even prefer to have) their day in court as part of litigation groups. Often, these groups form informally when claims are related, and the likelihood of their formation increases with the number of related claims. When the reality is that group-wide representation will occur in any event, the decision to formalize it seems less intrusive. "[T]he benefits of formal aggregation should be weighed against the reality of informal aggregation, rather than against an imaginary picture of uneconomical individualized litigation." Erichson, *Informal Aggregation*, 50 Duke L.J. at 466. See also Michael D. Green, *Bendectin and Birth Defects* 241 (1996) ("[T]he advantages of consolidation must be assessed against the alternative—which is not the individual-lawyer-with-separate-client-litigating-independently paradigm that some have employed.").

The relative efficiency of informal versus formal aggregation is difficult to assess. Some argue that informal aggregation can be as efficient as formal aggregation. See Richard L. Marcus, *Reassessing the Magnetic Pull of Megacases on Procedure*, 51 DePaul L. Rev. 457, 467–468 (2001) (questioning the need for a Coordinating Committee for Multiple Litigation to coordinate the handling of the 2000 separate private antitrust actions concerning price-fixing in the electrical equipment industry that were pending in 35 different federal district courts, and observing that "[d]uring roughly the same period of time, similar efficiencies were effected in [products-liability] litigation by informal arrangements created among counsel without organized judicial oversight").

Administrative aggregation and private aggregation can occur together and complement each other. "The line between formal and informal aggregation can become rather fuzzy, as when lawyer coordination in related cases is prompted by a court, or when it takes the form of judicially designated steering committees or lead and liaison counsel." Erichson, *Informal Aggregation*, 50 Duke L.J. at 397. A private aggregation may even

reflect a desire to facilitate an administrative aggregation or aggregate lawsuit. Lawyers handling thousands of asbestos claims have worked with respondent companies on prepackaged bankruptcy plans under § 524(g) of the Bankruptcy Code. The shared object is to enable a respondent to resolve all of its asbestos exposure by entering bankruptcy and exiting quickly, so normal business operations can continue without interruption or impairment. In the discussion of Settlement in Chapter 3, the experience under § 524(g) provides important lessons for the treatment of aggregate settlements in the context of private aggregations.

§ 1.03 General Principles for Aggregate Proceedings

Aggregation should further the pursuit of justice under law by advancing the following goals:

(a) enforcing substantive rights and responsibilities;

(b) promoting the efficient use of litigation resources;

(c) facilitating binding resolutions of civil disputes; and

(d) facilitating accurate and just resolutions of civil disputes by trial and settlement.

Comment:

a. Pursuit of justice under law. Courts exist to provide justice under law. As understood here, justice under law concerns the law on the books with both its strengths and its shortcomings. When a law is valid, courts provide justice under law by enforcing it and effectuating the policy it embodies. Aggregation is a means by which courts may promote justice under law more fully. Aggregation is not an end unto itself.

Identifying the pursuit of justice under law as the central purpose of aggregation respects the institutional position of courts within our political system. Except in common-law areas, courts are not formally empowered to select substantive policies. They are agents of legislatures and other bodies authorized to decide the direction of public policy.

Courts are empowered to create and revise adjudicatory procedures, however. Within broad limits, a court can enforce a statute using a procedure that was developed or amended after the statute's effective date, assuming the statute itself does not say otherwise. Improved aggregation techniques must be thought of in this light.

A policy of pursuing justice under law also creates stable and appropriate expectations within legislative bodies. These bodies must expect routine, expeditious, and steadily-improving enforcement of the laws they enact. When they desire something other than this, legislatures can, within broad limits, design procedures and require their application. Knowing how courts enforce laws and not wanting particular laws to be enforced in the usual way, Congress may establish special procedures intended to better serve its policies. Nothing in this Section requires courts to overrule or disregard special procedures embodied in particular pieces of legislation.

The four subordinate considerations identified in this Section may on occasion be in tension with each other. For example, it may always be possible to increase the accuracy of trials by expending greater resources, but the cost of the additional resources consumed must be weighed against the value of the gain in accuracy achieved and the burdens that will be imposed on litigants and the judicial system. Procedural justice requires reasonable compromises of competing goals and considerations. This is true of the decision to aggregate and of the conduct of aggregations as well. In any given context, the best available compromise depends upon the facts, but compromises are likely to be better when made transparently on the basis of the factors identified in this Section. Furthermore, such compromises should be challenged and reviewed based upon openly articulated considerations.

b. Efficient use of litigation resources as the central purpose of aggregation. All forms of aggregation have efficiency as a goal. Given this, it is unsurprising that many of the problems associated with aggregation and many of the shortcomings identified in existing procedures relate to efficiency as well. For example, existing methods of consolidating cases often miss many pending cases and always miss unfiled claims, allowing resources to be wasted. Efforts to extend the reach of consolidation, of which there are many, can be justified on efficiency grounds.

c. Other considerations. This Section identifies three other principles by means of which aggregate proceedings should further the pursuit of justice under law. These proceedings should enforce substantive rights and responsibilities, facilitate binding resolutions of civil disputes, and facilitate accurate resolutions of civil disputes by trial and settlement. Elsewhere in this project, these principles are referred to as fidelity, finality, and feasibility. Fidelity concerns the relationship of aggregate procedure to underlying substantive law. Finality refers to the aim of resolving disputes and thereby eliminating the need to revisit issues or claims in other proceedings. Feasibility refers to the institutional capacity of the courts to conduct aggregate proceedings, which includes the ability to try cases to verdicts that reflect the merits and to encourage settlements that do so.

Sometimes, the pursuit of efficiency also advances these other objectives, but not always. The pursuit of efficiency must often be tempered for the sake of other considerations. This Section identifies fidelity, finality, and feasibility as matters to be taken into account separately so the potential for conflicts between these considerations and efficiency will be clear.

d. Relationship of general principles to judicial discretion to permit aggregation. The principles stated in this Section are intended to guide the exercise of judicial discretion when opportunities to permit aggregation arise. This Section does not address and is not intended to affect the occasions on which judges have this discretion. For example, this Section does not affect the permissibility of agreements to allow or deny aggregation in arbitration proceedings. Rather, this Section provides principles to guide the exercise of discretion in judicial proceedings, including arbitrations, where aggregation is an available option. Nor does this Section affect the possibility of aggregation when members of a putative class reside in other countries.

e. Aggregation of claims arising under statutes with minimum-damages provisions. Statutes sometimes entitle persons to sue for liquidated or minimum damages—also known as statutory damages—for technical violations of law that result in either no actual loss or an actual loss too small to warrant conventional litigation. The statutory language that entitles persons to minimum damages is phrased in different ways: as an entitlement to a specific dollar amount ($1000 per violation, for example), to a dollar amount within a specified range (not less than $100 but not more than $1000 per violation), or to an amount that depends on the procedural posture of the litigation ($1000 per violation but with an aggregate cap of $500,000 in the event of a class action).

By authorizing minimum awards, statutes subsidize individual claims arising from technical violations of regulatory requirements and, thereby, encourage compliance with statutory provisions that might otherwise be ignored. However, because conduct regulated by statutes with minimum-damages provisions often affects large populations, technical violations can foster lawsuits with enormous potential damage awards if aggregation is permitted. It is sometimes obvious whether aggregation of cases brought under statutes with minimum damages awards should be allowed. When a statute explicitly provides an aggregate cap on minimum damages in a class action, for example, permitting aggregation within the limit described—and in accordance with the applicable requirements for class certification—plainly advances the statute's remedial scheme.

Difficulties arise when statutes providing for minimum damages make no reference to aggregate procedures. In cases brought under such silent statutes, judges have tried to mediate between the risk of under-deterrence, which a denial of aggregation might cause, and the risk of over-compensation and over-deterrence, which a decision allowing aggregation would encourage. Some courts have declined to certify class actions, despite the predominance of common questions of law and fact, finding that class litigation is not superior to ordinary litigation because it threatens defendants with insolvency, equips plaintiffs with excessive settlement leverage, encourages litigation too strongly, raises significant due-process concerns, and distorts the remedial scheme of the statute. For example, suppose a business that operates via a website uses identical documents in transactions with one million customers. Because the documents are the same, a single customer who believes the documents are unlawful could file a class action on behalf of all. With a $1000-per-violation minimum-damages provision in force, the potential damages are $10 billion, even if no customer can prove any actual loss from the violation alleged. Overall, the prospect of an outsized aggregate-damage award is thought to render the discretionary act of certifying a class unwarranted.

In the end, the decision to permit or deny aggregation under a silent statute turns on legislative intent. A judge must determine whether a decision to permit aggregation would advance or impede a statutory scheme. There cannot be a categorical answer that would apply across all statutory causes of action. A middle-ground position may be that judges have the option of certifying a class with a damages cap or some other procedural limiting device that would prevent the aggregation from transforming the remedial reach of the statute.

Another middle-ground position may also be open. Some judicial opinions refer in this regard to the absurdity doctrine of statutory interpretation, whereby a court may avoid an absurd result—remedial overreach in the aggregate—that would be produced by the combination of class certification and adherence to the statutory language. The absurdity doctrine, however, remains a matter of considerable debate within the realm of statutory interpretation generally. And, here specifically, it is unclear that the necessary predicate for application of the absurdity doctrine is present. Confronted with a choice between adherence to the authoritative language of the statute and the exercise of discretion to deny class certification, the court arguably can avoid the purportedly absurd result—certification with remedial overreach—through a discretionary selection of the latter option.

REPORTERS' NOTES

Comment a. Cases, treatise entries, and scholarly literature on class actions, voluntary joinder, and consolidation routinely identify efficiency as the main goal of aggregation. Manual for Complex Litigation (Fourth) § 21.131, at 250 (2004) ("Rule 23(b)(3) permits a class action [when] ... 'a class action is superior to other available methods for the fair and efficient adjudication of the controversy.'"); id. § 20.11, at 218 ("If the cases appear to involve common questions of law or fact, and consolidation may tend to reduce cost and delay, the cases may be consolidated under Federal Rule of Civil Procedure 42(a)."); Union Carbide v. Adams, 166 S.W.3d 1 (Tex. J.P.M.L. 2003) (finding that certain asbestos cases "involve[d] one or more common questions of fact, and that transfer of these cases and tag-along cases to one district judge [would] be for the convenience of the parties and witnesses and will promote the just and efficient conduct of the cases").

Commentators also routinely cite efficiency in support of proposed changes to aggregation procedures. See, e.g., Joan Steinman, *The Effects of Case Consolidation Part 1: Justiciability and Jurisdiction (Original and Appellate)*, 42 UCLA L. Rev. 717 (1995) (arguing that treating consolidated lawsuits as a single case rather than as separate proceedings would enable federal courts to hear additional claims that can efficiently be heard together, enable the courts to assert supplemental jurisdiction and

personal jurisdiction more effectively, and eliminate uncertainties concerning litigants' rights and obligations that currently waste trial and appellate resources). In the development and improvement of litigation procedures, the pursuit of efficiency has been important both historically and normatively. See also Complex Litigation: Statutory Recommendations and Analysis 16 (invoking Rule 1 of the Federal Rules of Civil Procedure's specification of "the just, speedy, and inexpensive determination of every action" as the "tripartite goal for the federal procedural system").

Statutes establishing special procedures for aggregated claims include the Private Securities Litigation Reform Act of 1995, 15 U.S.C. § 77z–1 (1998) (establishing a special pleading standard for securities-fraud cases and special requirements for securities-fraud class actions); Magnuson–Moss Act, 15 U.S.C. § 2301 (1975) (establishing special requirements for consumer class actions); Truth In Lending Act, 15 U.S.C. § 1601 (1976) (establishing special limit on damages for class actions); The Class Action Fairness Act, 28 U.S.C. § 1715 (2005) (establishing federal-court jurisdiction over mass actions involving 100 or more plaintiffs). On class actions in Canada, see Gordon McKee & Robin Linley, *The Evolving Landscape for Pharmaceutical Product Liability Litigation in Canada*, 73 Def. Couns. J. 242 (2006).

Comment b. On the courts' responsibility to enforce all valid laws, see Richard A. Nagareda, *Aggregation and Its Discontents: Class Settlement Pressure, Class–Wide Arbitration, and CAFA*, 106 Colum. L. Rev. 1872, 1878 (2006) ("There is no authority for courts, as distinct from legislatures or executives, to select which principles in substantive law warrant vigorous enforcement and which do not.").

Comment c. In casting the general principles of aggregate proceedings in terms of fidelity to substantive law, finality in adjudication, and feasibility in judicial administration, this Section draws on a similar typology developed in the class-action context in Allan H. Erbsen, *From "Predominance" to "Resolvability": A New Approach to Regulating Class Actions*, 58 Vand. L. Rev. 995 (2005).

Comment d. On waivers of class-action treatment in contractual arbitration clauses, see In re American Express Merchants' Litig., 554 F.3d 300 (2d Cir. 2009); Kristian v. Comcast Corp., 446 F.3d 25 (1st Cir. 2006); Discover Bank v. Superior Court, 113 P.3d 1100 (Cal. 2005); Nagareda, *Aggregation and its Discontents*, 106 Colum. L. Rev. at 1895–1909; Samuel Issacharoff & Erin F. Delaney, *Credit Card Accountability*, 73 U. Chi. L. Rev. 157 (2006); Myriam Gilles, *Opting Out of Liability: The Forthcoming, Near–Total Demise of the Modern Class Action*, 104 Mich. L. Rev. 373 (2005); Jean R. Sternlight, *Creeping Mandatory Arbitration: Is It Just?*, 57 Stan. L. Rev. 1631 (2005); J. Maria Glover, Note, *Beyond Unconscionability: Class Action Waivers and Mandatory Arbitration Agreements*, 59 Vand. L. Rev. 1735 (2006).

On the challenges presented for class certification in the securities context when members of the proposed class reside in different countries, see Morrison v. Nat'l Australia Bank Ltd., 547 F.3d 167 (2d Cir. 2008); In re Alstom SA Sec. Litig., 253 F.R.D. 266 (S.D.N.Y. 2008); In re Vivendi Universal, S.A. Sec. Litig., 242 F.R.D. 76 (S.D.N.Y. 2007); Stephen J. Choi & Linda J. Silberman, *Transnational Litigation and Global Securities Class–Action Lawsuits*, 2009 Wisc. L. Rev. 465; Hannah L. Buxbaum, *Multinational Class Actions under Federal Securities Law: Managing Jurisdictional Conflict*, 46 Colum. J. Transnat'l L. 14 (2007).

Comment e. For examples of the different ways statutory language provides for minimum damages, see, e.g., 47 U.S.C. § 551(f)(2)(A) (2001) (Cable Communications Policy Act, authorizing "actual damages but not less than liquidated damages computed at the rate of $100 a day for each day of violation or $1,000, whichever is higher"); 15 U.S.C. § 1681n(a)(1)(A) (2008) (Fair Credit Transaction Act, authorizing "actual damages sustained by the consumer as a result of the failure or damages of not less than $100 and not more than $1,000"); 15 U.S.C. § 1692k(a)(2)(A)–(B) (1977) (Fair Debt Collection Practices Act, authorizing "in the case of any action by an individual, such additional damages as the court may allow, but not exceeding $1,000" but additionally providing, in the event of a class action, that such damages are "not to exceed the lesser of $500,000 or 1 per centum of the net worth of the debt collector"); 15 U.S.C. § 1640(a)(2)(B) (2009) (creating similar damages provisions applying to individual actions and class actions brought to enforce 15

U.S.C. § 1635). See also Six (6) Mexican Workers v. Arizona Citrus Growers, 904 F.2d 1301 (9th Cir. 1990) (applying the Farm Labor Contractor Registration Act, 29 U.S.C. §§ 1801, 1854 (1983), which allows for damages of "up to $500" per plaintiff per violation, with no minimum). Many state statutes also provide for minimum-damage awards. E.g., Ala. Code § 8–19–10(a)(1) (2002) (allowing minimum statutory damages of $100); D.C. Code § 28–3905(k)(1) (2007) (allowing minimum statutory damages of $1500); Utah Code Ann. § 13–11–19 (West 1995) (allowing minimum statutory damages of $2000).

The U.S. Supreme Court upheld Congress's power to provide for minimum statutory damages in a series of cases beginning with Waters–Pierce Oil Co. v. Texas, 212 U.S. 86 (1909), which found that the penalty imposed was not grossly excessive. Recent cases addressing the constitutionality of punitive-damage awards suggest that the Court today might require a closer connection between statutory damages and actual losses. See, e.g., BMW of North America, Inc. v. Gore, 517 U.S. 559, 575 (1996) (characterizing St. Louis, I. M. & S. Ry. Co. v. Williams, 251 U.S. 63 (1919), which involved an award of statutory damages, as a case involving punitive damages). Still, as one author recently observed, "most courts refuse to apply the modern *BMW* guideposts to aggregate statutory damages." Sheila B. Scheuerman, *Due Process Forgotten: The Problem of Statutory Damages and Class Actions*, 74 Mo. L. Rev 103, 122 (2009).

The foundational case raising concerns about the combination of statutory minimum-damage awards and class certification is Ratner v. Chemical Bank New York Trust Co., 54 F.R.D. 412 (S.D.N.Y. 1972). An excellent discussion also appears in Parker v. Time Warner Entertainment Co., 331 F.3d 13 (2d Cir. 2003). For analysis of *Parker*, see Nagareda, *Aggregation and its Discontents*, 106 Colum. L. Rev. at 1885–1888. See also Andrews v. Chevy Chase Bank, 545 F.3d 570 (7th Cir. 2008) (analyzing availability in proposed class action of rescission remedy under Truth in Lending Act).

Concurring in *Parker*, Judge Newman commented that both (1) certifying a class that exposes a defendant to an outsized damage award and (2) allowing only individual lawsuits with minuscule awards "are unsatisfactory." 331 F.3d at 26. He argued that "a district court has discretion to certify a (b)(3) class with the aggregate amount of statutory damages limited substantially below what a literal application of the statute might seem to require." Id. at 23. In a footnote, he added,

[a]nother option would be for the judge to inform the plaintiffs, before deciding on the motion for certification but after having received argument on the subject from all parties, of the aggregate statutory amount above which (b)(3) superiority concerns would arise, and to permit the plaintiffs to amend their motion for class certification to seek reduced aggregate damages before a certification decision is rendered.

Id. at 28 n.7.

Due-process issues associated with aggregation of claims arising under statutes with minimum-damage provisions are identified or discussed in Scheuerman, *Due Process Forgotten*, 74 Mo. L. Rev 103; Catherine M. Sharkey, *Revisiting the Noninsura-*

ble Costs of Accidents, 64 Md. L. Rev. 409, 454 n.225 (2005); Blaine Evanson, Note, *Due Process in Statutory Damages*, 3 Geo. J.L. & Pub. Pol'y 601 (2005); and J. Cam Barker, Note, *Grossly Excessive Penalties in the Battle Against Illegal File–Sharing: The Troubling Effects of Aggregating Minimum Statutory Damages for Copyright Infringement*, 83 Tex. L. Rev. 525 (2004).

For an analysis of due-process issues arising in cases for statutory damages based on copyright infringement, see Pamela Samuelson & Tara Wheatland, *Statutory Damages in Copyright Law: A Remedy in Need of Reform*, 51 William & Mary L. Rev. 439 (2009); Pamela Samuelson, *Preliminary Thoughts on Copyright Reform*, 2007 Utah L. Rev. 551, 568 (2007). The U.S. Supreme Court has held that the Seventh Amendment entitles a defendant to a jury trial in a case seeking statutory damages under the Copyright Act. Feltner v. Columbia Pictures Television, Inc., 523 U.S. 340 (1998). Presumably, this right exists in cases brought under all federal statutes falling under the compass of the Seventh Amendment. One may therefore expect jury awards of statutory damages to be subject to the same scrutiny as other damage awards. It is not clear whether or how the jury-trial requirement may bear on the decision to certify a class.

Aggregation of claims with provisions for minimum statutory damages may also raise due-process issues under recent cases requiring punitive-damage awards to bear some relation to actual damages. Cf. Exxon Shipping Co. v. Baker, 128 S.Ct. 2605, 2633 (2008) (applying one-to-one ratio of punitive-to-compensatory damages

as "upper limit" in maritime cases as a matter of federal common law).

On the importance of legislative intent, see White v. E–Loan, Inc., No. C 05–02080 SI, 2006 WL 2411420, at *8 (N.D. Cal. Aug. 18, 2006) (rejecting due-process challenge to class certification under statute providing for minimum damages and observing that "to the extent any problem exists, it results from Congress's policy decisions and is therefore Congress's issue to address"). The same conclusion was reached in Murray v. GMAC Mortgage Corp., 434 F.3d 948, 953–954 (7th Cir. 2006) (reversing a district court's refusal to certify a class while observing that the potential for enormous damages stems not from "an 'abuse' of Rule 23" but from "the legislative decision to authorize awards as high as $1,000 per person. . . . [As long as such a] statute remains on the books, . . . it must be enforced rather than subverted.").

Some states prohibit class certification of claims arising under statutes with penalty-damage provisions, absent express statutory language permitting it. See Sperry v. Crompton Corp, 863 N.E.2d 1012 (N.Y. 2007) (holding that the treble-damages provision in New York's Donnelly Act constituted a penalty under section 901(b) of New York's Civil Practice Law & Rules, and that therefore, such damages would not be recoverable in class-action suits). The Supreme Court has recently granted certiorari on section 901(b) in Shady Grove Orthopedic Associates v. Allstate Insurance Co., 549 F.3d 137 (2d Cir. 2008), cert. granted, 129 S.Ct. 2160 (2009) (No. 08–1008) (presenting question whether New York statute is binding in proposed federal-court class action based on diversity jurisdiction).

For scholarly criticism of the absurdity doctrine of statutory interpretation, see John F. Manning, *The Absurdity Doctrine*, 116 Harv. L. Rev. 2387 (2003).

Many statutes authorize prevailing parties or plaintiffs to recover awards of attorneys' fees in addition to any damages they receive. In the absence of mandated minimum-damage awards, aggregating claims under these statutes ordinarily raises no special problems or difficulties. However, when a statutory minimum award per claimant is accompanied by a right to attorneys' fees, a court may consider the latter when deciding where to set the ceiling on aggregate damages. Because the law governing losing-defendants' responsibilities for prevailing-plaintiffs' attorneys' fees is exceptionally parsimonious, the existence of a fee-award right does not wholly negate the need to pay class counsel additional sums, which may be drawn from class members' damage recoveries. A court should consider the need to pay additional fees when deciding how large the cap on a class's total recovery will be.

§ 1.04 The Internal Objectives of Aggregate Proceedings

(a) A lawyer representing multiple claimants or respondents in an aggregate proceeding should seek to advance the common objectives of those claimants or respondents.

(b) Unless otherwise agreed by the claimants, the objectives of an aggregation of claimants include but are not limited to

(1) maximizing the net value of the group of claims;

(2) compensating each claimant appropriately;

(3) obtaining a judicial resolution of the legality of challenged conduct and stopping unlawful conduct from continuing;

(4) obtaining the broadest possible nondivisible remedies for past misconduct; and

(5) enabling claimants to voice their concerns and facilitating the rendition of further relief that protects the rights of affected persons as defined by substantive law.

(c) Unless otherwise agreed by the respondents, the objectives of an aggregation of respondents include but are not limited to

(1) minimizing the total loss attributable to litigation of the claims the group faces;

(2) obtaining a judicial resolution of the legality of challenged conduct and enabling lawful conduct to continue;

(3) allocating financial responsibility appropriately;

(4) restricting nondivisible remedies for prior wrongful acts as narrowly as possible; and

(5) enabling respondents to voice their concerns and enjoy the benefits of their substantive legal rights.

Comment:

a. Internal objectives. This Section focuses on the internal objectives of aggregate proceedings, that is, the objectives from the perspective of the claimants and respondents included in an aggregation. Section 1.05 identifies the management tools that can help accomplish these objectives.

This Section does not discuss the external objectives of aggregation, such as the desire to promote judicial efficiency or to treat equitably persons who might be treated inequitably if separate conventional lawsuits were to proceed. These issues are dealt with in Chapter 2.

b. A lawyer should advance the objectives of claimants or respondents. Because claimants and respondents may have difficulty controlling their agents in aggregate proceedings, this Section sets out a general duty on the part of lawyers to pursue their interests when representing them.

c. Unless otherwise agreed. Subsections (b) and (c) identify objectives to be pursued absent agreements to do otherwise by or among the relevant persons. Participants in litigation are free to identify other ends and may do so by any means allowed by relevant law. Participants may also rank ends in importance. For example, claimants may rank compensation ahead of voice and legal vindication or behind them. Respondents may express analogous preferences.

The possibility of altering the objectives to be pursued exists mainly in consensual group lawsuits and other proceedings where participants who enjoy high levels of control can meet face to face. See § 1.05, Reporters' Note to Comment *b*.

d. Aggregation of claimants. Plaintiffs hope to benefit themselves by suing. They want money, specific performance, or other valuable relief. Plaintiffs may also desire vindication or a day in court before an impartial arbiter of justice. Subsection (b) identifies these objectives and others. Although it does not rank the objectives, rankings can often be inferred from plaintiffs' complaints. When plaintiffs demand monetary relief, the objectives of obtaining compensation and allocating it appropriately normally carry the most weight. Vindicating rights and ending challenged conduct normally matter most when plaintiffs request injunctive or declaratory relief. It may be difficult or impossible to rank-order the objectives when both divisible and indivisible remedies are sought.

Even then, however, one can ordinarily rule out the objective of benefiting solely or primarily persons outside the aggregation, such as the general public or claimants' attorneys. Various doctrines imply that the primary objective of aggregate litigation must be to benefit claimants. To establish standing under federal law, claimants must seek relief from which they would benefit directly. To satisfy the requirement of adequate representation in class actions, representative plaintiffs must have the same interest in obtaining relief as absent class members. Interests must also overlap for group members to be bound in other representative proceedings.

    e. Maximize the net value of the group of claims. The net value of a group of claims for monetary relief is the portion of any payment remaining *after* litigation costs, including attorneys' fees, are paid. Maximizing this value is a central objective of aggregate litigation primarily because it is a matter claimants normally care about greatly when litigating. Claimants who directly hire attorneys through individual contractual negotiations typically promise contingent-percentage fees partly to reward lawyers for obtaining higher values. This is true both when claimants sue individually and when they sue in groups.

In representative proceedings and other aggregate lawsuits where representation arises by law, the objective of maximizing net-claim values reflects a policy commitment to mimic market arrangements in contexts where markets are prone to fail. Class actions are substitutes for voluntary group lawsuits, which is why their use is limited to contexts in which joinder by ordinary means is impracticable. As such, their objectives and those of voluntary group lawsuits should generally be the same. Other representative proceedings may also usefully be thought of as substitutes for consensual lawsuits when considering their preclusive effects. See § 1.02, Reporters' Notes.

It is often impossible to know, or to prove objectively, that the net value of a group of claims has been maximized. The best one can do is design procedures that reward actions likely to have this effect. Tools available for this purpose are identified in §§ 1.05 and 3.13.

    f. Compensate each claimant appropriately. Normatively, compensation is an important objective of most lawsuits brought to obtain monetary relief. The procedural system achieves corrective civil justice by requiring wrongdoers to pay compensation and by enabling victims to obtain it. Compensation also plays an essential practical role by making it profitable for persons with valid civil claims to sue for relief. Given the cost of litigation, it normally is economically disadvantageous to sue for vindication alone. This Section recognizes the normative importance of compensation and the practical need to maintain incentives for litigation by identifying compensation as an objective of aggregate lawsuits.

Ideally, the amount of compensation a claimant receives should reflect the merits of the claim itself, including the likelihood that the claimant would prevail at trial and the amount the claimant would win. Meeting this standard in an aggregate proceeding would ensure horizontal equity (similarly situated claimants receive similar amounts) and vertical equity (more deserving claimants receive larger payments than less deserving ones).

In practice, the ideal is rarely achieved. Rough justice is normal in aggregate proceedings. In these cases, settlements usually involve an element of "damages averaging," which occurs when an allocation plan ignores some features of claims that might reasonably be expected to influence claimants' expected recoveries at trial. For example, a mass-tort settlement might pay smokers and nonsmokers the same amounts, even though smokers have shorter life expectancies. In the limit, the administrative cost of apportioning payments may warrant a share-and-share-alike plan that treats all claimants equally.

Rough justice also occurs in conventional lawsuits, where bargaining allows risk aversion, the ability to endure delay, and other arbitrary factors to affect claim values. Payments in aggregate lawsuits need not be tuned more finely than payments in conventional lawsuits. However, in conventional lawsuits, claimants accept settlements voluntarily, and their consent gives rough justice a normative foundation. Consent to settlement can play a similar role in many aggregate proceedings, but attempts to elicit consent must reflect the peculiarities of these proceedings. In some aggregate lawsuits, consent cannot practicably be obtained, and the normative foundation for settlements must stem from judicial review and approval. See Chapter 3.

g. Enable claimants to voice their concerns and facilitate the rendition of further relief. Participants in aggregate proceedings often value the opportunity to express themselves and to participate in the legal process of vindication. However, the cost and value of expression may vary from one proceeding to another. When regulating opportunities for expression, it is appropriate to take account of both their costs and their benefits.

h. Aggregation of respondents. Defense-side aggregation can create issues and problems similar to those associated with claimant-side aggregation. These include control problems not present in ordinary litigation and allocation problems, the latter involving the allocation of litigation costs and potential liabilities rather than litigation costs and potential gains.

i. Minimizing losses and obtaining vindication. In conventional litigation, defendants (or their liability insurers) typically hope to minimize the total cost, including indemnity and defense, of responding to a claim. Aggregation, whether on the plaintiffs' side or the defendants', normally leaves this desire unchanged but may greatly alter the strategies available for achieving it.

In ordinary litigation, defendants often advance the legitimate desire to minimize losses and obtain vindication by asserting individualized defenses, such as statutes of limitation, res judicata, or counterclaims. In aggregate lawsuits, opportunities to raise individualized defenses in the aggregate proceeding itself should be preserved as fully as the form of aggregation permits. For example, counterclaims may be proper in consolidations (because all claimants are parties), even though counterclaims against persons other than named plaintiffs are ordinarily improper in class actions (because absent class members are represented nonparties). Opportunities for individualized discovery should be treated similarly (and may also depend on party status). When the form of aggregation prevents a defendant from asserting an available defense or a counterclaim, the defense or counterclaim is preserved, not lost, but must be raised in an alternative proceeding. See § 2.07(d) ("[T]he court shall ensure that aggregate treatment of related claims does not compromise the ability of any person opposing the aggregate group in the litigation to dispute the allegations made by claimants or to raise pertinent substantive defenses.").

Defendants in aggregate lawsuits may care about vindication or other values in addition to, or as alternatives to, cost minimization. For example, a church or other religious organization sued by a parishioner or member for sexual harassment might defend the lawsuit with the objective of minimizing the loss, or it might employ an approach calculated to honor the values, ideals, or beliefs for which the organization stands. The organization may think it more important to treat the member fairly and compassionately than to minimize the amount of compensation it pays. A business caught up in an aggregate lawsuit, such as being charged with having been one alleged patent infringer among many, may also desire vindication for straightforward financial reasons. Its sales, stock price, and credit rating may suffer until the cloud over its product is removed.

In ordinary litigation, a defendant (or its liability insurer) can choose its own objectives and pursue them. In most respondent aggregations, this may also be true. Defendants usually retain significant or complete control of litigation even when defendants (or claimants) are aggregated. For example, they decide whether to settle and, if so, on what terms. Control is not always complete, however. Although rare, defendant class actions, which have been used in patent-infringement cases and suits against public officials, may impede respondents' control of litigation affecting their interests. Control may also be limited in multidistrict consolidations, where judges may appoint lead and liaison counsel for defendants (as well as plaintiffs). In these instances, the default objectives apply, unless respondents agree otherwise.

j. Allocating responsibility among defendants. Aggregation should not impair, and may enhance, a defendant's legitimate interest in bearing only the fraction of the cost of compensating a claimant (or a group of claimants) that is appropriate under applicable law.

Courts should avoid using trial procedures that would prevent defendants from adjudicating their fractional liabilities, but such adjudications may be addressed independently of the trial of the main action. In some instances, issues of apportionment may better be reserved until the total liability of all defendants is established, at which point a verdict or ruling in favor of some or all defendants in the main action may simplify the adjudication of fractional responsibilities or eliminate the need for it entirely. In other instances, resolving issues of apportionment may facilitate settlement of some or all of the case. So long as the substantive rights of parties are respected, courts should have discretion to organize the proofs in a case in such manner as will facilitate the fair and efficient resolution of the dispute.

A settlement involving fewer than all defendants may raise knotty problems of contribution or indemnification. Settling defendants will typically desire complete insulation from subsequent proceedings; defendants still litigating will want to preserve their rights to extract payments from others. Courts have developed many techniques to address these problems, including, under some circumstances, issuing orders barring non-settling parties' claims for contribution. Usually, these orders contain provisions entitling non-settling parties to setoffs, the size of which may be based on the settlement payment or the settling defendants' adjudicated proportion of fault.

Aggregation of respondents may facilitate adjudication or settlement of defendants' respective shares by bringing more potentially responsible persons into the same forum. Concentrating defendants in a single court ensures that allocation issues are decided by an informed judge, reduces the likelihood of inconsistent rulings or adjudications, and permits unitary appeals. Defendants who are forced to work together also often enter into joint-representation agreements or cooperate in other ways that build trust, facilitating the amicable resolution of allocation disputes.

k. Restricting the scope and burdens of nondivisible remedies. In a proceeding brought to obtain injunctive relief, a defendant may advance the desire to minimize its loss by arguing for a narrower or less burdensome remedy. Aggregation, whether of claimants or respondents, neither weakens nor delegitimizes this interest. Aggregation of defendants may facilitate the imposition of appropriate injunctions, however, by bringing before a court more persons who are potentially subject to an injunction's costs or effects.

l. Enabling respondents to voice their concerns. See Comment *g.*

REPORTERS' NOTES

Comment a. The history of aggregate litigation (indeed, of all litigation) shows clearly that, in lawsuits brought for monetary relief, claimants prefer larger recoveries to smaller ones. Stories abound of claimants who tried to bargain up from low settlement offers. Stories of claimants who tried to bargain down from high offers are few and far between. No significant evidence shows that claimants prefer less money to more.

Because the net value of a group of claims is the money available for payment to claimants after all litigation costs are defrayed, maximizing this quantity satisfies as fully as possible claimants' overwhelming preference for the most money they can obtain. Maximizing the gross value of a group of claims would not necessarily accomplish this. A $10 million recovery diminished by $6 million in fees and costs leaves a net of $4 million available for distribution. A $7 million recovery diminished by $2 million in fees and costs leaves a net of $5 million. In this example, the smaller gross recovery generates $1 million more in funds for claimants than the larger gross recovery. Because claimants care about the money they keep,

the proper focus is the net value of claims, not the gross.

By maximizing the net recovery, aggregate lawsuits create incentives for potential wrongdoers to respect others' legal rights. In other words, they deter wrongdoing by attaching a price to it, just as conventional lawsuits do. Many commentators believe that the goal of deterring wrongdoing provides the strongest justification for claim aggregation.

The statement that aggregate lawsuits attach prices to wrongdoing implies neither that the prices are correct nor that the level of deterrence is optimal. Establishing these matters would require a theory of optimal deterrence and an empirical study of liability threats.

That said, any plausible theory of litigation-induced deterrence is likely to take the goal of maximizing the net value of claims as the objective of claimant representations, for a simple reason: litigants tend to pursue economic gains. Operating within constraints established by procedural statutes and rules and by other factors, such as claim size and personal wealth, claimants tend to select strategies with an eye to maximizing their expected net recoveries. Strategies can and do change (along with success rates) in response, for example, to amendments to procedural and substantive rules, but the objective continues to be to net the largest amount. Given this, any plausible theory of litigation-induced deterrence will take the pursuit of self-interest as a given and will design the litigation system, including the possible concerns about overdeterrence, on the assumption that claimants will seek to maximize their net recoveries.

Lawyers play a pivotal role in figuring out how to maximize recoveries on claims. Any system of litigation, individual or aggregate, must limit the means that can properly be invoked to achieve this goal. A discussion of these limits, which include prohibitions or restrictions on advertising and solicitation, abuse of process, maximum fees, and frivolous claims, falls largely outside the scope of this project. However, there are distinct issues that arise in aggregate proceedings because of the multiple layers of fiduciary duties that are presented. For example, ordinarily, a lawyer is a fiduciary to a claimant and to no one else, and no claimant owes a duty to any other. In class actions, however, named plaintiffs owe fiduciary duties to absent class members. See Blanchard v. Edgemark Fin. Corp., 175 F.R.D. 293, 298–300 (N.D. Ill. 1997) (holding that any individual settlement with a certified class representative must be submitted to the court for approval because the representative has voluntarily undertaken a fiduciary responsibility toward the class as a whole and the court has a commensurate duty to protect absent class members); 7A Charles Alan Wright et al.,

Federal Practice and Procedure: Civil 2d § 1751 (1986 & Supp. 2002).

Class counsel is a thus fiduciary to a client who is also a fiduciary. A similar relationship obtains between lead attorneys and other lawyers in a multidistrict litigation. The lead attorneys must "act fairly, efficiently, and economically in the interests of all . . . parties' counsel." Manual for Complex Litigation (Fourth) § 10.22, at 24 (2004). Because "parties' counsel" are fiduciaries of the clients they directly represent, in multidistrict litigations a double layer of fiduciary relationships also obtains. Finally, whenever a group of litigants works together, its members may owe each other duties by agreement or common law.

The complicated web of duties just outlined may require persons acting as fiduciaries to put others' interests ahead of their own. For example, a named plaintiff who is not personally interested in a particular form of relief may nonetheless in some circumstances have to pursue it if others stand to gain.

Comment b. The connection between corrective justice and litigation incentives is weaker in some aggregate lawsuits than in most lawsuits that involve solitary claimants. For example, incentives to file small-claim class actions could be maintained by compensating named plaintiffs and defraying attorneys' fees and litigation costs from common funds, even if absent class members received nothing in the way of payments. By contrast, but for the prospect of receiving a payment, no incentive would exist for a single aggrieved person to file a lawsuit.

Comment c. Agreements among litigants or between litigants and lawyers purporting to establish the objectives of litigation may be governed by contract law, the law governing lawyers, agency law, or other law. These Principles do not attempt to alter any such body of law.

Comment d. For support of the proposition that the primary concern of claimants is with net recovery, see In re Cendant Corp. Litig., 264 F.3d 201, 254–255 (3d Cir. 2001) (observing that "a rational, self-interested client seeks to maximize net recovery; he or she wants the representation to terminate when his or her gross recovery minus his or her counsel's fee is largest"); Lucian Arye Bebchuk, *The Questionable Case for Using Auctions to Select Lead Counsel*, 80 Wash. U. L.Q. 889, 890 (2002) ("From the perspective of the class, it would be desirable to select . . . a fee schedule so as to maximize the expected net recovery for the class. This expected net recovery is in turn equal to (i) the expected recovery in the case, minus (ii) the expected expenditure on legal representation."); Charles Silver, *Due Process and the Lodestar Method: You Can't Get There From Here*, 74 Tul. L. Rev. 1809, 1841 (2000) ("[J]udges should set percentages with an eye to encouraging lawyers to maximize the value of class members' claims. They should do what the sole holder of an entire set of claims would do, namely, select the fee formula that is expected to yield the largest net recovery after the lawyers are paid."). On adequate representation, see § 1.05.

Although the possibility of obtaining compensation provides an incentive to litigate, common-law courts in the United States do not generally take litigation costs into account when awarding compensation. They set compensation at the amount needed to undo the wrong on the merits. Thus, when a claimant lost $1 million as a consequence of a civil violation, a respondent is normally found liable for that amount, and each side is required to pay its own litigation costs, including attorneys' fees. The claimant typically winds up with far less than $1 million on net.

Because compensation standards are creatures of substantive law, the awards claimants stand to win at trial should be the same in conventional lawsuits and aggregate lawsuits. A defendant's total liability may vary as a function of the number of claims tried together, but a defendant's liability to an individual claimant should not. A claim that would justify a verdict of $1 million in a conventional lawsuit should also justify a verdict of $1 million for the particular claimant involved in an aggregate proceeding. That the two verdicts should be the same does not imply that exact equality is required. First, judges and juries do rough justice, even when lawsuits are tried individually. In aggregate lawsuits, no greater precision is needed. Second, a lawyer trying an aggregate lawsuit may develop a case differently than one trying an individual claim, for example, by devoting more resources to the location and presentation of evidence. If the choice of approaches influences the jury, the verdicts in the two contexts may differ. Finally, it usually is impossible to know whether exact equality was achieved, for one rarely has access to the necessary data.

Comment f. "Damage averaging" is the hallmark of mass proceedings, which we characterize under the sometimes pejorative term "rough justice." It occurs when an allocation plan minimizes the importance of differences between claims that could or would affect their expected value at trial, or ignores such differences entirely. John C. Coffee, Jr., *The Regulation of Entrepreneurial Litigation: Balancing Fairness and Efficiency in the Large Class Action*, 54 U. Chi. L. Rev. 877, 917 (1987). "Allocation plans used in class actions inevitably involve some degree of damage averaging." Charles Silver & Lynn A. Baker, *I Cut, You Choose: The Role of Plaintiffs' Counsel in Allocating Settlement Proceeds*, 84 Va. L. Rev. 1465 (1998). The same is true of mass-tort settlements, where allocation grids and formulas commonly lump together persons whose claims differ somewhat in size or strength. For example, the Vioxx Settlement Calculator, available at http://www.officialvioxxsettlement.com/calculator/ (last visited Jan. 20, 2010), contains only five categories for length of use of Vioxx, even though length of use is a continuous variable and could have been broken into much finer gradations.

The widespread use of allocation grids and formulas in class-action and mass-tort settlements is a practical effort to address the inherent tension between "the good of all" and "the good of the individual" in aggregate litigation. Although in theory it is possible to design fee formulas that encourage lawyers for groups to recommend settlement allocations that give each person a more precise share of the total proceeds, in practice information problems are overwhelming, as when individuals have exposures that may not yet be fully manifested or when there are subjective claims of particularized emotional distress. See Paul Edelman, Richard A. Nagareda & Charles Silver, *The Allocation Problem in Multiple–Claimant Representations*, 14 Sup.

Ct. Econ. Rev. 95 (2006). Therefore, other means are needed to ensure that the pursuit of the common good and justice for the individual receive appropriate weight. These means include fee awards tied to common-fund recoveries, subclasses (when intraclass conflicts are large), communication, and settlement voting rules, as discussed in Chapter 3. The two most common reasons for such damage averaging are that in small-value cases, the cost of distinguishing the value of each individual claim may not be cost justified, and in larger cases, it is difficult to get a precise calculation of each individual's exact entitlement without a full evidentiary hearing.

Although there is a tendency to think that justice is rougher in aggregate lawsuits than individual representations, in fact rough justice is the norm everywhere. In individual representations, plaintiffs who win at trial often receive far smaller amounts than juries award. A study of Texas closed claims found an average settlement discount exceeding 50 percent, and much larger discounts in tried cases with the largest awards. David A. Hyman, Bernard Black, Kathryn Zeiler, Charles Silver & William M. Sage, *Do Defendants Pay What Juries Award? Post–Verdict Haircuts in Texas Medical Malpractice Cases, 1988–2003* J. Empirical Legal Stud. 3 (2007). The process of monetizing claimants' losses inherently involves subjective judgments and approximations as well. One could reasonably contend that the grids and formulas used in aggregate settlements merely make more open and transparent a process that occurs in all representations that end with payments. Concerns about rough justice in aggregate lawsuits may often reflect the frankness with which discriminations are made in these proceedings.

Comment h. For discussions and examples of defendant class actions, see Robert R. Simpson & Craig Lyle Perra, *Defendant Class Actions*, 32 Conn. L. Rev. 1319 (2000); Note, *Defendant Class Actions*, 91 Harv. L. Rev. 630 (1978). On defensive strategies used by religious organizations, see Patrick J. Schiltz, *Defending the*

Church, 29 No. 3 Litig. 19 (2003). On the judicial power to appoint lead and liaison counsel for defendants, see Manual for Complex Litigation (Fourth) § 10.22 (2004).

Comment i. On strategies for handling problems of contribution and indemnification raised by partial settlements, see Manual for Complex Litigation (Fourth) § 13.13 (2004).

§ 1.05   Ensuring Adequate Representation

(a) **In aggregate proceedings, judges may limit the control parties and represented persons have over litigation of claims or defenses.**

(b) **When control of aggregate proceedings is limited, judges should ensure that parties and represented persons are adequately represented.**

(c) **To promote adequate representation, judges may:**

(1) **enforce parties' agreements regarding the conduct of litigation;**

(2) **give named parties with sizeable stakes control of litigation decisions;**

(3) **enforce fiduciary duties on named parties and their attorneys;**

(4) **appoint competent counsel;**

(5) **use financial incentives, including fee awards and incentive bonuses, to reward good performance;**

(6) **require notice and other communications;**

(7) **permit opt-outs; and**

(8) **employ case-management techniques, including severance, subclassing, coordination, and consolidation.**

Comment:

a. Scope. This Section focuses on a common structural feature of all aggregate proceedings: the loss of control of litigation by persons whose interests are at issue. All aggregate lawsuits enable managers, typically attorneys but sometimes also lead or representative parties, to influence or control the progress of litigation, affecting the interests of diverse participants other than themselves. Because the principals lose control when litigation managers are empowered, aggregate proceedings raise fears of inadequate representation. To address these fears, judges should use a variety of tools to encourage litigation managers to pursue principals' interests, while adhering to the usual and customary norms of judicial neutrality. This Section identifies some available tools and explains how they may be employed.

    b.   Judges may limit the control parties and represented persons have over litigation. Lawsuits with small numbers of plaintiffs and defendants (often with only one of each) make up the bulk of the filings in state and federal trial courts. Usually, these lawsuits are straightforward. Because they involve a single transaction and few contested issues, little discovery is likely to occur and resolving the cases is often easy.

    When parties are few in number, control of litigation usually proceeds straightforwardly as well. The parties decide how the lawsuit is run. The paradigm case may be a contract dispute involving two companies, both possessing established relationships with lawyers, experience in litigation, and sufficient wealth to bear the cost of the case. Here, the parties consider mainly their own self-interest, and the agents generally carry out their wishes. Control is not perfect. Lawyers' interests never match clients' interests exactly, and lawyers always have some freedom to manage lawsuits as they think best, if only because clients cannot supervise their every move. But litigation generally proceeds smoothly and the system relies on each party to police its own control problems. Judicial management occurs mainly when issues arise between opposing parties that the parties cannot work out themselves.

    When the number of parties or represented persons is large, problems requiring judicial management arise between persons whose interests are nominally the same. For example, when multiple related lawsuits are proceeding, duplication of effort may be a significant problem, but neither the parties nor their attorneys may be able to avoid it. In class actions, the problem of encouraging appropriate litigation investments arises, as does the problem of allocating recoveries fairly among represented persons.

    In aggregate proceedings, judges may address these problems and others by empowering certain parties or attorneys to control litigation, by rewarding them for appropriate behavior, by imposing duties on them, and by reviewing their work. For example, judges may appoint lead plaintiffs and lead attorneys, thereby subordinating other plaintiffs and attorneys to lesser roles. The extent of judges' power to manage litigation may vary from one type of proceeding to another. Historically, judges have had extensive power to manage class actions, but less power to manage other aggregations. In recent years, judges have expanded their authority to manage non-class aggregations, however, and differences between types of proceedings have been blurred. For example, judges have recently begun to import class-action management procedures into multidistrict litigations, including procedures relating to appointment of counsel and regulation of lawyers' fees. In so doing, they have drawn upon some of the parallels between multidistrict litigations and class actions. In this way, class-action-style procedures have come to be employed in mass-tort lawsuits where class actions could not ordinarily be certified.

    c. Judges should ensure that parties and represented persons are adequately represented. Aggregate proceedings can saddle parties and represented persons with inadequate representation. Many factors contribute to this. For example, because any individual participant accounts for a small percentage of the total recovery, an individual claimant may have little incentive to monitor the conduct of the litigation. Also because individual participants are a small part of the total litigation, a lawyer may have insufficient incentive to see that individual participants are fairly treated. Every participant must also share control with others and divide costs and benefits with others. The need to share may create conflicts of interests.

    Parties and claimants sometimes use contracts to decide how they want aggregate proceedings to be run. As a general matter, courts should respect their agreements. See §§ 3.15–3.18 (discussing aggregate settlements). In the absence of contracts or when contracts are deficient, judges should take steps to ensure adequate representation. Sometimes, statutes authorize judges to apply helpful procedures. In securities class actions, for example, there is a statutory preference for lead plaintiffs with large stakes, who must select and retain class counsel and monitor the progress of the suit. The statutory language creates a presumption in favor of the lawyer and compensation arrangement selected by the lead plaintiff, but also requires judges to review lead plaintiffs' decisions and guard against abuses. Procedural rules may also empower judges to improve the quality of representation. The federal rule governing class actions allows judges to appoint competent counsel and set fee terms at the outset of litigation (when fee awards are authorized by other law). Setting fees by judicial order at or near the start of litigation can motivate class counsel to provide zealous representation, just as setting contingent fees at the outset of ordinary tort cases does. See § 3.13, Comment *c*. Sometimes, judges use their inherent power to manage litigation. In federal multidistrict consolidations, no express rule or statute authorizes judges to appoint or compensate lead attorneys, but a custom of doing so has arisen. In all these situations, the objective is to ensure adequate representation, without which litigants cannot be bound, while pursuing justice under law more efficiently or fairly.

The requirement of adequate representation is a creature of due process that exists in class actions and other representational lawsuits where parties stand in judgment on behalf of others. A party can be bound when given notice and an opportunity to be heard. Speaking generally (and specifically excluding criminal prosecutions and special cases involving persons of deficient capacity), outside of representational lawsuits the law generally assumes that parties always adequately represent themselves. This assumption may be incorrect in non-class aggregate lawsuits because of deficient incentives, conflicts of interests, or other reasons. This Section does not change the law of due process, but it does encourage judges to ensure that all parties and represented persons are represented adequately.

d. *Tools available to encourage adequate representation.* The literature on corporate governance has identified many forces and mechanisms that can help encourage managers to run companies well, including stock markets, reputational damage stemming from business failure, efforts by agents to bond themselves closely to principals, the market for corporate control, fiduciary duties, financial incentives, oversight by third parties, and shareholder empowerment. Many of these forces and mechanisms have analogues that are or could be deployed in aggregate lawsuits with beneficial effects.

This Section identifies some of the tools judges can use in aggregate proceedings to encourage adequate representation. Not all tools are available in all cases. For example, in massive joinder actions, coparties hire lawyers directly. Judges are not ordinarily free to replace chosen lawyers with other lawyers. Nor do they ordinarily have the right to change the compensation terms coparties agreed to pay. These tools are limited to multidistrict consolidations, class actions, and other proceedings where judges are called upon to appoint attorneys or set compensation.

Illustration:

1. Buyer A files a class action alleging antitrust violations against Sellers X, Y, and Z. After news of the lawsuit spreads, Buyer B intervenes and asks to be appointed named plaintiff in place of A. Buyer B contends that it is the largest direct purchaser of the product at issue, suffered the largest damages, and has the largest financial stake in the success of the case. The court has discretion to appoint B, if the appointment would improve the quality of representation provided to the class.

e. When possible, put named parties with sizeable stakes in charge of litigation. The statute governing class-action litigation for securities fraud requires judges to give control of litigation to the "most adequate plaintiff." A presumption exists that the "most adequate plaintiff" is the person who suffered the largest loss.

In many class actions, claim size varies too little to affect the choice of lead plaintiff. This is true, for example, when all represented persons' claims are small. Sometimes, certain class members have much larger stakes than others. In this context, having a lead plaintiff with a large stake can be an advantage, especially if the lead plaintiff is sophisticated in business affairs. When claim size is known to vary, judges should encourage lawyers seeking appointment as lead counsel to obtain at least one client with a sizeable claim.

f. Fiduciary duties. Being agents at common law, lawyers owe clients fiduciary duties and act subject to their control. One consequence of this is that a lawyer cannot help one client by harming another. Another consequence is that a lawyer may not disregard a client's instruction and continue representing the client.

Aggregate representations strain the fiduciary duty and the duty to obey. A lead lawyer must act for the benefit of all parties and represented persons, including those who are not individual clients with whom the lawyer has a direct contractual relationship. A lead lawyer may also have to disobey an instruction from a signed client that, in the lawyer's professional judgment, conflicts with the best interests of the group. In a successful case, a lead lawyer may have to help fashion a plan for allocating the proceeds of a settlement among persons with conflicting interests.

To a degree, then, a lead lawyer in an aggregate proceeding may operate without the usual tethers of loyalty and obedience. Even so, the fiduciary duty retains some content. It requires a lawyer to take all steps that have reasonable potential to make one or more parties or represented persons better off without harming others. Bargaining for the largest possible settlement fund normally satisfies this criterion, as does preparing a case for trial in a manner likely to generate the largest possible award. It also forbids a lead lawyer from advancing his or her own interests by acting to the detriment of the persons on whose behalf the lead lawyer is empowered to act.

Illustrations:

2. Lawyers I, O, and P practice in Indiana, Ohio, and Pennsylvania, respectively. They represent hundreds of clients

with asbestos-related claims against Manufacturer. They then refer the cases to Lawyer T, who practices in Texas. They agree to share fees with T and satisfy all requirements relating to referrals. Unless otherwise agreed with the clients, Lawyers I, O, and P continue to owe the usual lawyerly duties to the clients, and Lawyer T owes the usual lawyerly duties to all the clients referred.

3. Same situation as in Illustration 2, except that instead of referring the cases to Lawyer T, Lawyers I, O, and P hire T to negotiate settlements with Manufacturer, agreeing to pay T five percent of their fees. Lawyers I, O, and P owe the usual lawyerly duties to the clients. Lawyer T may have duties to only the clients, to only Lawyers I, O, and P, or to both, depending on the nature and terms of his agreement with I, O, and P. Lawyers I, O, and P may hire T without establishing client–lawyer relationships between T and all their signed clients.

4. Same situation as in Illustration 2, except the cases being handled by Lawyers I, O, and P are consolidated in a single federal district court by order of the Judicial Panel on Multidistrict Litigation. Thereafter, the judge presiding over the transferee court appoints Lawyer T, who also has cases there, to the position of Lead Counsel. Lawyer T becomes a fiduciary to all plaintiffs and lawyers in the consolidated proceedings and may not use her position to enrich herself at their expense.

Insofar as the fiduciary duty is concerned, then, conventional lawsuits differ from aggregate proceedings in that the latter require lawyers to make some tradeoffs. For this reason, aggregate proceedings also typically contain safeguards not found in conventional lawsuits to help ensure that tradeoffs are made appropriately. In a class action, a lawyer who helps design an allocation plan must submit the plan for judicial approval and must allow class members to comment on it. In a mass lawsuit, a lawyer must obtain the approval of clients pursuant to an aggregate voting rule. See § 3.17. Recognizing that the duty of loyalty is necessarily strained in aggregate proceedings, other tools are employed.

Communication is an important tool for addressing the many departures or deviations from ordinary fiduciary duties that are commonplace in aggregate representations. For example, a lawyer representing many plaintiffs pursuant to separate retainer agreements may have the option of trying one of the cases first. The lawyer should select the case with the greatest potential to increase the value of the entire group of claims; that is, the lawyer should choose the case to be tried with the goal of pursuing the good of all. By doing so, the lawyer would not violate the fiduciary duty, even though the choice may involve a trade-off. Many clients may wish to be first (or may be advantaged by being first), but only one can be. The fiduciary duty does not prevent the lawyer from selecting for the first trial the client who, in the lawyer's reasonable judgment, is most likely to maximize the value of all claims in the group. However, the lawyer should ordinarily communicate with all clients regarding the need to select the test case and explain, insofar as is possible, the basis for the decision. By selecting the client for the first trial for a reason other than the one identified here, a lawyer could potentially breach a fiduciary duty by choosing among clients on a basis that does not benefit the clients in the aggregate. This might be true, for example, if the lawyer chose a client who promised an unusually high fee solely for that reason. A situation involving one plaintiff in a group with a right to trial preference due to ill health raises different considerations not addressed by this Comment.

g. Appoint competent counsel. Procedural rules and related case law require judges to evaluate the competency of attorneys who seek to be appointed class counsel. Although this requirement does not exist in other aggregate proceedings, the considerations that justify it in class actions also apply elsewhere, and judges understandably prefer to appoint outstanding lawyers to lead roles.

Many criteria bear on lead counsel's adequacy, including a track record of success in prior litigation, the number of clients represented and the size of their interests, and counsel's ability to fund litigation. Judges may reasonably require representations concerning these criteria and others, and may review them in camera to avoid disclosure of sensitive information in a manner that either embarrasses the attorney or compromises work product.

h. Fee awards and incentive bonuses. When hiring agents directly, principals often use compensation arrangements to motivate them to perform well. Clients shopping in the market for legal services do this when hiring lawyers. Frequently, clients seeking representation as plaintiffs offer lawyers contingent-percentage fees, while clients seeking representation as defendants pay lawyers by the hour or use other approaches. Plaintiffs' decision to use contingent fees reflects many factors, including the desire to align lawyers' interests with clients', to reduce the clients' need to monitor the conduct of the litigation, and to make lawyers responsible for risks associated with the use of legal services. These functions are especially important when plaintiffs have difficulty monitoring lawyers' conduct directly, as they often do.

In mass actions, clients set lawyers' fees directly and always pay contingent-percentage fees. Judges normally respect these agreements. In other aggregate proceedings, such as class actions, contracting is not possible. Yet, fees must be paid and costs must be reimbursed if lawyers are to represent others zealously. Others must set lawyers' fees when clients cannot. Historically, judges set compensation terms in aggregate proceedings. The federal class-action rule recognizes this responsibility explicitly. In securities class actions, Congress shifted primary control of fees to lead plaintiffs. It gave judges the back-up role of assuring that lead counsel is not overpaid.

Because fees have significant potential to harmonize the interests of lawyers and represented persons, judges can help ensure adequate representation by choosing fee formulas wisely. In this endeavor, judges should take guidance from the private market; they should attempt to employ the same fee and cost arrangements represented persons would use if they could hire lawyers directly. This requires the use of contingent-percentage compensation in claimant representations. It also argues strongly for setting fees as early as possible in litigation. See § 3.13(d).

No fee arrangement can align the interests of principals and agents perfectly, however, because an agent always receives only a fraction of the return on effort and may be able to force the principal to bear all or part of the cost of poor performance. Consequently, under any fee arrangement, opportunities may arise for an agent to benefit himself or herself by expending less effort or bearing less risk than a principal rationally wants. To ensure adequate representation, judges must use other tools in addition to thoughtful fee arrangements.

Named or lead parties must also be incentivized to represent others well. When these parties have large interests that overlap strongly with the interests of represented persons, self-interest should motivate good representation. By acting in ways that help themselves, these parties should help others automatically. Even then, however, it may be desirable to encourage them to bear burdens they would not ordinarily shoulder if only their own interests were at stake. Even a person with a large interest might not want to monitor counsel closely over litigation lasting for years.

Judges have encouraged lead parties to invest more heavily in litigation by reimbursing them for expenses incurred and time expended at reasonable hourly rates. This practice has a simple economic justification. Part of the justification is comparable to the practice, common in many states, of providing incentive bonuses for named plaintiffs and other class members whose participation contributes importantly to a successful result, and who must on occasion bear additional responsibilities and face the possibility of the adverse demands and consequences of being a named party to litigation. Such bonuses, however, should not be an incentive for securing the acquiescence of either the lead parties or the named class members on a basis adverse to the interests of the aggregated group as a whole.

i. Require notice and other communications. Technological advances have made it easier and less expensive for lawyers to communicate with clients and class members. Many lawyers now regard communicating by e-mail and via websites as standard practice techniques. They post important documents online, provide periodic updates on the progress of litigation, comment on press coverage, and disseminate other information broadly. It is often far more cost-effective to communicate with clients electronically than to do so by mail.

In large cases, lawyers also establish phone banks, enabling clients or class members to talk with operators trained to answer their questions. These operations are much more expensive than electronic communications. Consequently, lawyers usually reserve them for major developments, mainly settlements.

The duty to communicate requires lawyers to give clients all the information they reasonably need to make informed decisions. Lawyers who wish to lead aggregate proceedings must be prepared to satisfy this duty. Few communications may be warranted in class actions and other proceedings where individuals' claims are small and represented persons are generally passive. Higher levels of communication are appropriate in other contexts. See § 2.07, Comment *f.*

j. Permit opt-outs. Ordinarily, clients can discharge attorneys at will. Some aggregate proceedings impair this ability. For example, absent class members cannot fire class counsel. Nor can plaintiffs in consolidations fire attorneys other than their own who are appointed by judges to lead roles. Because the power to discharge counsel is impaired, lawyers are freed from the discipline imposed by the possibility of being discharged. The inability of clients to terminate their representation by lawyers requires that courts offer other means of escape from unwanted representation. The most common mechanism is to permit class members to opt out of the class action before being bound by litigation or settlement.

k. Use case-management techniques to ameliorate significant conflicts. Many procedures exist for improving the caliber of representation in aggregate lawsuits. Some, such as consolidation and cooperation among judges in different courts, work by broadening the scope of aggregate proceedings. Others, such as severance and subclassing, narrow that scope by separating issues or subgroups for independent consideration. Because the latter procedures reduce the economies of scale available in aggregate proceedings, judges must use them with caution. Severance and subclassing should generally be used only to address conflicts on central issues or to facilitate the development of issues that, being unique to certain individuals, are unlikely to be addressed otherwise.

REPORTERS' NOTES

Comment a. A foundational insight of the economic literature on agency relationships is that ownership of assets and control of their disposition must often be separated to achieve economies of scale, to take advantage of the division and specialization of labor, to bear risks efficiently, and to realize other advantages. Equally basic, however, is the understanding that when ownership and control of assets are divided, managers predictably lack incentives to maximize asset values and may even gain by acting to owners' detriment. On the advantages and disadvantages of the separation of ownership and control, see Eugene F. Fama & Michael C. Jensen, *Separation of Ownership and Control*, 26 J. Law & Econ. 301 (1983); Michael C. Jensen & William H. Meckling, *Theory of the Firm: Managerial Behavior, Agency Costs, and Ownership Structure*, 3 J. Fin. Econ. 305 (1976); Adolf A. Berle & Gardiner C. Means, *The Modern Corporation and Private Property* (1932). On agency problems related to contingent fees in conventional lawsuits, see Geoffrey Miller, *Some Agency Problems in Settlement*, 16 J. Legal Stud. 189, 198–202 (1987). On aggregate proceedings, see John C. Coffee, Jr., *Understanding the Plaintiff's Attorney: The Implications of Economic Theory for Private Enforcement of Law Through Class and Derivative Actions*, 86 Colum. L.

Rev. 669, 712–713 (1986). This Section addresses the problem of agency failure in aggregate proceedings by establishing adequate representation as a goal and by identifying tools that can be used to help ensure it.

Normally, lawsuits have preclusive effects only on parties. However, some proceedings also bind nonparties who are adequately represented. See, e.g., Hansberry v. Lee, 311 U.S. 32 (1940) (discussing requirement of adequate representation in class actions). See also § 1.02 (discussing overlap of interests required for parens patriae actions to preclude subsequent lawsuits by individuals). A duty of adequacy also exists in other proceedings where represented persons may be bound. This is true, for example, in suits brought by conventional fiduciaries, such as trustees. See Restatement Second, Judgments § 41, Reporter's Note ("[C]onventional fiduciaries have a duty of adequate representation comparable to that required in the class suit."); id. § 42 ("A person is not bound by a judgment for or against a party who purports to represent him if ... [t]he representative failed to prosecute or defend the action with due diligence and reasonable prudence, and the opposing party was on notice of facts making that failure apparent."); 18A Charles Alan Wright, Arthur R. Miller & Edward H. Cooper, *Federal*

Practice and Procedure § 4454, 444 (3d ed. 2005) ("A final limitation on preclusion by representation requires that the representative attain some minimal level of adequate representation.").

The recognition of the importance of adequate representation in diverse contexts suggests an underlying "theory of nonparty preclusion that is often identified as 'virtual representation[,]' " the broadest form of which "would preclude relitigation of any issue that had once been adequately tried by a person sharing a substantial identity of interests with a nonparty." Id. § 4457 at 512. The Reporter's Note to the Restatement Second of Judgments § 41 may be said to embrace this theory, and to identify class-action law as its source. For example, it contends that "the matter of representation of holders of future interests is integrated with class suits, in which the representative is recognized as such because of the similarity of his situation and that of the person represented."

In arguing that a deep procedural resemblance to class actions accounts for the practice of binding holders of future interests by the results in suits involving holders of current interests, the Restatement Second of Judgments purports to deviate from the path laid down by the first Restatement, the older document being said to attribute bindingness to the nature of property. See Restatement Second, Judgments § 41, Reporter's Note (contending that "[a] reexamination of the authorities [cited in the Restatement of Judgments § 87] ... indicates that the preclusion of holders of future interests was based on the representative concept rather than doctrine peculiar to future interests as such"). In fact, the position taken

in the Restatement Second is less novel than it may appear. The first Restatement also explicitly connected the class action and the ability to bind nonparties to the results of suits over land and other subject properties.

> [T]he same policy which permits class actions where there is a large class of possible litigants, in order to prevent multiplicity of actions and to give a person threatened with such actions security in acting in accordance with a judicial determination ... operates to permit the rules of res judicata to act for and against persons who have future interests and who cannot be made parties. In both situations persons who are not parties to the action are affected by the judgment. *If there are parties to the litigation who are in positions such that, in order to protect their own interests, they necessarily protect the interests of those not parties, those thus protected are bound by the judgment.*

Restatement of Judgments § 87, Comment *a* (emphasis added). The strong overlap of interests identified in the italicized sentence is a hallmark of adequate representation, which forms the core of class-action law and the general theory of virtual representation. See Hansberry v. Lee, 311 U.S. 32, 41–42 (1940) ("Where the interests of those not joined are of the same class as the interests of those who are, and where it is considered that the latter fairly represent the former in the prosecution of the litigation of the issues in which all have a common interest, the court will proceed to a decree."); id. at 44 ("Because of the dual and potentially conflicting interests of those who are putative parties to the agreement in compelling or resisting its performance, it is impossible to say . . . that any two of them are of the same class. Nor without more, and with the due regard for the protection of the rights of absent parties which due process exacts, can some be permitted to stand in judgment for all."). Evidently, the authors of the first Restatement also recognized the emergence of a general set of principles governing the ability to bind nonparties, the main requirement being adequate representation.

The leading procedure treatise views the general theory of virtual representation with suspicion and cautions against it, warning that "[a]doption of the theory" in its broadest form "could expand nonparty preclusion far beyond current practice." 18A Wright, Miller & Cooper, *Federal Practice and Procedure* § 4457 at 512. After noting that "[v]irtual representation theory has obvious ties not only to general nonparty preclusion doctrines but also to class-action preclusion," the treatise points out that "class-action procedure provides many explicit safeguards designed to ensure adequate representation" and that "[v]irtual-representation theory," by contrast, "has no explicit safeguards." Id. at 514. Other commentators agree. See, e.g., Howard M. Erichson, *Informal Aggregation: Procedural and Ethical Implications of Coordination among Counsel in Related Lawsuits*, 50 Duke L.J. 381, 458–464 (2000) (arguing against "expansive application of the virtual representation doctrine [against nonparties] based on informal aggregation," which would facilitate the "circumvention of protections built into formal aggregation mecha-

nisms, especially the class action rule").

By making adequate representation a goal in all aggregate proceedings, this Section does not create a free-floating, adequate-representation requirement. For example, it does not require judges to force notice procedures used in class actions upon parties to mass actions who have not chosen to employ them. Parties must generally rely on consensual arrangements with their own attorneys and common-law duties to provide representation of the caliber they desire. Nor does this Section encourage judges to override agreements among parties or between parties and lawyers that are intended to govern a representation's progress. A judge who believes that a particular consensual arrangement for handling a representation is unwise may certainly voice the opinion, but no duty to invalidate the arrangement arises under this Section. This Section does not address whether such a duty arises under other law, such as the law governing lawyers.

Comment b. In practice, when large numbers of related claims exist, the choice is not between individual lawsuits with high degrees of control and aggregations; it is between informal aggregations and formal aggregations, in both of which control is necessarily impaired. See Howard M. Erichson, *Informal Aggregation: Procedural and Ethical Implications of Coordination Among Counsel in Related Lawsuits*, 50 Duke L.J. 381, 465–466 (2000) ("Given the powerful drive to coordinate, evidenced by both plaintiffs and defendants in a wide variety of litigation, true litigant autonomy may be unattainable in many situations involving multiple related claims . . . . In other words, the benefits of formal aggregation may come without much loss of litigant autonomy, given the extent to which lawyers coordinate anyway.").

Control varies across forms of litigation.

[E]ach litigant in non-class litigation has an individual attorney-client relationship with a lawyer whom that client retained. In non-class litigation, the explanation goes, litigants and their lawyers make decisions about the conduct of the litigation and the course of settlement negotiations.... In theory, the client in non-class litigation can protect her own interests by stating her objectives, monitoring her lawyer's conduct, and above all, making her own decisions about whether and on what terms to settle. In a class action, absent class members lack the same ability to protect their own interests. Thus, class actions provide a number of procedural safeguards, including judicial supervision of settlement and fees, as well as a requirement of adequate representation: a court certifies the class only if the court is satisfied that the class representatives and class counsel will adequately represent the class as a whole.

Howard M. Erichson, *Beyond the Class Action: Lawyer Loyalty and Client Autonomy in Non–Class Collective Representation*, 2003 U. Chi. Legal F. 519, 523–524.

The following table classifies aggregate lawsuits according to their tendency to enable persons who stand to be bound to control the terms of their representation.

Table 1: Types of Lawsuits Arranged by Level of Control Exercised by Parties and Nonparty Claimants and Respondents

Extensive Control	Moderate Control	Minimal Control
Joinder Actions	Single District Consolidation	Class Actions
Interpleader	Multidistrict Consolidation	Parens Patriae
Representation by Agent	Representation by Trustee or Other Fiduciary	Virtual Representation

In aggregate lawsuits where the degree of control is high, participants possess the same powers and responsibilities as parties to conventional cases. In theory, they can set terms for collective action as well. When control is minimal, participants (sometimes including named parties) can decide neither how their individual claims or defenses will be litigated nor how the larger group will be run. Usually, represented persons can express themselves only by staying in or opting out, by filing or refusing to file claims, and by objecting or remaining silent. By comparison to the tools parties possess in conventional lawsuits, none of these options is especially efficacious. Cases with moderate control afford participants some important powers but deny them others. For example, they continue to be represented by their own attorneys, and they can accept settlement offers or reject them. But, in important respects, they are also at the mercy of others. They cannot escape aggregation, even when it occurs against their wishes, and, except when they serve as lead parties, they must accept services from and pay fees to lawyers and other persons they have little power to control.

The decision to permit aggregation often leads to other decisions that limit participants' control. For example, judges presiding over consolidated proceedings often appoint lead lawyers and give them control of pleadings, discovery, and settlement. This practice impairs the ability of parties represented by non-lead attorneys to control events, and forces all parties into groupings they did not choose. Even so, it is acceptable when and because it is advantageous.

Comment c. Quality representation is a critical component of the procedural system, without which the system cannot efficiently compensate injuries or deter misconduct. The adversarial process operates on two assumptions. The first, that trial outcomes will be unbiased, means that they will tend to attach legally appropriate values to claims and that deviations from appropriate values (errors) will not systematically favor particular interests. The second assumption is that the predictability of unbiased trial outcomes will enable opposing parties to settle "in the shadow of the law" at prices reflecting those courts would attach. When

these assumptions are met, the procedural system can generate appropriate levels of compensation and deterrence automatically, that is, with little active intervention by courts.

By saying that the procedural system operates on the assumption that claim values are unbiased, we do not mean to imply that the assumption is always correct. We are well aware of the literature arguing that the "haves" come out ahead, and do not deny that repeat players enjoy significant advantages in litigation. We also recognize that many claims are too small to justify the cost of litigation and that many claimants cannot afford to pay lawyers other than on contingency. Two important functions of aggregation are to level the playing field on which claimants and respondents compete and to make small claims viable by taking advantage of economies of scale.

The need to ensure adequate representation may be particularly great in judicial aggregations. For example, the procedures judges deploy in multidistrict consolidations, including procedures assigning responsibilities for services and allocating costs and fees, have the potential to influence representation quality and should be designed to encourage adequate representation.

Since the enactment of the Private Securities Litigation Reform Act of 1995, many courts have recognized a presumption arising in favor of a lead plaintiff's choice of counsel and compensation arrangement. See, e.g., In re Cendant Corp. Litig., 264 F.3d 201, 282 (3d Cir. 2001) (affording "a presumption of reasonableness to any fee request submitted pursuant to a retainer agreement that was entered into between a properly-selected lead plaintiff and a properly-selected lead counsel," thereby ensuring "that the lead plaintiff, not the court, functions as the class's primary agent vis-à-vis its lawyers"). See also In re AT & T Corp., 455 F.3d 160 (3d Cir. 2006); In re Rite Aid Corp. Sec. Litig., 396 F.3d 294 (3d Cir. 2005); In re EVCI Career Colleges Holding Corp. Sec. Litig., Nos. 05 Civ. 10240 (CM) et al., 2007 WL 2230177 (S.D.N.Y. July 27, 2007); Schwartz v. TXU Corp., Nos. 3:02–CV–2243–K et al., 2005 WL 3148350 (N.D. Tex. Nov. 8, 2005); In Re WorldCom Inc. Sec. Litig., 388 F.Supp.2d 319 (S.D.N.Y. 2005); In re Global Crossing Sec. & ERISA Litig., 225 F.R.D. 436 (S.D.N.Y. 2004); In re Lucent Tech., Inc. Sec. Litig., 327 F.Supp.2d 426 (D.N.J. 2004). Respect for agreements between sophisticated lead plaintiffs and attorneys "reflects the reality that prices are best set by buyers and sellers bargaining in competitive environments." Charles Silver, *Reasonable Attorneys' Fees in Securities Class Actions: A Reply to Mr. Schneider*, 20:3 The NAPPA Report 7, 7 (Aug. 2006).

On the judicial power to appoint and compensate lead attorneys in multidistrict consolidations, see Manual for Complex Litigation (Fourth) §§ 10.22 & 22.6 (2004). For a criticism of emerging judicial practices, see Charles Silver & Geoffrey P. Miller, *The Quasi–Class Action Method of Managing Multi–District Litigations: Problems and a Proposal*, 63 Vand. L. Rev. 107 (2010); for a defense of judicial oversight of non-class aggregation, see Samuel Issacharoff, *Private Claims, Aggregate Rights*, 2008 Sup. Ct. Rev. 183.

The judicial power to appoint lead counsel (or to ratify a lead plaintiff's choice of class counsel) should not entitle a judge to override a party's decision to hire a lawyer for him- or herself or serve as a general expansion of the scope of judicial control over the attorney–client relationship. Nor should the power ordinarily authorize a judge to discharge a lawyer who has been contractually engaged by a party. The power should be limited to the appointment and termination of lawyers who are to handle responsibilities for and on behalf of an aggregation.

Comment d. This Section identifies the tools that are available to promote adequate representation. The tools are costly to employ and imperfect in operation. Consequently, some positive level of opportunism will prevail even when all means of combating it are efficiently deployed.

The key difference between aggregations in which participants enjoy extensive, moderate, and minimal control concerns participants' ability to use the market for legal services and otherwise to plan for collective action in advance. In cases offering extensive control, participants can shop for lawyers and plan, and they can do so knowing that anyone can back out unless working arrangements satisfactory to all are designed. In moderate-control settings, participants can shop for good lawyers to represent them personally, but they are also thrust into groups from which they cannot withdraw. They and their lawyers retain some freedom to decide how these involuntary collective actions will run, but they must bargain with each other knowing that judges will impose order on them if they fail to agree. In minimal-control settings, participants cannot practicably use the market or plan for collective action in advance, because their claims are too small, because they are too widely dispersed, or for other reasons.

Agreements governing the rights and duties of the clients inter se have been reported in several cases. In Hayes v. Eagle–Picher Industries, 513 F.2d 892 (10th Cir. 1975), 18 clients who retained a common lawyer agreed to decide whether to settle as a group by a majority rule. In Abbott v. Kidder Peabody & Co., 42 F.Supp.2d 1046 (D. Col. 1999), a securities-fraud lawsuit involving more than 100 sophisticated investors, the retainer agreement provided for collective control of the lawsuit in many ways, including management by a steering committee, fee and cost sharing, a formula for dividing settlement proceeds, and penalties to discourage opt-outs and individual settlements. In Tax Authority, Inc. v. Jackson Hewitt, Inc., 873 A.2d 616 (N.J. Super. Ct. App. Div. 2005), 154 operators of tax-preparation franchises signed retainer agreements creating a steering committee for the litigation and providing that the decision to settle would be made by a weighted majority of the clients. This limited case experience may have helped provide a model for collective control and disposition of aggregate proceedings, as discussed in § 3.16 et seq. However, the decision below was reversed and remanded by the New Jersey Supreme Court in an interesting opinion. The court found the use of the plaintiffs' steering committee to violate the New Jersey application of the aggregate-settlement rule, but applied its ruling prospectively only, and upheld the enforcement of the settlement as a matter of equity. The court then referred the question of the continued application of the aggregate-settlement rule to the Commission on Ethics Reform for reconsideration of the entire rule, with a request for further review to be submitted to the court. The court expressly relied on the academic commentary and concerns addressed in § 3.15 et seq. as the basis for its request for reexamination. See Tax Auth., Inc. v. Jackson Hewitt, Inc., 898 A.2d 512, 521, 523 (N.J. 2006).

Comment e. The modern securities class action operates on the premise that self-interest will motivate sophisticated lead plaintiffs with sizeable stakes to reduce agency costs in class actions by selecting good lawyers, incentivizing them appropriately, and monitoring their performance. Other shareholders can then free-ride on lead plaintiffs' efforts, enjoying the benefits of well-run litigation conducted on behalf of all without incurring significant additional costs.

The insight that self-interest may cause named parties with sizeable stakes to run aggregate lawsuits well is not limited to securities class actions. See, e.g., Sandwich Chef of Texas, Inc. v. Reliance Nat'l Indem. Ins. Co., 202 F.R.D. 484, 493–494 (S.D. Tex. 2001) (RICO fraud class action in which court commented positively on the large size of the named plaintiff's claim), rev'd on other grounds, 319 F.3d 205 (5th Cir. 2003). Consequently, when suitable candidates are available, it may be desirable to put other aggregate lawsuits under their control as well. Obviously, this option will not exist in many consumer-protection lawsuits and other cases involving solely participants with small claims.

Comment f. Agents are subject to a variety of legal duties, some of which derive from contracts and some of which have other sources, such as agency law. See generally Restatement Third, The Law Governing

Lawyers. In aggregate lawsuits, lawyers and named parties always owe duties to clients and other participants, the sources of which may include (without limitation) contracts, agency law, rules of professional responsibility, rules of civil procedure, court orders, and statutes. Some of these duties give rise to claims for damages when breached. Others are enforced by courts, which may, for example, discharge noncompliant attorneys or reduce their fees. Some duties are mainly hortatory or aspirational. They establish norms to which lawyers as professionals are drawn even when these norms are not backed by penalties.

A lawyer who participates in an attorney–client relationship with every participant has the usual duties—including loyalty, obedience, communication, and confidentiality—unless an agreement limiting them is in place.

The matter is more complex when a lawyer participates in attorney–client relationships with some participants but not others. In the simplest such case, the lawyer owes the clients the customary duties and owes the nonclients whatever duties are voluntarily incurred. For example, a lawyer participating in a joint-defense group may have a duty not to share information received from a nonclient cooperating defendant or to refrain from using such information to the nonclient's detriment without its consent. These duties are spelled out in a contract and possibly supplemented by common law.

In other aggregate proceedings, lawyers' duties to nonclients have noncontractual sources. In consolidations, judges often appoint lawyers to positions of responsibility. These appointments both empower and obligate the chosen lawyers to act for other parties, such as by taking discovery that all parties can share. The source of these rights and responsibilities is the common law of consolidations, usually deriving ultimately from procedural rules or statutes, which enables judges to manage these proceedings. In class actions, lawyers appointed as class counsel become fiduciaries for all class members. They may even acquire responsibilities to absent claimants that trump their duties to their signed clients, the named parties. See Fed. R. Civ. P. 23(g)(1), advisory committee's note ("Appointment as class counsel means that the primary obligation of counsel is to the class rather than to any individual members of it. The class representatives do not have an unfettered right to 'fire' class counsel. In the same vein, the class representatives cannot command class counsel to accept or reject a settlement proposal. To the contrary, class counsel must determine whether seeking the court's approval of a settlement would be in the best interests of the class as a whole.").

Comment g. Lawyers handle aggregate proceedings on contingency: they must win to be paid. Because aggregate proceedings are expensive, they saddle lawyers with sizeable risks that are hard to diversify. A lawyer who handles conventional cases manages a portfolio of small risks each of which involves a small investment. Although the outcome in any particular case may be hard to predict, the cases as a group can be expected to generate a reliable income stream. By contrast, a lawyer involved in an aggregate lawsuit manages a single risk in which a great deal is at stake. Few lawyers can afford to run this risk and lose more than a few times. Failure should therefore drive less-able plaintiffs' lawyers out of the aggregate-lawsuit business and discourage many such lawyers from entering this practice area to begin with.

The law of class actions makes experience a factor for judges to consider when assessing the adequacy of class counsel. Some commentators have derided the experience criterion, pointing out (correctly) that the vast majority of lawyers who offer themselves as candidates for the position of class counsel have track records of success in large lawsuits. This criticism does not show that past successes are unimportant. It rather shows that litigation failure (or the threat thereof) is narrowing the pool of candidates by weeding out lawyers who fail (or fear they will).

The valid point of the criticism of the experience factor is that experience by itself often provides an insufficient basis for choosing among competing attorneys, all of whom will have settled sizeable cases or, much less often, won them at trial. A track record of success can be at most a necessary condition for appointment to the class-counsel post, not a sufficient one.

Lawyers involved in aggregate proceedings sometimes flounder. These attorneys can be replaced or supplemented by new counsel. In the famous "Agent Orange" case, the lawyers initially in charge of the purported class action ran out of money and sought the assistance of new investor-lawyers, who provided a much-needed infusion of litigation resources. In effect, the new lawyers bought control of the case from the old lawyers by assuming responsibility for the cash flow of the litigation. The purchase price consisted of (1) the agreed share of the eventual contingent-fee award (if any) the old lawyers would receive, plus (2) the resources (including both money and time) the new lawyers committed to the case (which made the case viable, increasing the expected size of (1)), minus (3) the resources (again including money and time) the old lawyers agreed to provide in the future (which also made the case viable and reduced the burden on the new attorneys). In practical effect, the new lawyers acquired control of the assets (the participants' claims and the existing work product) and determined how, going forward, they would be used. The particular fee-sharing agreement employed was struck down on conflict-of-interest grounds. See In re "Agent Orange" Prod. Liab. Litig., 818 F.2d 216 (2d Cir. 1987).

All aggregate lawsuits require claimants' lawyers to bear the risk of exhausting their resources and having to beg for help in the capital market. Because the market will predictably offer poor terms, lawyers have incentives to select large cases with care and to plan for their economic needs in advance. Typically, planning involves the creation of a team of attorneys who will provide diverse inputs, including financial resources sufficient to fund a case. To assemble a team, a lawyer must convince other attorneys that a case can be litigated to a successful resolution within the budget assigned. (Attorney teams also provide other advantages, including internal monitoring.)

Comment h. In many representations, fees provide the strongest inducement for lawyers to provide high-quality service. This seems plainly true in claimant representations where lawyers work for contingent-percentage fees. The attractiveness of this form of fee derives largely (but not exclusively) from the strength of the bond it creates between an agent's self-interest and a principal's wellbeing. This connection makes contingent-percentage fees especially attractive to clients, like many tort claimants, who cannot evaluate the quality of lawyers' efforts easily and for whom the burdens of monitoring what level of expenditure is necessary would be overwhelming. In effect, these clients pay a premium for high-quality service because it is better for them to do so than to bear the burden of monitoring that would exist if the premium were withheld.

In many aggregate proceedings, participants and lawyers agree on fees contractually. Judges should honor these private arrangements in the vast majority of cases. The market for legal services is highly competitive. "No law firm supplies more than a tiny fraction of the nation's legal services (even of the specialized submarket in big-stakes litigation)." In re Synthroid Marketing Litig., 325 F.3d 974, 979 (7th Cir. 2003) (Synthroid II). A strong presumption should therefore exist that the private market prices legal services efficiently.

This Section takes the position that judges should mimic the market when setting fees in class actions and other contexts where lawyer and clients cannot bargain directly. This recommendation follows existing precedent in the Seventh Circuit and other courts. See, e.g., *Synthroid II*, 325 F.3d at 975 ("A court must give counsel the market rate for legal services"); In re Synthroid Marketing Litig., 264 F.3d 712, 718 (7th Cir. 2001) (Synthroid I) ("[W]hen deciding

on appropriate fee levels in common-fund cases, courts must do their best to award counsel the market price for legal services, in light of the risk of nonpayment and the normal rate of compensation in the market at the time."); In re Continental Illinois Sec. Litig., 962 F.2d 566, 568, 572 (7th Cir. 1992) (Continental I) ("[I]t is not the function of judges in fee litigation to determine the equivalent of the medieval just price. It is to determine what the lawyer would receive if he were selling his services in the market rather than being paid by court order.... [C]lass counsel are entitled to the fee they would have received had they handled a similar suit on a contingent fee basis, with a similar outcome, for a paying client.").

In the private market where clients directly hire lawyers on contingency, contingent-percentage fees are standard. See Kirchoff v. Flynn, 786 F.2d 320 (7th Cir. 1986); see also Herbert M. Kritzer, *Risks, Reputations, and Rewards: Contingency Fee Legal Practice in the United States* (2004). Contingent-percentage-fee arrangements dominate the market because (1) they align the interests of claimants and lawyers by rewarding superior performance and punishing failure, (2) they minimize the need to evaluate the reasonableness of attorneys' efforts ex post, which is both time consuming and often difficult, and (3) they transfer the burden of financing lawsuits and other risks lawsuits entail from claimants to attorneys who are better able to bear them.

In keeping with the recommendation of the Seventh Circuit and the empirical evidence, this Section recommends the use of contingent-percentage compensation in aggregate proceedings where lawyers and clients cannot bargain directly. It also recommends that percentages be set as nearly as possible at market rates. To accomplish this, judges must consider empirical evidence on the size of percentage fees. Procedures and standards relating to fee awards are discussed in § 3.13.

On incentive bonuses for named plaintiffs, see Theodore Eisenberg & Geoffrey P. Miller, *Incentive Awards to Class Action Plaintiffs: An Empirical Study*, 53 UCLA L. Rev. 1303 (2006); Richard A. Nagareda, *Restitution, Rent Extraction, and Class Representatives: Implications of Incentive Awards*, 53 UCLA L. Rev. 1483 (2006); see also 15 U.S.C. § 78u-4(a) (Private Securities Litigation Reform Act of 1995, eliminating incentive bonuses in securities lawsuits, but allowing awards intended to reimburse lead plaintiffs' reasonable costs and expenses). Incentive bonuses vary greatly in amount, but can be sizeable. Reimbursements for legal plaintiffs in securities-fraud cases can also be large, especially when lead plaintiffs are sophisticated institutional investors with in-house legal staffs. Although standards for these bonuses and reimbursements are evolving, the purpose in awarding them should be to make it economically advantageous for potential named plaintiffs to volunteer to serve in class actions. Without these payments, potential lead plaintiffs often find it economically advantageous to wait for others to sue and free-ride on their efforts, or to file conventional lawsuits of benefit to themselves alone. Incentive bonuses and expense reimbursements provide selective incentives available only to named plaintiffs in class actions. See Jay W. Eisenhofer, *Institutional Investors as Trend–Setters in Post–PSLRA Securities Litigation*,

PLI Order No. 8588 579, 590–593 (July 2006) (discussing pros and cons for institutional investors of opting out of class actions and suing alone); James D. Cox & Randall S. Thomas with Dana Kiku, *Does the Plaintiff Matter? An Empirical Analysis of Lead Plaintiffs in Securities Class Actions*, 106 Colum. L. Rev. 1587, 1604 (2006) ("Institutional investors with large potential claims have sometimes found it more advantageous to act for themselves rather than on behalf of all other investors.").

Comment i. In many contexts, principals encourage agents to perform well by monitoring them. In aggregate proceedings, the utility of monitoring may be limited, for several reasons. First, the quality of lawyers' effort is often difficult to observe. Second, many aggregate proceedings, such as consumer-protection class actions, contain persons who lack the litigation experience needed to monitor lawyers effectively. Many aggregate lawsuits also involve solely or mainly persons whose claims are too small to justify the expense monitoring entails. Third, the private cost of monitoring may exceed the expected private return. The economically rational strategy for any individual may be to rely on others to monitor, so as to gain the benefit of improving agent performance without bearing the cost of the necessary monitoring. See Wayne Schneider, *An Obligation to Pursue Litigation? Really?*, NAPPA Report (1997); Wayne Schneider, *Objections to Attorneys Fee Requests in Securities Class Actions*, 19:1 NAPPA Report 9, 10 (Feb. 2005) (arguing that pension funds with large stakes in securities class actions should free-ride rather than serve as lead plaintiffs because the marginal cost of active involvement exceeds the marginal gain). Of course, if everyone free-rides, no monitoring occurs, and lawyers can underperform.

For monitoring to occur, interested persons must receive relevant information about the progress of litigation. When it is expensive to provide this information, the cost bears on the amount of communication that should occur. The likely effectiveness of communicating should also be considered. Communication should be encouraged when it is likely to enable recipients to make informed decisions and when it is likely to generate informed responses. Otherwise, communication is simply a burden. In aggregate proceedings involving large numbers of persons, lawyers should be encouraged to use low-cost methods of communicating routine information. Expensive methods should be employed only when fundamental matters are at hand, such as communications about settlement or required discovery responses.

Chapter 2

AGGREGATE ADJUDICATION

TOPIC 1. INTRODUCTORY PROVISIONS

TOPIC 1

INTRODUCTORY PROVISIONS

§ 2.01 Definition of Common Issues

Common issues are those legal or factual issues that are the same in functional content across multiple civil claims, regardless of whether their disposition would resolve all contested issues in the litigation.

Comment:

a. The basis for common issues. Modern industrial society and the active role of government give rise to complex relationships among individuals. These relationships extend beyond direct contractual interactions to relationships through commonly shared institutions, such as markets for goods or services or the institutions of government itself. As a result, conduct that results in civil wrongdoing as to one person has the potential to give rise to claims by other persons that exhibit both common and individual features.

b. Relationship to substantive law. The legal and factual issues involved in any individual civil claim are a function of applicable substantive law. Legal issues concern the elements that properly constitute the plaintiff's claim and applicable defenses. Factual issues concern disputes about whether the evidence at trial demonstrates, under the applicable standard of proof, the existence of a given element. In casting the definition of common issues in terms of whether they are "the same in functional content across multiple civil claims," this Section casts the inquiry in the manner of the familiar insistence upon the "same issue" for purposes of issue preclusion. At the same time, this Section emphasizes the connection in practical operation between factual issues and the proof that bears thereon. A factual issue may rise to the level of a common issue if, subject to the constraints of § 2.05 concerning choice of law, a common body of evidence to be presented on behalf of multiple claimants at trial is capable of proving the existence of a material fact as to all such claimants.

Illustrations:

1. Multiple persons, 1–100, have claims for fraud against the defendant. Applicable substantive law includes a reliance element as part of all claimants' cause of action for fraud, and no presumption of reliance arises from the fact of misrepresentation by the defendant. Applicable substantive law instead requires that each claimant prove actual reliance upon the defendant's alleged misrepresentations. All claimants nonetheless seek to prove actual reliance through a common body of evidence, and that body of evidence, if believed by the factfinder, is capable of proving reliance on the part of all claimants. The defendant disputes the common body of evidence offered by claimants but, in so doing, the defendant offers no individualized evidence of nonreliance on the part of particular claimants. The factual issue of reliance constitutes a common issue across all claimants.

Before affording aggregate treatment, however, the court should ensure that the additional constraints on aggregation stated in this Chapter are satisfied. In particular, the court should ensure that aggregate treatment does not compromise the ability of the defendant to dispute the allegations made by claimants or to raise pertinent substantive defenses. See § 2.07(d). The court also should ascertain whether the use of a common body of evidence to prove actual reliance would give rise to a structural conflict of interest among the claimants that could not be mitigated by appropriate case-management instructions or the ability to opt out. For example, some class members could be prejudiced if class treatment of their claims deprived them of an opportunity to strengthen their case on the reliance element through the invocation of individualized evidence. See generally § 2.07(a)(1)(B) (underscoring the need for judicial inquiry into the existence of structural conflicts of interest within the proposed class).

2. Same situation as in Illustration 1, except that the common body of evidence, even if accepted as true by the factfinder upon consideration of any contrary evidence offered by the defendant, is not capable of proving reliance on the part of all claimants. The factual issue of reliance does not constitute a common issue across all claimants. See also § 2.03, Illustration 2.

3. Same situation as in Illustration 1, except that the defendant offers individualized evidence of widespread nonreliance on the part of particular claimants. The factual issue of reliance does not constitute a common issue across all claimants.

c. *Relationship to individual issues.* The definition of common issues in this Section proceeds in contrast to individual issues. To be sure, multiple civil claims may exhibit recurring individual issues in the sense of the same legal elements that multiple civil claimants must satisfy. But those recurring individual issues nevertheless do not rise to the level of common issues within the meaning of this Section. Common issues both recur across multiple civil claims and are the same in functional content in the sense of calling for the same legal and factual determinations for their resolution. As a matter of broad generalization in light of accumulated, real-world experience with class actions, common issues will tend to arise more frequently with respect to "upstream" matters focused on a generally applicable course of conduct on the part of those opposing the claimants in the litigation rather than on "downstream" matters centered upon the individual situations of those claimants themselves. Similarly—again, as a matter of broad generalization from experience—common issues will tend to arise more frequently with respect to economic injuries from a generally applicable course of conduct than with regard to personal injuries, as to which the "upstream" inquiry likely would not materially advance the disposition of claims.

Illustration:

4. Multiple consumers, 1–100, have claims against defendants Alpha Corporation and Beta Corporation. The claims of all consumers rest upon allegations that Alpha and Beta entered into an agreement to fix the prices of their competing consumer products in violation of federal antitrust law and that the alleged agreement raised prices for all consumers above competitive levels. Whether Alpha and Beta, in fact, entered into such an agreement would constitute a common issue across all consumers. How to measure the damages suffered by consumers—that is, the method for the calculation of damages—also would constitute a common issue across all consumers. How much in the way of damages each consumer should receive in the event of a showing of unlawful price-fixing presents a recurring individual issue across all claimants in the sense that their respective causes of action all have damages as one of their elements. But that issue does not constitute a common issue. Rather, questions surrounding the calculation of damages for consumers turn upon the particular factual situation of each (such as the volume of purchases made) and thus do not call for the same factual determination across all consumers.

The contrast drawn between common issues and individual issues nonetheless remains distinct from the question whether to afford aggregate treatment for a common issue. As discussed in § 2.02(a), the aggregation decision turns not simply on the presence of a common issue as defined here but also on several additional inquiries, including whether aggregate treatment of that issue will materially advance the resolution of the implicated claims and whether such treatment will conform to the principles set forth in §§ 1.03–1.05. Subsequent Sections describe additional limitations on aggregation that warrant judicial attention before aggregate treatment is afforded.

d. Related claims. As Comment *c* implies and as the black letter of this Section underscores, the disposition of common issues need not necessarily resolve all contested issues in the litigation. Individual issues may remain. Multiple civil claims nonetheless are appropriately described as "related claims" when they exhibit overlapping legal and factual features that give rise to a common nucleus of operative fact.

Aggregate treatment of related claims may be appropriate, as described in § 2.07. Aggregate treatment of related claims nonetheless remains distinct from aggregate treatment as to only a common issue, a procedure discussed separately in § 2.08. Aggregate treatment of a common issue by way of a class action under § 2.08 would generate only issue preclusion, with the remaining issues in the litigation to be addressed in subsequent proceedings. By contrast, aggregate treatment of related claims by way of a class action under § 2.07 would generate both issue preclusion and claim preclusion, for the aggregate proceeding would encompass all contested issues in the litigation.

  e. Handling individual issues efficiently. Despite failing to qualify as common issues, individual issues nonetheless may possess features that facilitate their efficient handling on an aggregate basis. This may be true when a common scientific, economic, or other method exists for the calculation of damages, such as to reduce to a ministerial exercise the calculation for a given claimant. For further discussion, see § 2.03, Comment *c.* Situations in which individual issues may be handled efficiently on an aggregate basis are among the most frequently encountered settings for aggregate treatment of related claims, as described in § 2.07. Here, again, as a matter of broad generalization from experience, such situations tend to arise with regard to claims of economic injury rather than personal injury.

REPORTERS' NOTES

Comment b. Illustration 1 stems from the treatment in Klay v. Humana, Inc., 382 F.3d 1241, 1258–1259 (11th Cir. 2004), of common evidence capable of proving reliance on the part of all class members in connection with fraud-based claims under the federal Racketeer Influenced and Corrupt Organizations Act (RICO) in class-action litigation concerning the reimbursement practices of the managed-care industry. Illustration 2 stems from Poulos v. Caesars World, Inc., 379 F.3d 654, 667–668 (9th Cir. 2004), in which a common body of evidence—even if accepted as true by the factfinder—would not have proven reliance on the part of all class members in the context of RICO-based fraud claims concerning video gambling machines due to the individualized and perhaps idiosyncratic reasons why casino patrons might choose to gamble.

  Speaking to the use of common evidence in the context of a motion for certification of an antitrust class action, the Third Circuit succinctly captured the distinction drawn here between the results in *Klay* and *Poulos*:

> Plaintiffs' burden at the class certification stage is not to prove the element of antitrust impact.... Instead, the task for plaintiffs at class certification is to demonstrate that the element of antitrust impact is *capable of proof* at trial through evidence that is common to the class rather than individual to its members. Deciding this issue calls for the district court's rigorous assessment of the available evidence and the method or methods by which plaintiffs propose to use the evidence to prove impact at trial.

In re Hydrogen Peroxide Antitrust Litig., 552 F.3d 305, 311–312 (3d Cir. 2008) (emphasis added).

Illustration 3 stems from In re St. Jude Medical, Inc., 522 F.3d 836, 840 (8th Cir. 2008) ("Given the showing by [defendant] St. Jude that it will present evidence concerning the reliance or non-reliance of individual physicians and patients on representations made by St. Jude [concerning its prosthetic heart valve], it is clear that resolution of St. Jude's potential liability to each plaintiff under the consumer-fraud statutes will be dominated by individual issues of causation and reliance. The need for such plaintiff-by-plaintiff determinations means that common issues will not predominate the inquiry into St. Jude's liability.").

Comment c. On the contrast in suitability for aggregate treatment between "upstream" and "downstream" matters and between economic and personal injuries:

It is possible to divide the successful and unsuccessful class actions [in the sense of those that succeed in garnering aggregate treatment] by separating the cases involving economic harms on the one side from personal injuries on the other. Nonetheless, there is something more to be learned from this than simply the distinction between economic harms and personal injuries.

It turns out, perhaps not surprisingly, that courts are at their best in finding and handling facts. The further we stray from that basic role of courts as fact finders, the more problems we have. The reason that the economic harm cases are basically manageable [on an aggregate basis] by the courts is that there are only a few critical facts that dominate the whole case. These are what can be thought of as

the upstream cases; that is, cases when the harm is alleged to be some uniform course of conduct by the defendant, from which everything else follows. Usually the damages can be calculated administratively, with each plaintiff receiving a pro rata share of compensation for some particularized kind of harm should the plaintiffs prevail.

On the other hand, there are the personal injury cases. What distinguishes these is not that they sound in tort, but rather the fact that the upstream inquiry is not dispositive. In cases such as asbestos, for example, even if there is a common upstream inquiry into the fact that asbestos exposure causes asbestosis, there is an immediate need to shift downstream and find fact after fact with regard to each individual plaintiff. The caselaw history shows that no court has been able to handle that in one proceeding. The caselaw history cautions that the further we stray from that which courts could administer in their fact-finding capacity, the worse off we are. The general line of demarcation seems to be that the upstream liability cases are manageable as class actions; the downstream harm cases are not.

Samuel Issacharoff, *Class Action Conflicts*, 30 U.C. Davis L. Rev. 805, 831–832 (1997).

Comment d. The casting of "related claims" as those that exhibit a "nucleus of operative fact" borrows the locution historically used by procedural law to describe situations suited for the discretionary exercise of pendent jurisdiction by a federal court over state-law claims. United

Mine Workers of America v. Gibbs, 383 U.S. 715, 725 (1966) ("The state and federal claims must derive from a common nucleus of operative fact. But if, considered without regard to their federal or state character, a plaintiff's claims are such that he would ordinarily be expected to try them all in one judicial proceeding, then, assuming substantiality of the federal issues, there is power in federal courts to hear the whole.").

Effect on current law. The definition of "common issues" offered here is designed to reflect the emerging judicial understanding of the term in class-action and consolidated litigation.

§ 2.02 Principles for the Aggregate Treatment of Common Issues

(a) The court should exercise discretion to authorize aggregate treatment of a common issue by way of a class action if the court determines that resolution of the common issue would

(1) materially advance the resolution of multiple civil claims by addressing the core of the dispute in a manner superior to other realistic procedural alternatives, so as to generate significant judicial efficiencies;

(2) conform to the general principles for aggregate proceedings in §§ 1.03–1.05; and

(3) not compromise the fairness of procedures for resolving any remaining issues presented by such claims.

(b) Realistic procedural alternatives under subsection (a)(1) may, in a given situation, include

(1) coordinated discovery;

(2) pretrial rulings, such as on a motion for summary judgment or concerning the admissibility of evidence related to the common issue;

(3) trial of an individual claimant's case or multiple individual cases;

(4) an administrative aggregation within the meaning of § 1.02(b); or

(5) another class action already pending in another judicial system.

(c) Aggregate treatment of a common issue pursuant to subsection (a) should be subject to appellate review as provided in § 2.09.

(d) If factual development is warranted to inform the court's determination whether to authorize aggregate treatment pursuant to subsection (a), then the court should set forth a plan whereby claimants and respondents may undertake controlled discovery of facts pertinent to that determination.

    (e) As part of its obligation under § 2.12, the court should

        (1) identify the issues encompassed by aggregate treatment and

        (2) explain how aggregation will resolve fairly and efficiently the common issues identified and materially advance the resolution of any remaining issues or claims.

Comment:

    a. Materially advancing the resolution of multiple claims. Subsection (a) sets forth the animating principles for aggregate treatment under this Chapter. The focus here is on courts as the institutions with the authority and responsibility to determine whether litigation may proceed on an aggregate basis. Subsection (a) starts from the bedrock point that aggregate treatment in litigation is a matter of judicial discretion that flows from the general authority of courts to exercise early and effective supervision of litigation and, often, from the particular statute or rule authorizing aggregate treatment. In exercising this discretion, courts should consider whether aggregate treatment of a common issue by way of a class action will materially advance the resolution of multiple civil claims by addressing the core of the dispute in a manner superior to other realistic procedural alternatives such that aggregate treatment would generate significant judicial efficiencies. In a given situation, realistic procedural alternatives themselves may include administrative aggregation, as defined in § 1.02(b), or the use of nonaggregated alternatives, such as bellwether trials. In this manner, the present Section situates the class action in continuity with emerging procedures for administrative aggregation that some courts have denoted—with some degree of ambiguity—as "quasi-class actions." The terminology developed in these Principles seeks to lend greater precision to this notion.

    With the phrase "materially advance the resolution," subsection (a)(1) underscores the limited nature of the judicial authority recognized therein. This usage is in keeping with existing invocations of the phrase, or similar locutions, by courts. The application of subsection (a)(1) accordingly is not expected to make for substantial change in the law of aggregate litigation but, rather, to synthesize the application of that body of law that has emerged over decades of experience with the modern class action. This process of application is presently undertaken in terms of a predominance of common questions and the existing authorization for class actions confined to particular issues. The present Section draws upon experience with on-the-ground application of the existing law of class actions so as to frame both the predominance concept and the authorization for issue classes in a more coherent fashion. In particular, this Section as a whole—not just the phrase "materially advance" in subsection (a)(1)—delineates the multifaceted inquiries presently encapsulated under the predominance concept.

Section (a)(1) further confines aggregate treatment of a common issue in a class action to those situations in which that issue defines the core of the dispute presented by multiple civil claims, not merely its tangential or secondary dimensions. Identification of a common issue, the resolution of which will "materially advance the resolution" of such claims, thus goes significantly beyond identification of the minimal commonality that is among the general requirements for certification of a class action under current rules of civil procedure. The inquiry is qualitative, not one focused simply on the effort expected to be devoted to resolution of the common issue by counsel and the court. The reference to advancing "the resolution of multiple civil claims," moreover, is not intended to suggest that the tendency of aggregate treatment to make settlement more likely—simply as a descriptive matter—should operate, in itself, as a consideration in favor of aggregate treatment.

The phrase "materially advance the resolution" also operates in tandem with the principles for aggregate proceedings generally—hence, the cross-reference in subsection (a)(2) to §§ 1.03–1.05. As Comments c–f underscore, those general principles—particularly, the content and structure of applicable substantive law as well as preclusion principles and related practical considerations—constrain the situations in which aggregate treatment of a common issue will "materially advance the resolution" of multiple claims. Application of subsection (a) thus is informed by the many Illustrations in §§ 2.03–2.10. Given that those Illustrations speak to various constraints on aggregation, they are best encountered in their respective settings rather than replicated in their entirety here. As a matter of broad generalization, accumulated experience with the class-action device suggests that aggregate treatment of a common issue will materially advance the resolution of multiple civil claims more frequently when the issue concerns "upstream" matters focused on the generally applicable conduct of those opposing the claimants in the litigation, as distinct from "downstream" matters focused on those claimants themselves. See § 2.01, Comment c. Again, in keeping with the broad generalization from experience in § 2.01, aggregate treatment of a common issue concerning generally applicable conduct alleged to result in economic injury might materially advance the resolution of multiple claims by reducing to a ministerial task such individualized matters as the calculation of damages. See also § 2.03(b), Comment c. Experience with the class-action device suggests that aggregate treatment of common issues in personal-injury litigation is far less likely to materially advance the resolution of such claims, particularly by comparison to the procedural alternative of actual trial concerning all issues in individual cases.

The court undertaking the aggregate proceeding cannot predetermine, mandate, or guarantee that aggregation will "materially advance the resolution" of multiple claims in the words of subsection (a)(1) or that the aggregate proceeding will be binding on both claimants and respondents. Recognition of these points, however, does not mean that the court should shy from analysis of the potential preclusive effect of class treatment. To the contrary, the cross-reference to the notion of "facilitating binding resolutions" in § 1.03(c) reflects the centrality of the inquiry into potential preclusive effect as part of the initial determination whether to aggregate. In particular, when aggregate treatment by way of a class action would encompass only one or more issues within the constellation of all issues raised by related claims, substantial doubt about the capacity of the class action to yield issue preclusion should counsel strongly against aggregation by way of a class action in the first place.

b. Superiority to other realistic procedural alternatives. The judicial inquiry described in subsection (a)(1) is inherently comparative, calling for the court to consider the realistic procedural alternatives to aggregation by way of the class action and the degree to which they, too, would materially advance the resolution of the implicated claims. This is in keeping with the recognition that class actions are but one of several methods by which civil procedure may facilitate the resolution of related civil claims.

Considerations that bear on the comparative inquiry include, for example, the viability of claims in the absence of aggregate treatment and the degree of variation among claims. "Viability" refers to the prospect, in practice, that claimants would obtain representation in the market for legal services in the absence of aggregate treatment. "Variation" picks up the previous suggestion to focus aggregate treatment on common issues that define the core of the dispute. The degree of variation itself may vary, depending on whether aggregate treatment is to serve as the vehicle for the resolution of all contested issues raised by the underlying claims or of some subset composed of common issues. See §§ 2.03–2.04. "Variation" also will tend, in general, to track the distinctions noted earlier between upstream and downstream matters in the litigation and between economic and personal injuries. See Comment *a.*

85

Different combinations of viability and variation have different implications for aggregation. In situations of low viability in the absence of aggregation but also low variation between individual claims, procedural law has long regarded aggregation as important, as a practical matter, to the vindication of private rights of action. The initial choice whether to recognize such rights, however, remains up to the institutions of substantive law, not the law of aggregate litigation. By contrast, situations of both high viability and high variation present the weakest scenarios for aggregation, as there are likely to be realistic procedural alternatives to such treatment for the resolution of the underlying claims. Claims for personal injury frequently fit this description.

Personal-injury litigation involving high viability and high variation might well present one or more common issues within the meaning of § 2.01, but aggregate treatment confined to such a common issue carries a significant risk of an acontextual determination of that issue in isolation from other, related issues. This risk is unnecessary for the court to run when the economic viability of personal-injury claims on an individual basis makes individual trials under § 2.02(b)(3) a realistic procedural alternative—one that would present any common issue within its larger context, alongside the remaining issues. As elaborated in § 2.03, Comment b, individual trials additionally would avoid the practical need for evidence on the common issue in an aggregate proceeding to be substantially reconsidered in proceedings on the remaining issues. Finally, individual trials would avoid placing both claimants and respondents at risk of an all-or-nothing determination of the common issue on the merits in the aggregate. In some circumstances, the predominance-of-the-evidence standard for civil judgments may properly result in some claimants winning and others losing in the early stages of similar claims arising from mass harms. Multiple individual trials—proceedings that might reach different results—might reflect more accurately the degree of uncertainty associated with a given common issue, so as better to inform the resolution of the litigation overall.

In operational terms, principles for the aggregate treatment of common issues may be of most use for what one might call the mixed combinations. The principles set forth in this Chapter accordingly seek to lend greater precision to judicial analysis of aggregation questions, with particular attention to such settings. In situations of high viability but low variation, aggregation might materially advance the resolution of the underlying claims, but only if accompanied by the opportunity of claimants to exclude themselves from the proceeding on an individual basis. See § 2.07(a)(1). By contrast, in situations of low viability and high variation, aggregate treatment of all issues raised by the underlying claims is unlikely to drive claim resolution by comparison to alternative procedural avenues. The court, however, should consider whether aggregate treatment only of common issues would do so. See §§ 2.03–2.04.

Subsection (b) elaborates, by way of nonexclusive illustration, the "realistic procedural alternatives" that, in a given situation, may inform the court's inquiry into whether aggregate treatment of a common issue by way of a class action will materially advance the resolution of multiple civil claims. Several of the alternatives mentioned by way of example in subsection (b) are likely to be quite familiar to the court from the setting of ordinary, nonaggregate litigation. In that setting, the kind of coordinated discovery mentioned in subsection (b)(1) is commonplace across multiple civil claims in the federal judicial system that involve common questions of fact. The further references in subsection (b)(2) to rulings on motions for summary judgment (including partial summary judgment) and on the admissibility of evidence that pertains to a common issue serve as reminders that such rulings also might materially advance the resolution of multiple civil claims to such a degree as to make aggregate treatment by way of a class action inappropriate from a comparative standpoint.

As anticipated in the preceding discussion of personal-injury claims, subsection (b)(3) recognizes the potential usefulness of conventional trials, whether in an individual claimant's case or in multiple such cases, as a vehicle that might, in a given situation, materially advance the resolution of multiple civil claims. Such trials might consist of "bellwether trials," to which claimants and respondents in other cases might voluntarily consent to be bound. Even if not formally binding on other claimants or respondents, bellwether trials can inform both the court and other potential litigants on critical questions concerning both the benefits of other aggregative tools and the merits of the underlying disputes and can serve as the basis for preclusion against parties on issues that have been actually litigated. Bellwether trials, moreover, need not necessarily take place before a single trial-level court but, rather, may proceed across multiple courts in which individual cases are pending—potentially with informal coordination among the relevant judges or with a particular judge sitting by designation in the various locations where individual cases may be tried. The court should bear in mind, nonetheless, that the conduct of multiple bellwether trials is far from costless, both to the parties and to the judicial system, such that those costs are appropriately evaluated by comparison—again—to any efficiencies anticipated to be generated by aggregate treatment.

Subsection (b)(4) also draws attention to the prospect that, in a given situation, administrative aggregation may offer a plausible alternative to aggregate treatment by way of a class action. As defined in § 1.02(b), administrative aggregation consists of "related lawsuits, which may or may not be aggregate lawsuits, proceeding under common judicial supervision or control." In current law, courts on occasion have gone so far as to dub some forms of administrative aggregation as "quasi-class actions." The reference to administrative aggregation carries forward the considerations described in Comment *a* in connection with the viability of claims on an individual basis. If claims would be individually viable and are pending before a manageable number of courts, then common judicial supervision or control may reduce substantially the practical need for a class action. In a situation involving more than one court before which cases are pending, informal coordination among the judges involved can give rise to common judicial supervision in functional terms. Any such informal coordination should effectively inform all parties of all relevant procedural determinations.

As set forth in § 2.02(a)(1), the generation of "significant judicial efficiencies" lends additional force to the notion of material advancement by comparison to realistic procedural alternatives. Considerations pertinent to this inquiry include not only whether aggregate treatment would be more efficient, but also whether the proceedings on any remaining issues not resolved in the aggregate are likely to take place before the same court. When the same court stands to handle both the issue class proceeding and proceedings on any remaining issues in the litigation—as may be so when the dispute concerns matters of a geographically confined or localized nature—aggregate treatment of the common issue is more likely to give rise to significant judicial efficiencies than when the remaining issues stand to be addressed by far-flung courts. This observation elaborates on existing case law. Federal appellate courts that have overturned issue-class treatment in mass-harm litigation have nonetheless endorsed such treatment in environmental and employment-discrimination litigation focused on a particular geographic location or facility. Indeed, in some of the latter cases, federal appellate courts have held that the district courts abused their discretion in *not* certifying the proposed environmental or employment-discrimination class at issue.

Subsection (b)(5) addresses situations in which the proposed class action is merely one of multiple class actions that would encompass the same or closely overlapping claimants. As elaborated in § 3.02, Comment *a*, a situation of multiple class actions calls for close judicial attention to the possibility of what has come to be known as a "reverse auction," whereby the party opposing the class might seek to play off competing would-be class counsel against one another in search of a class settlement that would undervalue class members' claims. The court in the class action proposed solely for the purposes of settlement should consider whether to withhold certification there in light of the superiority of another, already-pending class action as a vehicle for resolution of the underlying claims.

    c. Applying general principles for aggregation. As anticipated in Comment *a,* subsection (a)(2) constrains the court's determination whether to authorize aggregate treatment of a common issue by reference to the principles for aggregation set forth in §§ 1.03–1.05. This constraint, too, does not anticipate substantial change in existing law but, rather, sets forth with greater precision considerations that currently inform the application of the predominance concept for class actions. As applied here, the principles of § 1.03 counsel that aggregation should respect the rights and responsibilities delineated by applicable substantive law; it should enable the determinations made as to any common issues on an aggregate basis to give rise to binding resolutions as to all claimants; and it should protect the interests of parties, represented persons, claimants, and respondents.

    d. Substantive law. Given that the existence of common issues is itself a function of underlying substantive law, as discussed in § 2.03, Comment *b,* the content of substantive law influences the decision whether to afford aggregate treatment. Substantive law defines the relationships among legal and factual issues—sometimes intertwining them and sometimes separating them cleanly so as to create a "joint" at which aggregate treatment may carve. See § 2.03(a). Aggregation must respect these substantive choices, for procedural rules generally exist to describe the available modes for adjudication of civil claims without themselves altering the content of substantive rights. One may understand this constraint on aggregate procedure in terms of a distinction between the amplification of civil claims as delineated by substantive law and the distortion of underlying substantive law. In accordance with § 1.03(b), the present Section envisions the aggregation of common issues in litigation as operating seamlessly with substantive law in the sense of providing for the fair and efficient resolution of those issues without altering their substantive content. Aggregate treatment thus is possible when a trial would allow for the presentation of evidence sufficient to demonstrate the validity or invalidity of all claims with respect to a common issue under applicable substantive law, without altering the substantive standards that would be applied were each claim to be tried independently and without compromising the ability of the defendant to dispute the allegations made by claimants or to raise pertinent substantive defenses. See § 2.01, Comment *b* (discussing the relationship of common factual issues to the evidence anticipated at trial). The existence of such common evidence is a manifestation of low variation between the claims to be aggregated.

e. Scope of preclusion. There is no point to the aggregate treatment of common issues in litigation if such treatment will not alleviate, as a practical matter, the need to revisit the same issues in other proceedings. The decision to pursue aggregate treatment accordingly must take place with close attention to both the potential claim-preclusive and issue-preclusive effects of determinations made in the aggregate proceeding. Cf. § 2.01, Comment *d* (noting that aggregate treatment of a common issue under § 2.08 will give rise only to issue preclusion, whereas aggregate treatment of related claims under § 2.07 will generate both issue and claim preclusion). If the determination of a given issue as to one claimant would not determine that issue as to all, or if a determination in the aggregate would occur only amidst doubts about its preclusive effect, then those concerns should stand as warning signs counseling strongly against aggregation in the first place. As § 2.07 elaborates, the scope of preclusion is closely related to dictates of constitutional due process and considerations of fairness to claimants and respondents, both of which form some of the most significant grounds to withhold preclusive effect from aggregate proceedings.

The emphasis here on preclusive effect lends additional clarity to the operation of subsection (a)(1). Aggregate treatment of common issues may materially advance the resolution of multiple civil claims by comparison to other realistic procedural alternatives by making more transparent and straightforward the determination of issue preclusion in subsequent proceedings concerning the remaining issues in the litigation. See § 2.03, Comment *b*; § 2.12, Comment *b*. This clarification of issue-preclusive effect—again, a matter for ultimate determination in subsequent proceedings—notably operates even when those opposing aggregation are prepared to concede the common issues for which aggregate treatment is sought. Consideration of preclusion is not limited to the time at which the court makes the aggregation determination. When the court authorizes aggregate treatment of a common issue, the court should revisit its analysis of potential preclusion at the conclusion of the proceeding, insofar as developments in the course of that proceeding have brought to light additional facts or considerations that bear on the scope of preclusion.

f. Protecting the interests of the participants. As Chapter 1 observes, aggregate lawsuits endow participants with different levels of control. See § 1.05, Reporters' Notes. In particular, some forms of aggregation, such as class actions, entail relatively limited control by participants. As control recedes, the framework for aggregation must itself assume a greater role in protecting the interests of all participants. Part of this protection involves respect for the rights and remedies delineated by applicable substantive law. See Comment *d*. Additional aspects of protection concern the individual rights of participants in the aggregate proceeding. As § 2.07 elaborates, these individual rights take a variety of forms, including notice, opportunities for participation, and judicial inquiry into the representational arrangements for the aggregate proceeding.

Subsection (a)(2) underscores the importance of one particular aspect of the general principle in § 1.04(a) that aggregate proceedings should take into account the objectives of both claimants and respondents. Aggregate treatment of a common issue should not compromise the fairness of procedures for resolution of the remaining issues raised by multiple civil claims. The fairness question nonetheless remains informed by applicable substantive law and accordingly should be analyzed by the court in that light.

Illustration:

> 1. Multiple employees, 1–100, have claims against Defendant, all based on the allegation the Defendant engaged in a pattern or practice of disparate treatment on the basis of sex in its workplace. Applicable substantive law provides that proof of such a pattern or practice gives rise to an inference of disparate treatment with respect to the particular adverse employment actions of which the respective employees complain. But Defendant contends that substantive law also requires that Defendant must be afforded an opportunity to rebut that inference with respect to particular employees. In order to determine whether to authorize aggregate treatment and the appropriate scope of any such treatment, the court should determine whether substantive law requires that Defendant be afforded the opportunity to rebut the inference of disparate treatment in individual instances. If substantive law so provides and if those instances do not present common issues across all employees for which aggregate treatment is sought, then the aggregate proceeding—if any—should not encompass the rebuttal process.

g. Appellate review. Subsection (c) of the present Section emphasizes at the outset the deep connection between the discretionary authority to aggregate described here and the framework for appellate review—both review of the aggregation determination itself, as already provided in the law of class actions and, if aggregate treatment encompasses only a common issue, review of the resolution of that issue on the merits. Section 2.09 elaborates with greater specificity the process for appellate review on the merits determination of a common issue in the aggregate.

h. Informing the court's aggregation determination. Subsection (d) speaks to the process by which the court should position itself to decide whether to authorize aggregate treatment. Application of the principles in this Chapter will often require the court to look beyond the pleadings. The attention in subsection (d) to the potential need for "controlled discovery" on factual matters pertinent to the aggregation determination stems from the emerging recognition that the question whether to aggregate presents a mixed question of fact and law, not a matter of pleading. The insistence in subsection (a) that the court affirmatively "determine" that aggregation would satisfy the criteria stated therein underscores the obligation of the court to resolve any such questions as a predicate to authorization of aggregate treatment. See also § 2.06 (underscoring the judicial obligation to decide all questions of law that bear on the aggregation determination).

The factual dimension of the decision may warrant controlled discovery in a given instance to inform the court's application of the principles set forth here. Discovery on the aggregation question is not a matter of right for claimants or respondents but, rather, turns on a discretionary ruling by the court in light of the nature of the factual matters that bear on aggregation. If the court determines that controlled discovery is warranted, then the court should set forth a plan to organize such discovery. The further phrase "pertinent to that determination" likewise reflects that controlled discovery, when authorized by the court, should not encompass all factual disputes presented by multiple claims but, rather, only those that bear on the appropriateness of aggregate treatment. Factual disputes that are not pertinent to aggregate treatment are appropriately engaged by the court under the ordinary framework for summary judgment or trial.

i. Identification of the scope of aggregate treatment. Subsection (e)(1) underscores the need for the court to identify the common issues or claims to be encompassed by aggregate treatment. This identification serves the immediate purpose of positioning the court to provide notice, as warranted under § 2.07(a)(3), concerning the matters that might be precluded as a result of the aggregate proceeding. Judicial precision in the identification of the scope of aggregation additionally facilitates the determination of preclusive effect in any subsequent proceedings on other issues presented by multiple claims. Identification of the scope of aggregation also facilitates the provision of meaningful notice to those whose claims or defenses the aggregate proceeding might operate to preclude. Finally, clear articulation of the basis for aggregation facilitates informed appellate review.

j. Explanation of the justification for aggregation. Subsection (e)(2) operates in tandem with the criteria set forth in subsections (a) and (b) by insisting that any judicial authorization of aggregation should be accompanied by explanation of how such treatment will resolve fairly and efficiently the common issues or claims identified and materially advance the resolution of any remaining issues or claims. The need for explanation on the court's part flows from the recognition in Comment *a* of the discretionary nature of the aggregation determination. Section 2.12 elaborates further on the adjudication plan that the court should develop along these lines.

REPORTERS' NOTES

Comment a. The discretionary nature of the decision to aggregate by way of class actions and consolidations is a well-recognized feature of existing law. See 7AA Charles Alan Wright, Arthur R. Miller & Mary Kay Kane, *Federal Practice and Procedure* § 1785, 370–371 (3d ed. 2005) ("The trial court has broad discretion in deciding whether to certify a class action and its decision will be reversed only if an abuse of discretion is shown."); 9A Charles Alan Wright & Arthur R. Miller, *Federal Practice and Procedure* § 2383, 437–438 (3d ed. 2005) ("The district court is given broad discretion to decide whether consolidation ... would be desirable and the district judge's decision inevitably is highly contextual. ..."). The reference to the general authority of courts to exercise "early and effective supervision" over litigation stems from the Manual for Complex Litigation (Fourth) § 10 (2004).

Existing law recognizes the possibility of class treatment for all issues within a larger "controversy" if "the court finds that the questions of law or fact common to class members predominate over any questions affecting only individual members, and

that a class action is superior to other available methods for fairly and efficiently adjudicating the controversy." Fed. R. Civ. P. 23(b)(3). At the same time, existing law also recognizes the possibility that a court, "[w]hen appropriate," may accord class treatment "with respect to particular issues" within a larger constellation of issues raised by a given controversy. Fed. R. Civ. P. 23(c)(4).

This Section proceeds on the premise that both the predominance requirement of Rule 23(b)(3) and the authorization for issue classes in Rule 23(c)(4) are worthwhile components of the law of aggregate litigation. The framework set forth here contemplates neither the abandonment of these provisions in existing law nor, for that matter, the necessity of rule amendment. Rather, in casting the aggregate treatment of common issues in terms of whether such treatment will materially advance the resolution of multiple civil claims, this Section elaborates on current practices in a more systematic fashion. The objective is to assist both courts and lawyers by identifying with greater precision the considerations reflected in the interplay between

Subsections (b)(3) and (c)(4) of Rule 23, as set forth in existing case law.

Courts are divided over the precise relationship between the predominance requirement of Rule 23(b)(3) and the authorization for issue classes in Rule 23(c)(4). Compare, e.g., Castano v. Am. Tobacco Co., 84 F.3d 734, 745 n.21 (5th Cir. 1996) ("Reading rule 23(c)(4) as allowing a court to sever issues until the remaining common issue predominates over the remaining individual issues would eviscerate the predominance requirement of rule 23(b)(3); the result would be automatic certification in every case where there is a common issue, a result that could not have been intended."), with, e.g., In re Nassau County Strip Search Cases, 461 F.3d 219, 227 (2d Cir. 2006) ("[A] court may employ subsection (c)(4) to certify a class as to liability regardless of whether the claim as a whole satisfies Rule 23(b)(3)'s predominance requirement."). This division in the courts, in turn, has generated divergent recommendations from commentators. Compare Laura J. Hines, *Challenging the Issue Class Action End–Run*, 52 Emory L.J. 709 (2003) (criticizing the use of issue classes as undermining the requirements of Rule 23(b)(3)), with Jon Romberg, *Half a Loaf is Predominant and Superior to None: Class Certification of Particular Issues Under Rule 23(c)(4)(A)*, 2002 Utah L. Rev. 249 (advocating expanded use of issue classes).

By its terms, the predominance requirement of Rule 23(b)(3) calls for a comparison of "the questions of law or fact common to class members" and "any questions affecting only individual members." Advocates of class certification have an incentive to frame legal and factual issues at high levels of generality so as to argue for their commonality, whereas opponents of class certification have an incentive to catalogue in microscopic detail each legal or factual variation suggesting the existence of individual questions. The specification that common questions must "predominate" over individual ones, moreover, is susceptible of being misread to suggest that the piling up of common questions somehow can justify class certification, even in the presence of individual questions that will disable the proceeding from yielding common answers with respect to the matters encompassed. The language of Rule 23(c)(4), in turn, gives comparably little guidance on the considerations that should determine when partial certification comes within the "when appropriate" rubric. For a discussion of factors relevant to the decision to certify a class as to particular issues only, see Hohider v. United Parcel Service, Inc., 574 F.3d 169, 200–202 (3d Cir. 2009).

In seeking to understand both Rule 23(b)(3) and Rule 23(c)(4) as an integrated whole, the current Manual for Complex Litigation recognizes that courts should undertake aggregate treatment of common issues "only if it permits fair presentation of the claims and defenses and materially advances the disposition of the litigation as a whole." Manual for Complex Litigation (Fourth) § 21.24, at 273 (2004). See also Barbara J. Rothstein & Thomas E. Willging, *Managing Class Action Litigation: A Pocket Guide for Judges* 10 (2d ed. 2009) ("The test is whether the resolution of common issues advances the litigation as a whole, as opposed to leaving a large number of issues for case-by-case adjudication."). The same locution appears in case law. See, e.g., McLaughlin v. Am. Tobacco Co., 522

F.3d 215, 234 (2d Cir. 2008) (declining to authorize issue class action because it would not "materially advance the litigation"). The language of subsection (a)(1) of this Section incorporates this notion of material advancement, as distinct from only marginal or trivial advancement. A broadly similar notion of material advancement is part of existing law concerning the authorization of interlocutory appeals. See 28 U.S.C. § 1292(b) (providing that district courts may authorize interlocutory appeals from nonfinal orders, in the discretion of the relevant court of appeals, with respect to a "controlling question of law" such that "immediate appeal" therefrom "may materially advance the ultimate termination of the litigation"). The formulation "materially advance" in this Section is designed to convey a similar sense of central importance to the overall litigation.

The further specification in subsection (a)(1) that a common issue appropriate for aggregate treatment should be a "core" issue in the litigation, as distinct from a tangential or secondary issue, reflects the class-certification analysis under Rule 23(b)(3) in Klay v. Humana, Inc., 382 F.3d 1241, 1254–1255 (11th Cir. 2004). There, the court assessed the desirability of class certification based, in large part, on whether the resolution of common issues in the aggregate would advance the overall disposition of the underlying claims. See id. at 1254 (noting that, in making its class-certification decision, a court should "assess the degree to which resolution of the classwide issues will further each individual class member's claim against the defendant"). Still, the class certification in Klay did not encompass all issues in the underlying litigation. The certification encom-

passed only the federal civil RICO claims of the class members, not their state-law breach-of-contract claims. The resolution of only the federal civil RICO claims nonetheless, in the Klay court's analysis, would materially advance the overall disposition of the class members' claims.

The determination of what amounts to a "core" issue in the litigation nonetheless remains sensitive to the particular substantive area involved. In keeping with the recognition in this Section of the difficulty of class certification for downstream personal injuries, the district court responsible for consolidated federal-court product-liability litigation over the prescription drug Vioxx declined to certify a class action on the issue of general causation. The court noted that "[r]esolution of general causation is unlikely to affect the course of this litigation," because "[l]ittle or no time and expense will be saved in these individual trials by virtue of the preceding mass trial on general causation." In re Vioxx Prods. Liab. Litig., 239 F.R.D. 450, 462 (E.D. La. 2006) (internal quotation marks omitted). See also Roger L. Trangsrud, Mass Trials in Mass Tort Cases: A Dissent, 1989 U. Ill. L. Rev. 69, 79 ("Rarely ... will a mass trial [on general causation] lead to the prompt entry of judgment in favor of a large group of plaintiffs against one or more defendants because even if the jury finds, for example, that the defendant's product could have caused the plaintiff's injury, individual trials will still be necessary to determine specific causation, whether any affirmative defenses are available to the defendant, and the extent of the plaintiff's damages. Little or no time and expense will be saved in these individual trials by virtue of the preceding mass trial on general causation."). A Canadian appellate court came to a similar conclusion in Vioxx class litigation brought in that nation. See Wuttunee v. Merck Frosst Canada Ltd., [2009] 5 W.W.R. 228 (Can. Sask. C.A.).

The rejection of issue-class certification with respect to general causation in the Vioxx litigation carries forward the approach seen elsewhere in product-liability litigation and may indicate a further concern over the inability to render accurate judgments reflecting disparate individual claims. See, e.g., *Castano*, 84 F.3d at 741, 746 (rejecting proposed class-wide issues trial on "core liability issues" because the aggregation of claims "magnifies and strengthens the number of unmeritorious claims"); In re Rhone–Poulenc Rorer Inc., 51 F.3d 1293, 1297 (7th Cir. 1995) (reversing class-wide issues trial on general question of negligence, noting "the district judge's commendable desire to experiment with an innovative procedure for streamlining the adjudication of [a] 'mass tort' " but holding that in practice the issues trial would exceed the "permissible bounds of discretion in the management of federal litigation").

Nonetheless, courts have recognized the propriety of issue classes in circumstances outside the product-liability setting. See Mejdrech v. Met–Coil Systems Corp., 319 F.3d 910 (7th Cir. 2003); Allen v. Int'l Truck & Engine Corp., 358 F.3d 469 (7th Cir. 2004). The specifics of *Mejdrech* and *Allen* bear elaboration later, in §§ 2.03 and 2.04, respectively. The point for purposes of the present Section is that, in *Mejdrech* and *Allen*, the Seventh Circuit overturned for abuse of discretion the refusals of district courts to certify issue classes

in environmental-contamination and employment-discrimination litigation, respectively, in contrast to the same court's rejection of issue-class certification in product-liability litigation. See *Rhone–Poulenc*, 51 F.3d 1293.

At the same time, Comment *a* cautions that the tendency of aggregate treatment to increase the pressure toward settlement should not, in itself, increase support for a determination by the court that aggregation would materially advance the litigation. This caution is in keeping with the recognition that the descriptive reality of settlement pressure brought about by aggregation is distinct from the normative question of whether such pressure is desirable or undesirable in light of substantive law. See Richard A. Nagareda, *Aggregation and its Discontents: Class Settlement Pressure, Class–Wide Arbitration, and CAFA*, 106 Colum. L. Rev. 1872, 1879–1895 (2006).

Comment *a* likewise cautions against inquiry cast simply in terms of the amount of "effort" that counsel and the court expect to devote to a given common issue as the touchstone for aggregation. It is difficult at the threshold stages of litigation to attempt to quantify the amount of trial time needed for issues that may be resolved by pretrial motions, discovery, or otherwise. In general, such a quantitative inquiry does not appear likely to be fruitful. One state court appears to have adopted such a view of its opt-out class-action rule. See, e.g., Sw. Refining Co. v. Bernal, 22 S.W.3d 425, 434 (Tex. 2000) (casting the predominance inquiry in terms of " 'whether common or individual issues will be the object of most of the efforts of the litigants and the court' ") (quoting Central Power & Light Co. v. City of San Juan, 962

S.W.2d 602, 610 (Tex. Ct. App. 1998)). Anticipated allocation of "effort," to be sure, might shed light on whether a given common issue proposed for aggregate treatment would indeed "materially advance the resolution" of multiple claims. In fact, immediately before its reference to "the efforts of the litigants and the court," the *Bernal* court itself cast the predominance inquiry in terms of "the substantive issues of the case that will control the outcome of the litigation." Id. The language of subsection (a)(1) is designed to emphasize the qualitative nature of the inquiry, one potentially informed but not necessarily dictated by the anticipated allocation of effort as among the implicated issues.

On the familiar proposition that a court, as part of class certification, cannot predetermine the preclusive effect of its own judgments but, rather, that the preclusion question is one for ultimate determination in the context of other proceedings, see, e.g., Fed. R. Civ. P. 23, advisory committee's note (1966 amendment); Matsushita Elec. Indus. Co. v. Epstein, 516 U.S. 367, 396 (1996) (Ginsburg, J., concurring in part and dissenting in part); see also Complex Litigation: Statutory Recommendations and Analysis § 5.05, Comment *b*, 285 ("[T]he court deciding a complex case will not determine the exact scope of preclusion for the judgments in the litigation."). A court faced with whether to authorize aggregate treatment nonetheless should inquire with specificity into the *potential* preclusive effect of such a proceeding. Cf. Fed. R. Civ. P. 23, advisory committee's note (1966 amendment) ("The court, . . . in framing the judgment in any suit brought as a class action, must decide what its extent or coverage shall be, and if the matter is

carefully considered, questions of *res judicata* are less likely to be raised at a later time and if raised will be more satisfactorily answered."); Tobias Barrington Wolff, *Preclusion in Class Action Litigation*, 105 Colum. L. Rev. 717, 722 (2005) ("No court can legitimately rule on a request for certification in a class action—at least, a class action that may proceed to a litigated outcome—without achieving a clear understanding of the likely preclusive effect that a judgment in the case would have upon the members of the class and the options that the court has at its disposal for altering or constraining those effects.").

Comment b. Existing law recognizes the importance of a comparative inquiry into whether a class action "is superior to other available methods for fairly and efficiently adjudicating the controversy," the locution used by current law. Fed. R. Civ. P. 23(b)(3). The Supreme Court has reinforced this point, noting that "class actions constitute but one of several methods for bringing about an aggregation of claims, i.e., they are but one of several methods by which multiple similarly situated parties get similar claims resolved at one time and in one federal forum." Sprint Communications Co. v. APCC Services, Inc., 128 S.Ct. 2531, 2545 (2008).

As in § 2.01, the references in the present Section to the distinctions between upstream and downstream matters and between economic injury and personal injury stem from Samuel Issacharoff, *Class Action Conflicts*, 30 U.C. Davis L. Rev. 805, 831–832 (1997). See § 2.01, Reporters' Notes. The framing of this inquiry in Comment *b* in terms of such additional considerations as the viability of claims in the absence of aggregation and the variation between claims draws on a similar approach in scholarly commentary, albeit with somewhat different terminology:

	Low Variance Between Individual Claims	High Variance Between Individual Claims
Low Value of Individual Claims	Class actions indispensable for private prosecution	Private enforcement difficult because of manageability concerns
High Value of Individual Claims	Class actions necessary but greater concern for individual opt-out and other right of control	Aggregate treatment not essential and class actions held suspect

Samuel Issacharoff, *Group Litigation of Consumer Claims: Lessons from the U.S. Experience*, 34 Tex. Int'l L.J. 135, 149 (1999). The strength of the justification for class certification in the low-viability and low-variation scenario is well recognized in the law of class actions. See Amchem Prods., Inc. v. Windsor, 521 U.S. 591, 617 (1997) (" 'The policy at the very core of the class action mechanism is to overcome the problem that small recoveries do not provide the incentive for any individual to bring a solo action prosecuting his or her rights. A class action solves this problem by aggregating the relatively paltry potential recoveries into something worth someone's (usually an attorney's) labor.' ") (quoting Mace v. Van Ru Credit Corp., 109 F.3d 338, 344 (7th Cir. 1997)).

Coordinated discovery across multiple claims in the federal courts takes place through the Multidistrict Litigation Act, 28 U.S.C. § 1407(a) ("When civil actions involving one or more common questions of fact are pending in different districts, such actions may be transferred to any district for coordinated or consolidated pretrial proceedings."). See also Complex Litigation: Statutory Recommendations and Analysis, 21–24 (describing the process surrounding, and problems with transfer of, multidistrict litigation under § 1407).

Pretrial rulings on the admissibility of evidence that pertains to a common issue across multiple claims have emerged as an important dimension of federal litigation consolidated by the Judicial Panel on Multidistrict Litigation (MDL). See, e.g., In re Ocean Bank, 481 F.Supp.2d 892, 896 (N.D. Ill. 2007) (granting in part and denying in part plaintiffs' motion to strike certain expert testimony in Fair Credit Reporting Act actions); In re Fedex Ground Package System, Inc. Employment Practices Litigation, No. 3:05–MD–527 RM (MDL–1700), 2007 WL 3027405, *1 (N.D. Ind. Oct. 15, 2007) (overruling plaintiffs' motion to strike portions of defendant's expert reports on admissibility grounds).

For discussion of conventional individual trials as a means to materially advance the resolution of multiple claims in the context of MDL consolidation, see DeLaventura v. Columbia

Acorn Trust, 417 F.Supp.2d 147, 156 (D. Mass. 2006) (praising efforts of district judge in Vioxx litigation "to push plaintiffs and drug makers to the settlement table, by *trying* representative cases and letting their outcomes *in court* set a price tag for an overall settlement"). See also Edward F. Sherman, *The MDL Model for Resolving Complex Litigation If a Class Action is Not Possible*, 82 Tul. L. Rev. 2205 (2008). As another court explains:

> A bellwether trial ... allows a court and jury to give the major arguments of both parties due consideration without facing the daunting prospect of resolving every issue in every action. It must be remembered that a defendant is not liable merely because it has been sued by a large group of plaintiffs. And every experienced litigator understands that there are often a handful of crucial issues on which the litigation primarily turns. A bellwether trial allows each party to present its best arguments on these issues for resolution by a trier of fact. Moreover, resolution of these issues often facilitates settlement of the remaining claims.

> Of course, bellwether trials cannot exceed the limits imposed by the Constitution, but they do not necessarily pose an uncommonly high risk of doing so.

In re Methyl Tertiary Butyl Ether (MTBE) Prods. Liab. Litig., No. 1:00–1898, MDL 1358(SAS), M21–88, 2007 WL 1791258, *2 (S.D.N.Y. June 15, 2007). See also Morgan v. Ford Motor Co., No. 06–1080 (JAP), 2007 WL 1456154, *6–7, *9–10 (D.N.J. May 17, 2007); Alexandra D. Lahav, *Bellwether Trials*, 76 Geo. Wash. L. Rev. 576 (2008).

The district judge responsible for MDL-consolidated federal litigation over Vioxx explains that bellwether trials can generate information that may facilitate the resolution of related, untried cases, even when those trials do not yield preclusive effect with regard to those remaining cases:

> A typical bellwether case often begins as no more than an individual lawsuit that proceeds through pretrial discovery and on to trial in the usual binary fashion: one plaintiff versus one defendant. Such a case may take on "bellwether" qualities, however, when it is selected for trial because it involves facts, claims, or defenses that are similar to the facts, claims, and defenses presented in a wider group of related cases.... [T]he results of bellwether trials need not be binding upon consolidated parties with related claims or defenses in order to be beneficial to the MDL process. Instead, by injecting juries and fact-finding into multidistrict litigation, bellwether trials assist in the maturation of disputes by providing an opportunity for coordinating counsel to *organize* the products of pretrial common discovery, *evaluate* the strengths and weaknesses of their arguments and evidence, and *understand* the risks and costs associated with the litigation. At a minimum, the bellwether process should lead to the creation of "trial packages" that can be utilized by local counsel upon the dissolution of MDLs, a valuable by-product in its own right that supplies at least a partial justification for the traditional delay associated with MDL practice.

But perhaps more importantly, the knowledge and experience gained during the bellwether process can precipitate global settlement negotiations and ensure that such negotiations do not occur in a vacuum, but rather in light of real-world evaluations of the litigation by multiple juries.

Eldon E. Fallon, Jeremy T. Grabill & Robert Pitard Wynne, *Bellwether Trials in Multidistrict Litigation*, 82 Tul. L. Rev. 2323, 2325 (2008).

On the emergence of administrative aggregation that courts have regarded as rising to the level of a "quasi-class action," see In re Zyprexa Prods. Liab. Litig., 424 F.Supp.2d 488, 491 (E.D.N.Y. 2006) (noting "the large number of plaintiffs subject to the same settlement matrix approved by the court" in MDL-consolidated litigation). For similar views, see In re Vioxx Prods. Liab. Litig., 574 F.Supp.2d 606, 611 (E.D. La. 2008); In re Guidant Corp. Implantable Defibrillators Prods. Liab. Litig., MDL No. 05–1708 (DWF/AJB), 2008 WL 682174, *17–18 (D. Minn. Mar. 7, 2008). Administrative aggregation may present significant procedural questions. For analysis with reference to the mass-tort context, see Elizabeth Chamblee Burch, *Procedural Justice in Non-class Aggregation*, 44 Wake Forest L. Rev. 1, 16–23 (2009) (distinguishing between attitudes of "group-oriented individuals" and "individuals-within-the-collective" in non-class aggregation).

With respect to court-to-court communication to coordinate the handling of related civil claims, one might look—by analogy—to guidance developed for court-to-court communication in the context of transna-

tional insolvencies. See Guidelines Applicable to Court-to-Court Communications in Cross-Border Cases, http://www.ali.org/doc/Guidelines.pdf (last visited Jan. 21, 2010), As Adopted and Promulgated by The American Law Institute in 2000, and included as Appendix B in Transnational Insolvency: Principles of Cooperation Among the NAFTA Countries (2003). The further reference to the possibility that a particular judge might sit by designation in the various locations in which bellwether trials of individual cases may occur is designed to reflect emerging practice in MDL consolidated litigation. In that setting, the benefits of bellwether trials serving to inform the MDL transferee court may be realized, even within the constraints imposed by Lexecon Inc. v. Milberg Weiss Bershad Hynes & Lerach, 523 U.S. 26 (1998) (holding that MDL transferee court has authority to conduct only pretrial proceedings under 28 U.S.C. § 1407(a) and accordingly must remand the cases so consolidated to the relevant transferor courts for trial). See also Complex Litigation: Statutory Recommendations and Analysis § 3.06, Comment *g*, 125 ("[O]nce the transferee judge severs the common and individual issues . . . [t]he most common solution is likely to be that unresolved individual issues, such as damages, will be remanded to the transferor courts for adjudication.").

The discussion above about the ability of a court in an aggregate proceeding also to handle proceedings on remaining issues is linked to the divergent case law mentioned above on issue-class certification. A series of decisions from the Seventh Circuit reflects the distinction between judicial skepticism over issue-class certification in the mass-tort context and judicial endorsement of such treatment in some areas of environmental and employment-discrimination litigation. Compare In re Rhone–Poulenc Rorer, Inc., 51 F.3d 1293 (7th Cir. 1995) (mass-tort litigation over contaminated blood products), with *Mejdrech*, 319 F.3d 910 (environmental contamination); *Allen*, 358 F.3d 469 (employment discrimination).

Comment d. On aggregation in the class-action context as both a useful vehicle for amplification and a potentially troubling source of distortion in substantive law, see Richard A. Epstein, *Class Actions: Aggregation, Amplification, and Distortion*, 2003 U. Chi. Legal F. 475. The proposition that aggregate treatment of common issues in litigation must respect the divisions between issues made by applicable substantive law stems from the admonition that courts, in authorizing class-action treatment of particular issues, "must carve at the joint." *Rhone–Poulenc*, 51 F.3d at 1302. For more extensive discussion, see § 2.03, Comment *a*. The metaphor of joints created by substantive law appropriately focuses attention upon the existence and nature of the divisions made between various issues, as delineated by the elements of a cause of action or defense. Other kinds of joints might stem not so much from different legal elements as from the organization of proof at trial, such as the distinctions drawn in the law of employment discrimination between components of the plaintiff's prima facie case and responsive matters on which the defendant bears the burden of production. See, e.g., Griggs v. Duke Power Co., 401 U.S. 424, 432 (1971) (describing prima facie case for plaintiffs and burden of production for defendants in employment-discrimination actions under disparate-impact theory).

Comment e. The preclusive effect of aggregate treatment has generated considerable discussion in the class-action context. For two illustrative articles among the many discussions of this subject, see, e.g., Samuel Issacharoff, *Preclusion, Due Process, and the Right to Opt Out of Class Actions*, 77 Notre Dame L. Rev. 1057 (2002); Geoffrey C. Hazard, Jr. et al., *An Historical Analysis of the Binding Effect of Class Suits*, 146 U. Pa. L. Rev. 1849 (1998). For previous treatment of this topic by The American Law Institute, see Complex Litigation: Statutory Recommendations and Analysis § 5.05 and Comments.

On the special problems that may be presented when a proposed class action encompasses only some of the claims capable of being adjudicated on a classwide basis, see Citizens Ins. Co. of Am. v. Daccach, 217 S.W.3d 430 (Tex. 2007). There, the Texas Supreme Court held that its state class-action rule "requires the trial court, as part of its rigorous [class-certification] analysis, to consider the risk that a judgment in the class action may preclude subsequent litigation of claims not alleged, abandoned, or split from the class action." Id. at 457. "The trial court abuses its discretion if it fails to consider the preclusive effect of a judgment on abandoned claims, as res judicata could undermine the adequacy of representation requirement." Id. (citing Wolff, *Preclusion in Class Action Litigation*, 105 Colum. L. Rev. at 722).

On the desirability of aggregate treatment for common issues by way of a class action, even when the party opposing aggregation is prepared to concede those issues, see *Nassau*

County Strip Search Cases, 461 F.3d at 227–229. There, the Second Circuit linked the appropriateness of aggregate treatment to the issue-preclusive effect that such treatment would have in subsequent proceedings concerning the remaining issues in the litigation. Absent aggregate treatment of common issues via a class action concerning the defendants' conceded liability for an unconstitutional search policy, said the Second Circuit, courts in subsequent proceedings "might differ as to whether ... the requirements of collateral estoppel were met." Id. at 228.

Comment f. The need to safeguard the interests of participants due to the reduction in their control of litigation on an aggregate basis has long been recognized. See, e.g., Hansberry v. Lee, 311 U.S. 32, 42 (1940) (casting constitutional due process in class actions in terms of whether the procedure adopted "fairly insures the protection of the interests of absent parties who are to be bound by [the litigation]"). As § 2.07(d) observes, the need to protect the interests of the participants in aggregate proceedings is not confined to the persons aligned on the claimants' side but extends as well to persons opposing the claimants in the litigation.

Illustration 1 is drawn from the situation presented in Dukes v. Wal-Mart, Inc., 509 F.3d 1168 (9th Cir. 2007). The Illustration, however, takes no position on the legal question whether the substantive law of employment discrimination requires the defendant in a pattern-or-practice case involving alleged disparate treatment to be afforded an opportunity to rebut an inference of such treatment with respect to individual employees in the class. Nor does the Illustration

take a position on the ultimate aggregation question presented in *Dukes.* The Illustration simply underscores the central importance of the legal question concerning the opportunity to rebut for the capacity of aggregate treatment to avoid compromising the fairness of the rebuttal process, as delineated by substantive law.

Comment h. Current law in the class-action area recognizes that "[t]ime may be needed to gather information necessary to make the certification decision." Fed. R. Civ. P. 23(c)(1), advisory committee's note (2003 amendment). "[C]ontrolled discovery" under "[a]ctive judicial supervision" may be warranted to "identify the nature of the issues that actually will be presented at trial." Id. On the significance of the 2003 amendment, see Oscar Private Equity Investments v. Allegiance Telecom, Inc., 487 F.3d 261, 267 (5th Cir. 2007) ("These subtle changes ... recognize that a district court's certification order often bestows upon plaintiffs extraordinary leverage, and its bite should dictate the process that precedes it. These changes are the product of years of study by the Advisory Committee on Civil Rules, including many open hearings and symposia. This collective wisdom must not be brushed aside. That there are 'important due process concerns of both plaintiffs and defendants inherent in the certification decision,' cannot be gainsaid.") (quoting Unger v. Amedisys Inc., 401 F.3d 316, 320 (5th Cir. 2005)). See also Geoffrey P. Miller, *Review of the Merits in Class Action Certification*, 33 Hofstra L. Rev. 51, 87 (2004) (concluding that courts should "investigate the merits provided that doing so is convenient and useful to analyzing the [applicable class] certification requirements").

The characterization of the aggregation decision as presenting a mixed question of fact and law—with the factual dimension implying the need, in particular instances, for controlled discovery—stems from the dominant trend in recent decisions on the appropriate scope for the judicial inquiry into class certification. See In re IPO Sec. Litig., 471 F.3d 24, 40 (2d Cir. 2006) ("Although there are often factual disputes in connection with Rule 23 requirements, and such disputes must be resolved with findings, the ultimate issue as to each requirement is really a mixed question of fact and law. A legal standard, e.g., numerosity, commonality, or predominance, is being applied to a set of facts, some of which might be in dispute."); id. at 41 ("To avoid the risk that a Rule 23 hearing will extend into a protracted mini-trial of substantial portions of the underlying litigation, a district judge must be accorded considerable discretion to limit both discovery and the extent of the hearing on Rule 23 requirements. But even with some limits on discovery and the extent of the hearing, the district judge must receive enough evidence, by affidavits, documents, or testimony, to be satisfied that each Rule 23 requirement has been met."); In re Hydrogen Peroxide Antitrust Litig., 552 F.3d 305, 324 (3d Cir. 2008) (quoting preceding passage from *IPO*); *Oscar Private Equity*, 487 F.3d at 268 ("[The Supreme Court's decision in] *Eisen* [v. Carlisle & Jacquelin, 417 U.S. 156, 177–178 (1974)] did not drain Rule 23 of all rigor. A district court still must give full and independent weight to each Rule 23 requirement, regardless of whether that requirement overlaps with the merits."); Szabo v. Bridgeport Machines, Inc., 249 F.3d 672, 676 (7th Cir. 2001) ("A judge would

not and could not accept the plaintiff's assertion [as to numerosity] as conclusive; instead, the judge would receive evidence (if only by affidavit) and resolve the disputes before deciding whether to certify the class."); Dukes v. Wal–Mart, Inc., 509 F.3d 1168, 1181 (9th Cir. 2007) (calling for a "finding [by the district court] that, based on all the evidence presented, there exist[] common questions of fact sufficient to justify class certification").

For the specific insight that compliance with class certification does not present a question of proper pleading, see *Hydrogen Peroxide*, 552 F.3d at 316 ("[T]he requirements set out in Rule 23 are not mere pleading rules.").

Comment i. Existing law in the class-action area likewise recognizes that the court, as part of a class-certification order, "must define the class and the class claims, issues, or defenses...." Fed. R. Civ. P. 23(c)(1)(B). Judicial practice has tended, on occasion, to focus more attention on the former and less on the latter. The Third Circuit observes that "[c]ertification orders tend to treat the parameters of the class itself much more clearly and deliberately than the class claims, issues, or defenses." Wachtel v. Guardian Life Ins. Co., 453 F.3d 179, 184 (3d Cir. 2006). Parsing the language of Rule 23(c)(1)(B), the Third Circuit insists that "the precise parameters defining the class and a complete list of the claims, issues, or defenses to be treated on a class basis" must be "readily discernible from the text either of the certification order itself or of an incorporated memorandum opinion." Id. at 185. See also id. at 187–188 (insisting on "a readily discernible, clear, and complete list of the claims, issues or defenses to be treated on a class basis"). Subsection (e) and Comment *i*, in turn, elaborate the functional justification for insistence that the common issues to be determined on an aggregate basis must be "readily discernible" from the outset of the aggregate proceeding. See id. at 185 ("Clear and complete treatment of both the class and the class claims, issues, or defenses at the class certification stage will unquestionably facilitate the timely execution of what is almost always the next step ... in class litigation, namely the court-supervised distribution of class notice to class members.").

Notice of the specific claims to be pursued on a classwide basis is especially important when there is a potential for claim preclusion to arise as to other claims of absent class members that the class representative has chosen to abandon for strategic reasons in the class proceedings. Here, specific delineation of the claims to be encompassed by the class proceedings may be necessary in order to afford putative class members "an opportunity to exclude themselves from the class form of proceeding so that they may preserve individual claims that may otherwise be barred from subsequent litigation." *Citizens Ins.*, 217 S.W.3d at 457.

Effect on current law. The approach offered here is designed to lend precision to the inquiry presently undertaken by courts within the vocabulary of existing procedural law, particularly the predominance requirement and the authorization for issue classes found in Rule 23. For the most part, no change in existing procedural rules would be required in order for courts to implement the approach of this Section. As explained in greater depth in § 2.09, legislation would be needed to authorize the kind of interlocutory appeal from any merits determination of a common issue in a class action—an appeal in addition to the existing interlocutory appeal under Rule 23(f) with respect to the class-certification determination.

TOPIC 2

SUBSTANTIVE LAW AS A CONSTRAINT ON AGGREGATION

§ 2.03 **Issues of Liability Versus Issues of Remedy in Certifying a Class Action**

Subject to the general principles in § 2.02 and the additional limitations in §§ 2.07–2.08, the court

(a) may authorize aggregate treatment of a common issue concerning liability by way of a class action when substantive law separates that issue from the choice and distribution of appropriate remedies and from other issues concerning liability; and

(b) may authorize aggregate treatment of both common issues of liability and individual issues of remedy by way of a class action when resolution of the liability issues in claimants' favor will, in practical effect, determine both the choice

of remedy and the method for its distribution on an individual basis.

Comment:

a. Distinguishing liability from remedy. This Section applies the efficiency principle of § 1.03(b) to the distinction between issues of liability and issues of remedy, permitting class-action treatment when applicable substantive law creates a "joint" at which to separate a common issue concerning liability from issues of remedy. Issues of liability are often common across multiple claimants in that they call for the same legal or factual determinations for each claim. See § 2.01. Identity of the legal or factual inquiry across all claimants gives rise to the potential for class-action treatment to serve the general principles of aggregation identified in § 1.03 while leaving issues of remedy for treatment on an individual basis.

Class-action treatment of a common liability issue nonetheless remains a matter of judicial discretion. The court should consider whether aggregate treatment of a common liability issue will materially advance the resolution of multiple claims by addressing the core of the dispute in a manner superior to realistic procedural alternatives, so as to generate significant judicial efficiencies (see § 2.02(a)(1)), and will conform to the general principles for aggregation (see § 2.02(a)(2) (referencing §§ 1.03–1.05)). Once again, the broad-brush distinctions between upstream and downstream matters and between economic-injury claims and personal-injury claims (see § 2.01, Comment *c*) as well as the interplay between the viability of claims on an individual basis and the variation in those claims (see § 2.02, Comment *b*) bear attention.

Nothing in the identification of a common issue of liability overrides substantive law concerning the allocation of decisionmaking power with regard to that issue—for example, a right to jury trial with respect to the underlying claims. This constraint is consistent with the general admonition that aggregation should respect the content of substantive law. See § 1.03(a).

b. Identifying liability issues. Liability issues suitable for class-action treatment under subsection (a) might encompass the entire range of elements necessary to establish the defendant's liability to all claimants or only particular elements of claims. With regard to liability issues as a whole or particular elements of liability, the question for the court remains whether there are common issues that are the same in functional content across all claims to be aggregated, see § 2.01—a question closely tied to substantive law. Further, a court must identify with specificity the elements whose aggregate evaluation will materially advance the overall resolution of the litigation by addressing the core of the dispute; and the court must allow for final determination and appellate review as to those issues, as described in § 2.09. Special verdicts in the aggregate proceeding on the liability issues are one means by which the court may implement this specific identification. In this regard, the court is constrained by the practical need for other factfinders or other courts in proceedings on remaining issues to determine the issue-preclusive effect of the class-action proceeding on liability as a whole or on particular elements thereof. When the class-action proceeding would not yield such issue-preclusive effect, the practical justification for aggregation disappears. See § 1.03(c) (specifying that aggregation should "facilitat[e] binding resolutions of civil disputes").

Subsection (a) adds the significant limitation that the court should consider whether substantive law cleanly separates the common issue from remedial questions and from other issues concerning liability. Class-action treatment of a common issue would not materially advance the resolution of related claims when that common issue remains intertwined under applicable substantive law with other issues that are not common, including individualized defenses. At the very least, such intertwining is likely to give rise to a practical need for evidence presented on the common issue in the aggregate proceeding to be reconsidered in other proceedings to address the remaining issues in the litigation. The prospect for substantial duplication of effort for both the parties and the courts amounts to a danger signal that counsels strongly against aggregate treatment of the common issue in the first place.

The potential for reconsideration of evidence stems from the recognition that substantive law in many areas does not delineate the elements of a given cause of action or of applicable affirmative defenses in such a manner that those elements are entirely discrete and distinct from one another. Rather, elements may overlap conceptually, with the result that evidence relevant to one might also bear on others. In other words, when applicable substantive law does not delineate distinct "joints" between these various elements, evidence thereon may tend to overlap. In the parlance of § 2.02(a)(1), aggregate treatment of a common issue does not materially advance the resolution of multiple claims when the evidence in the aggregate proceeding would need to be substantially reconsidered in subsequent proceedings on other issues.

Given the tendency of evidence in many instances to be relevant to multiple aspects of a claim, it is not realistically possible to insist that no reconsideration of evidence whatsoever may occur across the aggregate proceeding and subsequent proceedings. The question is one of degree and, as such, calls for the exercise of judicial discretion, in keeping with the discretionary nature of the determination whether to authorize aggregate treatment. See § 2.02, Comment *a*. The greater the practical need for reconsideration of evidence, the lesser the likelihood that aggregate treatment would materially advance the resolution of multiple claims by comparison to other realistic procedural alternatives.

In addition, in litigation to which the Seventh Amendment right to jury trial applies, the reconsideration of evidence across the aggregate proceeding and subsequent proceedings must respect the limitations of the Reexamination Clause, which provides that "no fact tried by a jury, shall be otherwise reexamined in any court of the United States, than according to the rules of the common law."

An additional constraint on aggregate treatment of a common issue flows from the procedural consequence on which § 2.09(a)(2) elaborates. In authorizing aggregate treatment, the court also must authorize interlocutory appeal of any determination of the common issue on the merits, with consideration of the appeal remaining discretionary on the part of the relevant appellate court. This interlocutory appeal on the merits is in addition to the appellate process available with respect to the initial judicial decision to aggregate. As elaborated in § 2.09, Comment *b*, the prospect of an interlocutory appeal on the merits of the common issue is designed to function as an additional backstop to guard against aggregate treatment of trivial or insignificant issues that are nonetheless common in a given litigation. One may see this additional backstop as imparting a degree of self-policing to efforts to seek aggregate treatment, for little will be gained by any party to litigation in directing the attention of courts to issues that are not central to the disposition of the case at hand. Moreover, this Section reinforces the role of third-party oversight exercised by both trial-level and appellate courts in the application of the principles in this Chapter.

Illustrations:

1. Multiple persons, 1–100, have claims against Defendant in tort, all based on Defendant's alleged lack of reasonable care in connection with a standardized product consumed by such persons. All claims against Defendant arise under the same body of substantive law, but that law subjects actions in tort for negligence to an affirmative defense of comparative negligence. The factfinder ultimately must evaluate any lack of reasonable care on Defendant's part by comparison to any lack of reasonable care on the part of a given claimant. Whether Defendant failed to under-

take reasonable care with regard to the disputed product constitutes a common issue, but aggregate treatment of that common issue would not materially advance the resolution of the implicated claims. Evidence concerning Defendant's lack of reasonable care would have to be substantially reconsidered in subsequent proceedings on the remaining issues in the litigation, including the comparative-negligence inquiry for particular claimants. As a practical matter, the comparative inquiry could not occur without reconsideration of such evidence. In accordance with § 2.02(b), the court nonetheless should consider whether coordinated discovery, trials in individual cases, or administrative aggregation would materially advance the resolution of the claims involved.

2. Multiple persons, 1–100, have claims against Defendant, all based on alleged misrepresentations concerning the odds associated with the playing of Defendant's video gambling machines. Whether Defendant in fact misrepresented the gambling odds is a common issue, but aggregate treatment of that issue would not materially advance the resolution of the underlying claims. Evidence as to the nature of the alleged misrepresentations would have to be substantially reconsidered in subsequent proceedings to address issues of reliance and proximate causation with respect to particular claimants—persons who might have chosen to gamble, and to do so on Defendant's machines, for reasons having nothing to do with the misrepresentations concerning the gambling odds.

3. Multiple persons, 1–100, have claims against Defendant in tort, all premised on the allegation that an industrial facility operated by Defendant released a hazardous substance into the local community that, in turn, seeped into the soil beneath the claimants' respective properties. All claims against Defendant arise under the same body of substantive law. The liability, if any, of Defendant to all claimants turns upon whether Defendant's facility released the substance in question and where any such release ultimately went. Aggregate treatment of the fact and the geographic scope of seepage would be permissible, with further inquiry into the magnitude of seepage beneath any given claimant's property—to the extent relevant to liability or remedy—to be handled, if necessary, through subsequent individual proceedings. Aggregate treatment of the geographic scope of seepage would materially advance the resolution of the claims by defining the group of persons who then may proceed against Defendant with regard to the remaining liability and remedy issues, such as specific causation and extent of damages.

4. Multiple consumers, 1–100, have claims against Defendant, all premised on the allegation that Defendant fraudulently misrepresented the financial terms associated with insurance policies sold through its agents to each consumer. The alleged misrepresentations consist of varying sales techniques used by individual insurance agents across the country with regard to the implicated policies. All claims against Defendant arise under the same body of substantive law, but that law calls for proof of individual reliance on the alleged misrepresentations of Defendant's agents as part of each consumer's cause of action. There is, moreover, no common body of evidence by which claimants seek to prove reliance. Aggregate treatment would not be permissible as to either the issue of misrepresentation or the issue of reliance, because neither qualifies as a common issue. Determination of whether misrepresentation occurred would entail inquiry into the particular sales techniques used by the agent who sold the relevant policies to each consumer. Determination of reliance depends upon the facts surrounding each consumer's alleged reliance, not upon the same factual inquiry for all consumers.

5. Same situation as in Illustration 4, except that the alleged misrepresentations consist exclusively of a strictly standardized sales pitch prescribed by Defendant for use by insurance agents with regard to the implicated policies. Aggregate treatment of the misrepresentation issue would be permissible, even though aggregate treatment of the reliance issue would remain inappropriate.

6. Same situation as in Illustration 5, except that all claimants rely on a common body of evidence that, if believed by the factfinder, is capable of proving reliance as to all claimants. Defendant disputes the common body of evidence offered by claimants but, in so doing, points to no individualized evidence of nonreliance on the part of particular claimants. Aggregate treatment of both the misrepresentation issue and the reliance issue would be permissible.

7. Same situation as in Illustration 6, except that Defendant points to individualized evidence of widespread nonreliance on the part of particular claimants. Aggregate treatment of the misrepresentation issue would be permissible, but aggregate treatment of the reliance would not due to the need for individualized inquiry into the situation of particular claimants.

8. Same situation as in Illustration 5, except that applicable substantive law uses an objective, reasonable-person standard for reliance, presumes reliance upon proof of a material misrepresentation, or otherwise recognizes a basis for establishing reliance

upon proof of a common issue of fact. Aggregate treatment of both the misrepresentation issue and the reliance issue would be permissible if neither would entail individualized inquiry into each consumer's particular transaction. The need for individualized inquiry may be affected by substantive defenses raised as to the misrepresentation or reliance issue.

9. Multiple consumers, 1–100, have claims for economic injury against Defendant, all premised on the allegation that Defendant breached the implied warranty of merchantability under applicable commercial law by selling a product that did not conform to accepted standards of merchantable quality. Aggregate treatment of the breach issue—whether Defendant's product, in fact, did not conform to accepted standards of merchantable quality—would be permissible, as that issue is a common issue concerning liability that may be determined without reference to the selection or distribution of any remedy. The present Illustration in the context of economic injury does not speak to the context of personal-injury claims concerning an alleged breach of the implied warranty of merchantability, which may pose additional complications that may prevent aggregate treatment from materially advancing the resolution of such claims. See § 2.02, Comment a (noting, by way of broad generalization from experience to date with class actions, the greater suitability of claims for economic injury for aggregate treatment by comparison to claims for personal injury).

Substantive defenses or particular elements thereof may themselves constitute common issues as to liability suitable for determination on an aggregate basis. Some substantive defenses—for instance, some forms of setoffs to back-pay awards in employment discrimination—may not entail inquiry into the situations of particular claimants but, rather, may be amenable to determination across all claimants in the aggregate.

c. *Liability leading to ministerial administration of remedy.* Issues of remedy frequently entail individualized consideration of claimants—for example, the extent and nature of their loss, as necessary for the calculation of damages. The nature of liability in some contexts, however, is such that a finding of liability effectively will determine both the choice of remedy and the methodology for its distribution. When the nature of the injury suffered by claimants stems from their relationship both to the defendant and to each other through a market mechanism, as in much litigation concerning economic injuries, a finding of liability often will determine that the remedy for any given claimant should take the form of damages to be calculated by reference to some underlying benchmark reflecting the claimant's position within the relevant market.

Illustrations:

10. Multiple consumers, 1–100, have claims against defendants Alpha Corporation and Beta Corporation, all premised on the allegation that Alpha and Beta entered into an unlawful conspiracy to fix prices for their competing consumer products to direct purchasers. All claims arise under federal antitrust law. Aggregate treatment of both liability issues and remedy issues would be appropriate if a finding of liability—centered upon the existence and nature of any price-fixing by Alpha and Beta and antitrust injury on the part of all consumers—effectively will dictate that claimants receive retrospective relief in the form of damages and will determine the method for distribution of damages to individual claimants (e.g., based on a formula keyed to an estimate of the per-unit increase in price attributable to the price-fixing agreement). Other remedies, such as an injunction against Alpha and Beta to refrain from conspiring to fix prices in the future, may also be available, but aggregate treatment of damages would be permissible in any event.

11. Multiple investors, 1–100, have claims against Defendant, all premised on the allegation that Defendant made misleading statements concerning its business operations that artificially inflated the price at which Defendant's shares traded on an efficient capital market on which the plaintiff investors purchased those shares. All claims arise under federal securities law. Aggregate treatment of both liability issues and remedy issues would be appropriate insofar as a finding of liability—centered on whether the statements in question were misleading within the meaning of securities law, with no individualized defenses involved—effectively will dictate that investors receive relief in the form of damages and will determine the method for distribution of damages to individual investors (for example, based upon an estimate of the difference in share price during relevant time periods).

d. Settlement of a common liability issue. In providing for aggregate treatment of a common issue concerning liability, this Section does not assume that determination of that issue necessarily will proceed by way of trial rather than settlement. In authorizing a class action for aggregate treatment of a liability issue in keeping with

§ 2.02(a), this Section disturbs neither the requirement that the court approve any class settlement, see § 3.05, nor any of the other procedural requirements in current law concerning class actions. When a settlement stems from a class action restricted to a particular issue of liability, however, the settlement generally should encompass only that issue. The court should scrutinize closely a proposed class settlement that would set terms for subsequent individual proceedings on questions of remedy or that would extinguish aspects of claims other than the common liability issue. See Comment *e*. Courts likewise should scrutinize closely the expansion of the claims encompassed in the ultimate class settlement by comparison to the initial class complaint. The treatment of classes certified for settlement is addressed at length in § 3.06.

    e. Preclusion as to only the identified common issues. Complaints often contain claims that can properly be litigated in the aggregate (because they present common issues of law or fact) and claims that cannot (because they lack such common issues). In such a situation, a court may adjudicate some issues in the aggregate while severing the remaining issues or claims for separate trial or trying them concurrently but on a nonaggregate basis. In either event, preclusion from the aggregate proceeding extends only to the issues selected to be tried in the aggregate and only as to those claimants who have not elected to exclude themselves from the common resolution.

Illustration:

    12. Multiple claimants, 1–100, have claims for economic injury against Defendant, all premised on allegations that Defendant's product did not conform to accepted standards of merchantable quality and that all claimants suffered consequential damages because the product was defective. The court determines that the merchantability of Defendant's product constitutes a common issue based on satisfaction with the definition in § 2.01 in the circumstances presented but also that the product-defect claim does not present a common issue, because the latter claim depends upon the ways in which the product was used and the damage caused. If the court finds that the other conditions for aggregation are met, then an aggregated trial may proceed on the merchantability claim alone. Whatever the outcome of that trial, claimants would not be precluded from raising product-defect claims in other proceedings. Again, as for Illustration 9, the present Illustration speaks only to claims for economic injury, not to claims for personal injury as to which additional complications

in substantive law may prevent aggregate treatment from materially advancing the resolution of such claims.

REPORTERS' NOTES

Comment b. Illustration 1 builds on the analysis of comparative negligence and the difficulties it may present for classwide treatment of the breach issue raised by negligence claims in the product-liability context. In re Rhone–Poulenc Rorer, Inc., 51 F.3d 1293, 1303 (7th Cir. 1995). The analysis in Illustration 1, however, characterizes the difficulties presented for aggregation in this setting as ones of practicality, not problems of a constitutional dimension. See these Reporters' Notes, infra (distinguishing practical problems posed by the need to reconsider evidence in later proceedings from constitutional problems under the Reexamination Clause of the Seventh Amendment).

Illustration 2 is drawn from the situation in Poulos v. Caesars World, Inc., 379 F.3d 654, 665–666 (9th Cir. 2004) ("[G]ambling is not a context in which we can assume that potential class members are always similarly situated. Gamblers do not share a common universe of knowledge and expectations—one motivation does not 'fit all.' ").

Illustration 3 builds on the analysis of issue-class certification concerning localized environmental contamination in Mejdrech v. Met–Coil Systems Corp., 319 F.3d 910 (7th Cir. 2003). Illustrations 4–8 present factual variations on the series of lawsuits concerning so-called vanishing premiums in the insurance industry. See, e.g., In re Prudential Ins. Co. Am. Sales Practice Litig., 148 F.3d 283 (3d Cir. 1998). See also Fed. R. Civ. P. 23, advisory committee's note (1966 amendments) ("[A]lthough having

some common core, a fraud case may be unsuited for treatment as a class action if there was material variation in the representations made or in the kinds or degrees of reliance by the persons to whom they were addressed."). The same Illustrations also draw on the comparative treatment of reliance issues across consumer-protection, commercial, tort, and securities law in Samuel Issacharoff, *The Vexing Problem of Reliance in Consumer Class Actions*, 74 Tul. L. Rev. 1633 (2000). Illustration 7, in particular, reflects that evidence of widespread nonreliance offered by the party opposing the aggregate unit can defeat the existence of a common issue on the reliance element. See § 2.01, Illustration 3; In re St. Jude Medical, Inc., 522 F.3d 836, 840 (8th Cir. 2008); Sandwich Chef of Texas, Inc. v. Reliance Nat'l Indem. Ins. Co., 319 F.3d 205, 220 (5th Cir. 2003).

For scholarly discussion of additional possibilities for "polyfurcation"—the identification of "one or more elements of the cause of action, defenses, or damages" for treatment on a class-wide basis—see Laurens Walker, *A Model Plan to Resolve Federal Class Action Cases by Jury Trial*, 88 Va. L. Rev. 405, 412–415 (2002). See also Complex Litigation: Statutory Recommendations and Analysis § 3.01(d), 38 and § 3.01, Comment *f*, 61 (directing the aggregation inquiry to whether issues, not entire lawsuits, contain commonality sufficient to warrant aggregation).

For the authority in existing law for the use of written questions with a general verdict, see, e.g., Fed. R. Civ. P. 49(b).

In casting as a practical limitation the need for reconsideration of evidence across the aggregate proceeding and subsequent proceeding, Comment *b* generalizes to issue-class certifications as a whole a concern raised with respect to litigation that triggers the Seventh Amendment right to jury trial. The Seventh Amendment right to jury trial extends only to "suits at common law." U.S. Const. amend. VII. See also Ross v. Bernhard, 396 U.S. 531, 533 (1970) (holding that the Seventh Amendment "entitle[s] the parties to a jury trial in actions for damages to a person or property, for libel and slander, for recovery of land, and for conversion of personal property."); Curtis v. Loether, 415 U.S. 189, 194 (1974) (holding that the Seventh Amendment also extends "to actions enforcing statutory rights, and requires a jury trial on demand, if the statute creates legal rights and remedies, enforceable in an action for damages in the ordinary courts of law.").

Judicial attention to the application of the Reexamination Clause in aggregate litigation stems from In re Rhone–Poulenc Rorer, Inc., 51 F.3d 1293, 1303 (7th Cir. 1995), and Castano v. American Tobacco Co., 84 F.3d 734, 751 (5th Cir. 1996), both of which concerned mass-tort litigation. But see Robinson v. Metro–North Commuter R.R. Co., 267 F.3d 147, 169 n.13 (2d Cir. 2001) (rejecting Reexamination Clause challenge to certification of Rule 23(b)(2) class for liability in employment-discrimination litigation). None of these courts, however, consider closely the text or historical context of the Reexamination Clause. For such an analysis in a prominent defense-side journal, see W. Russell Taber, *The Reexamination Clause: Exploring Bifurcation in Mass Tort Litigation*, 73 Def. Counsel J. 63 (2006). For a pre-*Rhone–Poulenc* analysis of bifurcation of liability and damages issues, see Complex Litigation: Statutory Recommendations and Analysis § 3.06, Comment *e*, 118.

Comment *b* reflects the concerns expressed by the *Rhone–Poulenc* and *Castano* courts about the practical difficulties that attend the aggregate treatment of liability issues when applicable substantive law does not cleanly separate issues of liability from disputed affirmative defenses. Drawing specifically on the situation presented in *Rhone–Poulenc*, Illustration 1 reflects that the inquiry into comparative negligence for purposes of individual trials would, as a practical matter, involve substantial reconsideration of evidence concerning the defendant's alleged breach presented in the aggregate trial. As such, aggregate treatment of the breach issue would not materially advance the resolution of multiple claims but, rather, would involve the rehashing of evidence across the aggregate proceeding and subsequent proceedings.

Whether—and, if so, when—the reconsideration of evidence rises to the level of a constitutional violation under the Reexamination Clause remains uncertain as a matter of Supreme Court precedent. In a decision outside the aggregate-litigation context, the Supreme Court in Gasoline Products Co. v. Champlin Refining Co., 283 U.S. 494, 500 (1931), noted that a partial new trial in conventional one-on-one litigation "may not properly be resorted to unless it clearly appears that the issue to be retried is so distinct and separable from the others that a trial of it alone may be had without injustice." The *Gasoline Products* Court nonetheless added that the Seventh Amendment "does not prohibit the introduction of new methods for ascertaining what the facts are in issue, ... or require that an issue once correctly determined, in accordance with the constitutional command, be tried a second time, even though justice demands that another distinct issue, because erroneously determined, must again be passed on by a jury." Id. at 498. The Court simply held that "the question of damages" on a contractual counterclaim was "so interwoven with that of liability that the former cannot be submitted to the jury" by way of a partial new trial "independently of the latter." Id. at 500. The concern in *Gasoline Products*, in short, focused on relitigation of the liability issue—one as to which no error occurred in the original trial—not the reconsideration of evidence presented initially as to an issue *different* from those now for determination by the factfinder.

Comment c. Illustrations 10–11 stem from the treatment of both liability and remedy issues in such settings as securities and antitrust class actions. "The determination of damages sustained by individual class members in securities class action suits is often a mechanical task involving the administration of a formula determined on a common basis for the class, and these necessary mechanics do not bar class certification." 3 Herbert R. Newberg et al., *Newberg on Class Actions* § 10.8, 492 (4th ed. 2002). See, e.g., Blackie v. Barrack, 524 F.2d 891, 905 (9th Cir. 1975). For similar recognition that the calculation of damages in anti-

trust class actions may amount to a ministerial task in light of the liability determination, see, e.g., In re Cardizem CD Antitrust Litig., 200 F.R.D. 297, 324 (E.D. Mich. 2001); In re NASDAQ Market–Makers Antitrust Litigation, 169 F.R.D. 493, 521 (S.D.N.Y. 1996); In re Domestic Air Transp. Antitrust Litig., 137 F.R.D. 677, 692–693 (N.D. Ga. 1991).

Calculating damages in cases brought under other statutes may be equally ministerial or even more so. See, e.g., Roper v. Consurve, Inc., 578 F.2d 1106, 1116 (5th Cir. 1978), aff'd on other grounds, 445 U.S. 326 (1980) (use of computers to determine overcharge in credit-card fees under state usury law). Statutory damages may "flow directly" from a determination of liability so as to be "readily calculable on a classwide basis." Young v. Meyer & Njus, P.A., 183 F.R.D. 231, 235 (N.D. Ill. 1998) (discussing Federal Debt Collection Practices Act). In some instances, however, applicable law may impose limitations on statutory damages. See Shady Grove Orthopedic Assoc. v. Allstate Ins. Co., 549 F.3d 137 (2d Cir. 2008), cert. granted, 129 S.Ct. 2160 (2009) (No. 08–1008) (presenting question whether state legislation generally barring class-action treatment for statutory damages under New York law is binding in proposed federal-court class action based on diversity jurisdiction).

In authorizing aggregation to encompass both liability and remedy issues when determination of the former sets the basis for ministerial calculation of the latter, subsection (b) bears a resemblance to the "predominance" concept in the current law of class actions. See Fed. R. Civ. P. 23(b)(3). As noted earlier, however, § 2.02 lends greater precision to the predominance inquiry and coordinates it with the authorization for issue classes. See § 2.02, Reporters' Notes. Subsection (b) of the present Section clarifies that aggregation of liability and remedy issues in civil litigation should turn not upon a piling up of the common issues favoring aggregation and the individual issues to the contrary but, instead, upon an inquiry into whether the determination of liability will reduce to a ministerial task the distribution of relief.

Comment d. The requirement of judicial approval for a class settlement is well established in current law. See Fed. R. Civ. P. 23(e). On the importance of enabling class counsel to conduct settlement negotiations against the backdrop of a threat to take the issues that are the subject of those negotiations to trial in some meaningful fashion, even if not necessarily in the particular form of the proposed class action, see Reynolds v. Beneficial Nat'l Bank, 288 F.3d 277, 280–281 (7th Cir. 2002); Epstein v. MCA, Inc., 179 F.3d 641, 652–653 (9th Cir. 1999) (Thomas, J., dissenting); Samuel Issacharoff, *Governance and Legitimacy in the Law of Class Actions*, 1999 Sup. Ct. Rev. 337, 390; Marcel Kahan & Linda Silberman, Matsushita *and Beyond: The Role of State Courts in Class Actions Involving Exclusive Federal Claims*, 1996 Sup. Ct. Rev. 219, 235.

Comment e. Existing law in the class-action area recognizes that the preclusive effect of an aggregate proceeding extends only to the common issues addressed therein. For example, a class-wide finding that a defendant did not engage in a general pattern or practice of employment discrimination will not preclude employees from maintaining actions alleging individual instances of prohibited discrimination. See Cooper v. Federal Reserve Bank of Richmond, 467 U.S. 867, 880–881 (1984). This approach is consistent with general principles of preclusion positing that "a litigant should not be penalized for failing to seek unified disposition of matters that could not have been combined in a single proceeding." 18 Charles Alan Wright, Arthur R. Miller & Edward H. Cooper, *Federal Practice and Procedure* § 4412, 276 (3d ed. 2005).

Effect on current law. The discussion in this Section of the relationship between issues of liability and remedy is not designed to call for amendments to existing rules of civil procedure. As reflected in the Reporters' Notes to § 2.02, judicial decisions generally have not certified proposed issue classes in the product-liability and personal-injury contexts. No change to existing-rule language would necessarily be required for courts to implement this Section.

§ 2.04 Indivisible Remedies Versus Divisible Remedies

(a) **Divisible remedies are those that entail the distribution of relief to one or more claimants individually, without determining in practical effect the application or availability of the same remedy to any other claimant.**

(b) **Indivisible remedies are those such that the distribution of relief to any claimant as a practical matter determines the application or availability of the same remedy to other claimants.**

(c) The court may authorize aggregate treatment of common issues concerning an indivisible remedy by way of a class action, with no requirement under § 2.07 that claimants must be afforded an opportunity to exclude themselves from such treatment. Aggregate treatment as to an indivisible remedy may be appropriate even though additional divisible remedies are also available that warrant individual treatment or aggregate treatment with the opportunity of claimants to exclude themselves as to divisible remedies, as specified in § 2.07.

Comment:

a. Amenability of indivisible remedies to aggregate treatment. The present Section refines the terminology used by existing law in some areas of aggregation, such as class actions, by distinguishing between remedies based upon their divisibility. In doing so, this Section seeks to lend greater precision to inquiries presently conducted by reference to the law–equity distinction.

The line drawn here between divisible and indivisible remedies directs attention to matters of functionality and practical operation rather than inherited categorical labels. The contrast drawn between divisible and indivisible remedies in subsections (a) and (b) accordingly focuses on whether the distribution of relief to one claimant will "as a practical matter" determine the application or availability of relief to other claimants. As a general matter, "indivisible remedies" are those handled primarily under Rules 23(b)(1) and (b)(2) of the Federal Rules of Civil Procedure. By contrast, "divisible remedies" are claims typically handled under Rule 23(b)(3).

When a claimant seeks a prohibitory injunction or a declaratory judgment with respect to a generally applicable policy or practice maintained by a defendant, those remedies—if afforded—generally stand to benefit or otherwise affect all persons subject to the disputed policy or practice, even if relief is nominally granted only as to the named claimant. Even in litigation against governmental entities, to which limitations on preclusion may apply as a formal matter, the generally applicable nature of the policy or practice typically means that the defendant government will be in a position, as a practical matter, either to maintain or to discontinue the disputed policy or practice as a whole, not to afford relief therefrom only to the named claimant. Litigation seeking prohibitory injunctive or declaratory relief against a generally applicable policy or practice is already aggregate litigation in practice, because the relief that would be given to an individual claimant is the same as the relief that would be given to an aggregation of such claimants. To afford aggregate treatment of these indivisible remedies as a procedural matter is to bring procedure into line with that practical reality. Aggregate treatment has the further advantages of giving all persons with interests in the disputed policy or practice an opportunity to be heard and enabling the court to fashion the indivisible remedy with all relevant interests in mind. For the defendant, aggregate treatment eliminates the possibility of multiple claimants repeatedly litigating the same issues in successive proceedings, thereby reducing the likelihood of conflicting remedies and inconsistent outcomes, as well as the wasteful transaction costs associated with repeated litigation of the same issues. Aggregate treatment also can help to ensure that a denial of an indivisible remedy will redound to the disadvantage of all affected claimants, consistent with the kind of two-way preclusion contemplated for the modern class action.

Indivisible remedies also may arise with regard to the distribution of a limited fund. In this situation, any distribution as to one claimant invariably affects all other claimants' potential recovery. Here, too, aggregate treatment does not so much impose a relationship among the claimants as it recognizes the preexisting interdependence of their claims. Aggregate treatment, moreover, is likely to be preferable to serial litigation in its capacity to provide for equitable distribution of the limited fund among all claimants.

This Section clarifies that aggregate treatment of common issues concerning indivisible remedies is permissible even though divisible remedies are also available—such as damages outside the scenario of a limited fund—that warrant individualized treatment or, conceivably, aggregate treatment with the opportunity for claimants to exclude themselves. The court nonetheless should bear in mind the scenario described in § 2.03(b). If the determination of common issues with respect to indivisible remedies will determine, in practical effect, the methodology for distribution of divisible remedies, then the court should afford aggregate treatment as to both categories of remedy.

The decision whether to afford aggregate treatment remains distinct from the further question whether the aggregate proceeding should be mandatory in nature. The latter question implicates considerations of constitutional due process addressed separately in § 2.07. As explained there, considerations of due process generally require that the court determine the distribution of divisible remedies on an aggregate basis only upon affording claimants an opportunity to escape the preclusive effect of that determination. See § 2.07(a)(2). No such opportunity need be provided, however, with regard to indivisible remedies. The black letter of this Section anticipates and cross-references the more extensive treatment in § 2.07(c).

In contemplating aggregate treatment for an indivisible remedy that would not aggregate as to divisible remedies, this Section carries forward the general observation in § 2.02, Comment *e*, that an aggregate proceeding confined to particular issues stands to yield only issue preclusion with respect to the issues encompassed, whereas an aggregate proceeding that encompasses all issues stands to yield both claim preclusion and issue preclusion. There is an important scenario, however, in which the issue-preclusive effect of aggregate treatment for indivisible remedies may, in practical effect, extend more broadly.

Substantive law frequently provides for both indivisible and divisible remedies based on common issues concerning liability. In these circumstances, aggregate treatment of indivisible remedies—in particular, aggregate treatment on a mandatory basis—raises the potential for issue preclusion to result as to a common liability issue that, in turn, would preclude the pursuit of divisible remedies. The preclusion exerted, nonetheless, remains in the nature of issue preclusion from actual litigation and determination of the common liability issue in the mandatory class action. Recognition of the potential for issue preclusion to operate with respect to the pursuit of divisible remedies in this scenario is in keeping with the aspiration of aggregate procedure to yield two-way preclusion—here, for a defense victory on a common liability issue in a mandatory aggregate proceeding for indivisible remedies to be binding vis-à-vis all class members, just as a victory on the same issue by the plaintiff class could be invoked as issue preclusive by all class members against the defendant.

b. Problems of characterization. The distinction drawn in this Section between divisible and indivisible remedies focuses on structural characteristics of the remedies themselves. In characterizing a particular remedy for purposes of deciding whether to afford aggregate treatment, the court should look to the practical operation of the remedy rather than to its categorization along the law–equity divide. Prohibitory injunctions generally fit the description of an indivisible remedy, but other kinds of injunctions such as those that affirmatively compel specific remedial action may pose more difficult questions of characterization in a given situation. The specific remedial action required by an affirmative injunction may be such that it realistically can be undertaken only in such a way that does not differentiate among persons affected by the underlying conduct on the defendant's part. Again, the important point is for the court to focus on the practical operation of the injunction in the particular situation presented.

The court also should remain alert to the possibility that a given remedy might be mischaracterized as indivisible in an attempt to facilitate aggregation, even though the remedy, in practical operation, will function as a divisible one. Careful judicial examination along these lines may have a secondary benefit, in some instances, of avoiding the inadvertent foreclosure of divisible remedies through the operation of claim-preclusion principles.

Illustrations:

    1. Multiple beneficiaries of a retirement plan have claims against the plan administrator. All beneficiaries allege that the formula governing benefits has been misapplied, and all demand a declaratory judgment fixing the application of the formula for all beneficiaries. If the request for a declaratory judgment succeeds, then the beneficiaries will demand damages in the form of supplemental payments to cover the shortfalls they suffered in prior years. Aggregate treatment of the claim for a declaratory judgment would be permissible, because the remedy sought is indivisible. Any resulting change in the method for calculating plan benefits would inevitably affect all beneficiaries, because the retirement plan could not realistically be administered so as to apply different calculation methods to beneficiaries who are similarly situated. In accordance with § 2.03(b), the court should consider whether any further request for damages also would be suitable for aggregate treatment, insofar as the requested declaratory judgment, if granted, would make the calculation of damages a ministerial task.

    2. Multiple persons, 1–100, allege that each of them is at a significantly elevated risk of future disease as a proximate result of wrongful exposure in excess of background exposure levels to a toxic substance for which Defendant is legally responsible. As relief, all such exposed persons seek the establishment and funding by Defendant of a court-supervised program whereby all will receive medical monitoring. The question of liability, however, will turn on particular facts of each individual's claimed exposure—for instance, the magnitude of their respective exposures (relative to the level that would warrant medical monitoring), the warnings (if any) provided to them, or whether such individuals bear some degree of legal responsibility for the exposure under principles of comparative negligence. This individual inquiry will control the outcome of the proceedings, regardless of whether applicable substantive law requires physical injury beyond exposure alone, or, alternatively, recognizes an entitlement to medical monitoring in the absence of physical injury. Because the liability inquiry turns on the individual circumstances of exposure for the particular persons involved, aggregate treatment is unwarranted.

The availability of medical monitoring as a remedy, or as an independent claim, in the absence of physical injury, is an issue that has divided the courts. Initial acceptance of medical monitoring has waned, and the last decade has seen more states decline to recognize it than adopt it. The Institute has never taken a position on whether recovery for medical monitoring should be permitted in these circumstances, and these Principles similarly take no position on medical monitoring as a matter of substantive law, except that adjudications should be conducted with fidelity to applicable substantive law, as provided in § 1.03(a).

Illustration 2 describes a common outcome when class certification has been sought for medical-monitoring claims. Even when medical-monitoring claims are allowed, there is no basis for aggregating claims that ultimately rely on individual considerations to prove liability.

Illustration:

3. Same situation as in Illustration 2, except: (1) the evidence to be offered by persons 1–100 consists of epidemiological or other aggregate proof applicable to all those exposed to the disputed toxic substance, (2) the connection between the elevated risk of future disease and exposure to the substance for which Defendant is legally responsible does not involve individualized inquiry into the circumstances of particular persons, (3) all persons allege that, in light of such exposure, a reasonable physician would prescribe a medical-monitoring regime above and beyond the medical services that such a physician otherwise would recommend, and (4) such monitoring will be instrumental in guiding medical intervention to mitigate the effects of disease manifestation, should disease ultimately occur. If the requested remedy respects applicable substantive law as discussed in § 2.05, then the court should find that the requested relief demands a form of performance other than the distribution of money. Medical monitoring with the capacity to guide medical intervention to mitigate the effects of disease differs from the distribution of money to compensate for past harm, because the basis for the claimed program stems from a shared risk among similarly situated persons. In accordance with § 1.03, the court has discretion to characterize such a remedy as indivisible and, hence, capable of treatment on an aggregate basis. Such a characterization would operate irrespective of whether applicable substantive law treats medical monitoring as a legal or equitable remedy. The position of

medical monitoring along the law–equity divide may be important for other purposes, but it does not affect the characterization of the remedy for purposes of the court's aggregation decision.

Court supervision underscores the binding quality of the medical-monitoring program vis-à-vis exposed persons, who receive the indicated additional medical services, not an award in the nature of damages that such persons may use as they choose. Judicial discretion as to characterization nonetheless is appropriate due to the considerable variations in underlying facts and details of requested medical-monitoring programs.

Illustrations:

4. Same situation as in Illustration 3, except that the requested relief amounts to creation of a fund with a fixed sum of money equivalent to the anticipated cost of appropriate medical services, and ongoing court supervision to ensure that exposed persons actually obtain the indicated medical services is minimal. The court should characterize the requested relief as divisible and thus not suitable for aggregate treatment under this Section. Though nominally cast as a demand for medical monitoring, the requested relief operates in practice in the manner of conventional damages.

5. Multiple employees, 1–100, have claims against Defendant, all based on the allegation that Defendant engaged in a pattern or practice of discrimination on the basis of race in its workplace. Applicable substantive law provides that, in the event of a determination of unlawful employment discrimination, employees are entitled to injunctive relief, declaratory relief, and back pay. Applicable substantive law also recognizes the possibility of emotional-distress damages upon further individualized proof as to the nature of Defendant's unlawful discrimination with respect to particular employees. The employees' claims for injunctive and declaratory relief—which may include promotions, additional hires, job training, and other programs on Defendant's part—qualify as indivisible remedies, such that aggregate treatment of those claims would be permissible, if the allegations of pattern-or-practice discrimination are otherwise suited for aggregation. The employees' claims for back pay constitute demands for divisible remedies in that they would entail the distribution of back pay to individual employees. In accordance with § 2.03(b), the court should consider whether aggregate treatment of any

common issues concerning Defendant's liability will determine, in practical effect, the availability and method for the distribution of back pay. If so, then the employees' claims for back pay may be treated on an aggregate basis. The employees' remaining demands for emotional-distress damages also seek divisible remedies. In accordance with § 2.03(a), the court should consider whether there are any common issues of liability bearing upon those divisible remedies that are suitable for aggregate treatment. Distribution of emotional-distress damages for any particular claimant, however, must await individualized treatment.

REPORTERS' NOTES

Comment a. The present Section builds on, but also simplifies, the existing categories of aggregation by way of class actions. See Fed. R. Civ. P. 23(b). The distinction drawn here between divisible and indivisible remedies seeks to remain true to the functional insights behind the Rule 23(b) categories, unburdened by the historical categories of legal and equitable remedies. For an argument along broadly similar lines, see Brian Wolfman & Alan B. Morrison, *What the* Shutts *Opt–Out Right is and What it Ought to Be*, 74 UMKC L. Rev. 729, 747–750 (2006).

Existing law recognizes the appropriateness of class treatment for claims seeking injunctive or declaratory relief. Rule 23(b)(2) says as much by its terms. See Fed. R. Civ. P. 23(b)(2) (authorizing mandatory class treatment when "the party opposing the class has acted or refused to act on grounds that apply generally to the class, so that final injunctive relief or corresponding declaratory relief is appropriate respecting the class as a whole"). In practical operation, courts have come to much the same view of Rule 23(b)(1)(A), which authorizes mandatory class treatment when "prosecuting separate actions by . . . individual class members

would create a risk of . . . inconsistent or varying adjudications with respect to individual class members that would establish incompatible standards of conduct for the party opposing the class." Describing "the type of class action context most likely to qualify for class treatment under Rule 23(b)(1)(A)," one leading treatise points to "a broad spectrum of class actions seeking declaratory or injunctive relief against a party opposing the class." 2 Herbert B. Newberg et al., *Newberg on Class Actions* § 4:8, 31–32 (4th ed. 2002). The same source adds that "[m]ost of these examples, particularly in the civil rights area, will also qualify as Rule 23(b)(2) class actions." Id.

Courts, in short, have not succeeded in giving any distinct meaning to Rule 23(b)(1)(A) by comparison to Rule 23(b)(2). The present Section accordingly regards the category of claims suitable for class treatment under the two rules as the same in functional terms. The important question under either rule remains whether the class is seeking an indivisible remedy.

Considerable uncertainty has arisen over the advisory committee's note on Rule 23(b)(2), which states that the class treatment authorized under that subsection "does not extend to cases in which the appropriate final relief relates exclusively or predominantly to money damages." Fed. R. Civ. P. 23(b)(2), advisory committee's note. Similar language appears in discussions of Rule 23(b)(1)(A). See, e.g., Newberg et al., *Newberg on Class Actions* § 4:8, 32–33 (noting that "[m]onetary damages may be a major if not predominant form of relief sought" in Rule 23(b)(1)(A) classes that are "seeking primarily declaratory or injunctive relief"). The suggestion that a class action under either Rule 23(b)(1)(A) or Rule 23(b)(2) might include some manner of claims for money damages, as long as they do not predominate over claims for injunctive or declaratory relief, tends to cast the class-certification inquiry along lines akin to Rule 23(b)(3), under which courts must ask whether common issues predominate over individual ones. The present Section directs attention to the suitability of aggregate treatment for each specific type of relief rather than to questions about which type of relief predominates over the implicated claims as a whole.

Existing law also recognizes the appropriateness of class treatment for claims against a limited fund, describing the justification for such treatment in terms of the relationship among such claims "as a practical matter." See Fed. R. Civ. P. 23(b)(1)(B) (authorizing mandatory class treatment when "adjudications with respect to individual class members . . . , as a practical matter, would be dispositive of the interests of the other members not parties to the individual adjudications or would substantially impair or impede their ability to protect their interests").

On the special limitations on preclusion in the context of litigation against governmental entities, see, e.g., United States v. Mendoza, 464 U.S. 154, 162 (1984) (holding "nonmutual offensive collateral estoppel" inapplicable against the United States as a party).

Comment b. Illustration 1 comes from Berger v. Xerox Corp. Retirement Income Guarantee Plan, 338 F.3d 755 (7th Cir. 2003). There being only one formula governing benefits for all retirees, a declaratory judgment in favor of the named plaintiffs for the *Berger* class would necessarily have required the plan administrator to adjust the manner of benefit calculation for all similarly situated persons. The further demand for damages was both a natural follow-on to the declaratory-judgment request and required only a ministerial calculation once that request was granted. See id. at 764 ("The declaration established the right of each of the class members, and the computation of the damages due each followed mechanically.").

Illustrations 2–4 are designed to convey the main issues concerning the certification of class actions for medical monitoring. As a matter of substantive law, courts are split on the viability of, and proper approach to medical-monitoring actions. See Manual for Complex Litigation (Fourth) § 22.74, at 425–426 (2004) (explaining, for example, that "[some] courts have not, to date, required plaintiffs to show that [an] increase in risk constitutes the proximate cause of any injury that might follow, . . . [other] courts have adopted a lesser standard for evaluating how much of an increase in risk plaintiffs must show to trigger the medical monitoring remedy, . . . [while still other] courts have found that ... applicable state law precludes medical monitoring claims if the claimants have no present injury"). See also Metro–North Commuter R.R. Co. v. Buckley, 521 U.S. 424, 440–444 (1997) ("[T]he cases authorizing recovery for medical monitoring in the absence of physical injury do not endorse a full-blown, traditional tort law cause of action for lump-sum damages.... Rather, those courts, while recognizing that medical monitoring costs can amount to a harm that justifies a tort remedy, have suggested, or imposed, special limitations on that remedy [such as] 'a court-supervised fund to administer medical-surveillance payments.' "); In re Welding Fume Prods. Liab. Litig., 245 F.R.D. 279, 291–292 (N.D. Ohio 2007) ("The law of medical monitoring varies from state to state. Some states recognize medical monitoring as an element of damages when liability is otherwise established, while other states recognize medical monitoring as an independent cause of action; some states require proof of a present, physical injury to obtain medical monitoring, and some do not; and some states do not provide for medical monitoring at all."); James A. Henderson, Jr. & Aaron D. Twerski, *Asbestos Litigation Gone Mad: Exposure–Based Recovery for Increased Risk, Mental Distress & Medical Monitoring*, 53 S.C. L. Rev. 815, 841 (2002) ("On any fair assessment of the relevant precedent, American courts have not reached consensus regarding the legitimacy of ... medical monitoring claims."). Illustrations 2–4 take no position on medical monitoring as a matter of substantive law but, instead, analyze the implications for class-action treatment of several commonplace scenarios in which the requested relief takes such a form.

Illustration 2 addresses a common outcome in class-certification decisions involving medical monitoring in recent years. As a leading opinion described the problem:

> While 23(b)(2) class actions have no predominance or superiority requirements, it is well established that the class claims must be cohesive.... [B]y its very nature, a (b)(2) class must be cohesive as to those claims tried in the class action. Because of the cohesive nature of the class, Rule 23(c)(3) contemplates that all members of the class will be bound. Any resultant unfairness to the members of the class was thought to be outweighed by the purposes behind class actions: eliminating the possibility of repetitious litigation and providing small claimants with a means of obtaining redress for claims too small to justify individual litigation.... We believe that [nicotine] addiction, causation, the defenses of comparative and contributory negligence, the need for medical monitoring and the statute of limitations present too many individual issues to permit certification.... These disparate issues make class treatment inappropriate.

Barnes v. Am. Tobacco Co., 161 F.3d 127, 143 (3d Cir. 1998) (internal citations and quotation marks omitted) (applying Pennsylvania law). But see Donovan v. Philip Morris USA, Inc., 914 N.E.2d 891 (Mass. 2009) (allowing medical-monitoring claim on behalf of smokers for increased cancer risk). Illustration 2 also draws on the extensive treatment in In re Welding Fume Products Liability Litigation, in which the court explained:

[I]n medical monitoring cases stemming from toxic spills or radioactive releases, the question of increased risk of injury ... is virtually the same as the question of exposure—if the plaintiffs were exposed to a toxic material released by the defendant, then their risk of illness is higher....

In this case, however, the allegedly hazardous substance to which the plaintiffs were exposed (manganese fumes) is released by a commonly-used and extremely useful product (welding rods), the sale and use of which requires no governmental dispensation. The parties [sic] experts agree, moreover, that not every exposure to manganese fumes is toxic; the level of exposure is critical to the question of whether an increased risk of illness occurs. And, the product came with warnings. Thus, whether the defendants were negligent ... depends not simply on whether any given plaintiff suffered exposure, but on whether the warning supplied by the defendant sufficiently apprised the plaintiff of the risk of exposure. Similarly, whether a given plaintiff suffers an increased risk of illness ... depends not simply on the fact of welding fume exposure, but on the *degree* of exposure, and whether there was more exposure than might have otherwise occurred *due to the failure of the warning*. These circumstances change dramatically the degree of typicality of evidence and issues among plaintiffs in this case, because of the great variety of products, manufacturers, warnings, employers, and workplaces involved.

245 F.R.D. 279, 309–310 (N.D. Ohio 2007) (footnote omitted) (emphasis in original).

Particularly after *Barnes*, courts often have withheld class certification for medical monitoring due to the presence of individualized issues of the sort in Illustration 2. See, e.g., In re St. Jude Medical, Inc., 425 F.3d 1116, 1122 (8th Cir. 2005) (class certification inappropriate when class members' respective need for medical monitoring entails "individualized inquiry depending on that patient's medical history, the condition of the patient's heart valves at the time of implantation, the patient's risk factors for heart valve complications, the patient's general health, the patient's personal choice, and other factors"); Wilson v. Brush Wellman, Inc., 817 N.E.2d 59, 66 (Ohio 2004) (class certification inappropriate notwithstanding injunctive nature of requested medical-monitoring relief due to "multiple individual questions of fact requiring examination for different plaintiffs within the proposed class"); Rhodes v. E.I. Du Pont de Nemours & Co., 253 F.R.D. 365, 380 (S.D. W. Va. 2008) (declining to certify medical-monitoring class when significant exposure, significant increased risk of future disease, and need for medical monitoring could not be shown on class-wide basis).

Illustration 3 recognizes that medical-monitoring classes can be certified when individualized issues are not present, often because the standards for the relevant medical monitoring are undisputed. See *Welding Fumes*, 245 F.R.D. at 314 n.186 (citing illustrative federal cases). Whether a proposed medical-monitoring remedy is indivisible has often turned on "the fine distinction between a medical monitoring claim that seeks monetary relief in the form of compensatory damages and a medical monitoring claim that seeks injunctive relief in the form of a court-supervised medical monitoring program." Arch v. Am. Tobacco Co., 175 F.R.D. 469, 483 (E.D. Pa. 1997). As one court explained through a series of examples:

> Relief in the form of medical monitoring may be by a number of means. First, a court may simply order a defendant to pay a plaintiff a certain sum of money. The plaintiff may or may not choose to use that money to have his medical condition monitored. Second, a court may order the defendants to pay the plaintiffs' medical expenses directly so that a plaintiff may be monitored by the physician of his choice. Neither of these forms of relief constitute[s] injunctive relief. . . .

> However, a court may also establish an elaborate medical monitoring program of its own, managed by court-appointed court-supervised trustees, pursuant to which a plaintiff is monitored by particular physicians and the medical data produced utilized for group studies. In this situation, a defendant, of course, would finance the program as well as being required by the court to address issues as they develop during program administration. Under these circumstances, the relief constitutes injunctive relief. . . .

Day v. NLO, Inc., 144 F.R.D. 330, 335–336 (S.D. Ohio 1992), rev'd on other grounds, 5 F.3d 154 (6th Cir. 1993). Other courts have reached similar results. See, e.g., Olden v. La-Farge Corp., 383 F.3d 495, 508 (6th Cir. 2004) (upholding class certification when questions "[w]hether the defendant's negligence caused *some* increased health risk and . . . whether it tended to cause the class minor medical issues can likely be determined for the entire class"); In re Diet Drugs Prods. Liab. Litig., No. CIV. A. 98–20626, 1999 WL 673066, *13 (E.D. Pa. Aug. 26, 1999) (certifying medical-monitoring class in fen-phen litigation when "the individual issues which [the defendant] raises . . . are more susceptible to subclass treatment than the claims relating to tobacco use [in *Barnes*]").

Illustration 4 reflects cases in which courts have concluded that the requested medical-monitoring relief operated in functional terms as window dressing for a demand for money damages. See, e.g., *Day*, 144 F.R.D. at 335–336; Zinser v. Accufix Research Inst., Inc., 253 F.3d 1180, 1194 (9th Cir. 2001) (rejecting certification when "[i]t is apparent that the requested 'medical monitoring fund' is in essence a request for monetary relief"). The distinction between indivisible medical-monitoring relief and divisible-damage relief bears close attention, given the insistence upon opt-out rights for class members as to the latter as a matter of constitutional due process. See Phillips Petroleum Co. v. Shutts, 472 U.S. 797, 811–812 (1985).

On the relationship between aggregate treatment of claims for medical monitoring and the underlying characterization of such claims along the law–equity divide, see Samuel Issacharoff, *Preclusion, Due Process, and the Right to Opt Out of Class Actions*, 77 Notre Dame L. Rev. 1057, 1073–1080 (2002); John C.P. Goldberg & Benjamin C. Zipursky, *Unrealized Torts*, 88 Va. L. Rev. 1625, 1712 (2002); Pankaj Venugopal, Note, *The Class Certification of Medical Moni-*

toring Claims, 102 Colum. L. Rev. 1659, 1664–1670 (2002); Manual for Complex Litigation (Fourth) § 22.74 (2004).

Illustration 5 speaks to class treatment of divisible and indivisible remedies in the employment-discrimination context. Before 1991, courts routinely certified employment-discrimination class actions under Rule 23(b)(2), encompassing not only claims for injunctive and declaratory relief but also claims for back pay. The back-pay remedy seeks to account for the wages and other economic benefits lost as a result of unlawful discrimination. Courts countenanced the inclusion of back-pay claims in Rule 23(b)(2) class actions before 1991 by characterizing those claims as equitable—specifically, as seeking a remedy that follows, as a matter of course, from the underlying determination of unlawful discrimination. See, e.g., Pettway v. Am. Cast Iron Pipe Co., 494 F.2d 211, 256–258 (5th Cir. 1974); Senter v. Gen. Motors Corp., 532 F.2d 511, 525 (6th Cir. 1976); Robinson v. Lorillard Corp., 444 F.2d 791, 802 (4th Cir. 1971). The characterization of back pay as an equitable remedy in the years immediately after the Civil Rights Act of 1964 had the further consequence of avoiding the triggering of the Seventh Amendment right to jury trial—something that plaintiffs at the time might well have wished to avoid as a strategic matter. For commentary questioning the categorization of back pay as an equitable remedy, see Colleen P. Murphy, *Misclassifying Monetary Restitution*, 55 SMU L. Rev. 1577, 1633 (2002). For purposes of this Section, the historical classification of back pay as an equitable remedy is not

relevant. Because a demand for back pay, if honored, would result in a judgment directing the defendant to distribute money to particular individual claimants, back pay is a divisible remedy and should be so analyzed for purposes of aggregation. Whether back-pay remedies trigger jury trials as legal rather than equitable claims is not germane to the distinction between the divisible or indivisible character of the remedy.

The Civil Rights Act of 1991 added to the repertoire of remedies for employment discrimination both conventional compensatory damages (such as for emotional distress) and punitive damages. 42 U.S.C. § 1981a(a)(1) (2000). In the aftermath of the 1991 amendments, courts have struggled to adhere to precedents authorizing the inclusion of back-pay claims within Rule 23(b)(2) classes but, at the same time, to resist the wholesale inclusion of all damage claims. Compare, e.g., Allison v. Citgo Petroleum Corp., 151 F.3d 402, 425 (5th Cir. 1998) (permitting inclusion of back-pay claims in Rule 23(b)(2) class but disallowing inclusion of claims for additional monetary relief authorized by 1991 amendments), with Robinson v. Metro–North Commuter R.R. Co., 267 F.3d 147, 164 (2d Cir. 2001) (calling for "ad hoc balancing" to identify predominant claims within putative Rule 23(b)(2) class). For commentary on the divergent judicial approaches, see, e.g., Daniel F. Piar, *The Uncertain Future of Title VII Class Actions After the Civil Rights Act of 1991*, 2001 BYU L. Rev. 305; Lesley Frieder Wolf, Note, *Evading Friendly Fire: Achieving Class Certification After the Civil Rights Act of 1991*, 100 Colum. L. Rev. 1847 (2000). By authorizing new forms of damages in employment-discrimination actions, Congress added little to the managerial challenges already facing the courts with regard to aggregation. Like claims for back pay, claims for emotional-distress damages seek divisible remedies and should be analyzed accordingly. On the treatment of punitive damages, see § 2.07, Reporters' Notes.

The approach to aggregation outlined in Illustration 5 draws on the analysis of class certification in the employment-discrimination context in Allen v. Int'l Truck & Engine Corp., 358 F.3d 469 (7th Cir. 2004). In *Allen*, the Seventh Circuit overturned a district court's refusal to certify a Rule 23(b)(2) class for injunctive relief in a pattern-or-practice case, noting the benefits of aggregate treatment as compared to the pursuit of separate trials and forecasting the issue-preclusive effect that would flow from jury determinations of factual disputes surrounding the availability of injunctive relief. See id. at 472. The Seventh Circuit remanded to the district court the further question whether at least some issues bearing upon the defendant's liability for damages might warrant aggregate treatment, a stance consistent with § 2.03(b). Illustration 5 takes this analysis one step further, speaking specifically to the treatment of back-pay claims, a matter not discussed in *Allen*.

Effect on current law. The vocabulary of this Section—focused on the functional distinction between divisible and indivisible relief rather than on the formal categories of law and equity—is designed to explicate with greater precision the approach taken in recent years by courts under the auspices of Rules 23(b)(1)(A) and (b)(2). Rule amendment might be helpful eventually to incorporate the vocabulary of this Section into the text of the rule, but amendment is not necessary for courts to implement the approach of this Section.

§ 2.05 Choice of Law

(a) **To determine whether multiple claims involve common issues, the court must ascertain the substantive law governing those issues.**

(b) **The court may authorize aggregate treatment of multiple claims, or of a common issue therein, by way of a class action if the court determines that**

(1) **a single body of law applies to all such claims or issues;**

(2) **different claims or issues are subject to different bodies of law that are the same in functional content; or**

(3) **different claims or issues are subject to different bodies of law that are not the same in functional content but nonetheless present a limited number of patterns that the court, for reasons articulated pursuant to § 2.12, can manage by means of identified adjudicatory procedures.**

Comment:

　　a.　Obligation to undertake a choice-of-law analysis. Subsection (a) underscores the obligation of the court to ensure that aggregate treatment will materially advance the resolution of multiple claims. See also § 2.02(a)(1). When claims have connections to more than one jurisdiction, a court may need to undertake a choice-of-law analysis as a precondition for the identification of common issues. This need for a threshold determination of the governing substantive law flows logically from, and reinforces, the definition of common issues in § 2.01. A given issue will not qualify as a common issue if its determination does not call for the resolution of a question that is the same in functional content across all claims to be aggregated. One obstacle stems from differences in applicable substantive law across the claims for which aggregate treatment is sought.

　　When the choice-of-law analysis required by subsection (a) would entail consideration of foreign law, moreover, the court may consider the option of appointing an expert or special master to assist the court in that inquiry.

　　Subsection (a) contemplates no change in the body of choice-of-law principles that govern the court's usual selection of applicable substantive law. Thus, for example, under the legal principles now well established, a federal court considering whether to afford aggregate treatment for claims arising under state law should apply the choice-of-law rules of the state in which that federal court sits. As for this Chapter generally, the objective is for aggregate treatment to operate seamlessly with substantive law—here, by leaving the decision whether to innovate in the area of choice-of-law principles to the institutions with the authority to set those principles themselves. A decision to aggregate should not alter the law that would apply to any party's rights from the law that would be applied were the claims to be pressed individually.

　　The court's obligation to undertake a choice-of-law analysis nonetheless extends only to matters that bear on the legal and factual questions actually contested by the parties. The court need not and should not decide a hypothetical choice-of-law question. The failure of a party to demonstrate the need to decide a choice-of-law question can provide a basis for the court to determine that the question is hypothetical and, therefore, not pertinent to its decision whether to afford aggregate treatment.

Illustration:

　　1.　In a fraud case involving consumers located in diverse states, Defendant opposes aggregation by noting that a particular level of knowledge on the part of consumers with respect to the alleged fraudulent misrepresentations constitutes a defense to liability for fraud under the laws of some states but not those of others. Defendant further contends that individual inquiries will be needed to determine whether particular consumers possessed the requisite level of knowledge and that aggregate treatment accordingly is inappropriate. Before undertaking a choice-of-law analysis as to the knowledge defense, the court should require Defendant to offer evidence that some consumers located in relevant states lacked the level of knowledge required. The court should permit limited discovery for the purpose of enabling Defendant to make this showing.

b. Existing approaches. Choice of law has posed considerable challenges in the context of class actions involving members located in multiple jurisdictions whose claims arise under state law. Courts have used five basic approaches, three of which remain permissible under current law. The organization of this Section is designed to reflect the permissible approaches that exist in current doctrine rather than to set forth new choice-of-law principles for aggregate litigation.

The first approach applies the laws of the respective jurisdictions in which class members are found. Such a choice of law might stem from categorical principles that point to the various jurisdictions in which class members find themselves based upon the nature of the claims involved. The same choice of law might flow from a contextual determination that the jurisdiction in which each class member is found has the most significant interest in controlling the resolution of that class member's claim or, similarly, has the most significant relationship to the underlying dispute.

The second approach also looks to the laws of the jurisdictions in which class members find themselves but groups those laws into a limited number of patterns. The third approach involves the application of choice-of-law principles to select for the class action a body of law that is not arbitrary—that is, one that would not subject the defendant to a legal standard of which it lacked fair notice at the time of its primary conduct as to each class member.

Two additional approaches pose formidable difficulties. The fourth approach involves the application of forum law to all claims—even those that bear no relationship to the forum apart from the location of the aggregate litigation—in the presence of a conflict of laws. This fourth approach is foreclosed by considerations of constitutional due process that guard against arbitrariness in the choice of law. The fifth approach involves the application to all claims of a body of law that appears common only when considered at such a high level of generality that the law chosen does not reflect the actual law of any particular jurisdiction. This fifth approach is foreclosed by the recognition that each body of substantive law derives from a particular sovereign and that courts lack authority to resolve choice-of-law disputes in class actions through amalgamation of the laws of multiple sovereigns. Such an approach risks exposing the defendant to a legal standard for which it did not have notice at the time of the underlying conduct.

Subsection (b) of this Section does not seek to provide an exhaustive typology of permissible approaches to choice of law in aggregate litigation. Subsection (b), instead, pursues the more limited goal of identifying three situations on which a substantial consensus has emerged in existing law that choice-of-law considerations should pose no insurmountable barrier to aggregation.

c. *Single body of substantive law.* Subsection (b)(1) states what is, at first glance, an obvious point: that choice-of-law considerations should not defeat aggregate treatment, if other conditions for aggregation are met, when the application of choice-of-law principles points to a single body of substantive law as governing all claims. In accordance with Comments *a* and *b*, subsection (b)(1) leaves for development by appropriate institutions the choice-of-law principles to determine the situations, if any, in which a court may apply a single body of law—for example, the law of a common defendant's principal place of business—to a group of claims held by persons located in multiple states. At the present time, choice-of-law principles that point toward application of the law of the defendant's principal place of business remain quite rare across the various states. More typically, use of a single governing law based on the defendant's home state is a matter of the underlying substantive law, rather than a question of resolving conflicts of laws. For example, matters of corporate governance routinely are subject to the law of the corporation's state of incorporation, but that approach generally stems from the state's law concerning corporations, not from choice-of-law principles. Any such selection of a single body of law by state choice-of-law principles, moreover, remains subject to constitutional constraints of due process.

d. *Multiple bodies of substantive law that are the same in functional content.* Subsection (b)(2) extends the principle of subsection (b)(1) by noting that aggregate treatment may be proper even when a court finds that nominally different bodies of law govern the claims held by different individuals. The phrasing of subsection (b)(2) carries forward to the choice-of-law context the definition of common issues in § 2.01. The real question for the court is not a formal one (whether multiple bodies of law apply to the claims for which aggregate treatment is sought) but, rather, a functional one (whether those bodies of law are relevantly the same in functional content). If so, then the situation is appropriately treated in the same manner as one in which a single body of law applies to all claims—in practical effect, as a situation involving no conflict in substantive law.

In the legislative arena, significant pressure has long existed for states to make their statutes more uniform, and many efforts to promote uniformity have succeeded. In areas of common law as well, courts often take guidance from the case law of other states (and from federal courts), and that practice too has increased uniformity in some areas. When nominally different bodies of law apply but are the same in their functional content, common issues may be found so as to permit aggregate treatment.

The inquiry into substantive law remains distinct from the question about the desirability of aggregation. It is possible in some cases that nominally different bodies of law might be the same in functional content. This may not, however, be used to avoid resolving the functional content of applicable substantive law so as to facilitate class certification. Rather, just as in nonaggregate litigation when applicable law is uncertain in content, courts should ensure fidelity to state substantive law. See Comment *a* ("A decision to aggregate should not alter the law that would apply to any party's rights from the law that would be applied were the claims to be pressed individually.").

e. Manageable patterns. Subsection (b)(3) recognizes that choice-of-law considerations should not defeat aggregate treatment when the court determines that a manageable number of patterns exist in the relevant bodies of substantive law and explains their suitability for treatment on an aggregate basis as part of its adjudication plan under § 2.12. That 50 different states' laws might apply to a set of claims does not necessarily mean that 50 radically different variations in functional content exist. Subsection (b)(3) recognizes that different states' laws can form manageable clusters or groupings, even when they are not entirely uniform. Common issues may exist within the respective clusters so as to make aggregate treatment permissible.

Subsection (b)(3) nonetheless counsels caution, requiring that the court not only identify the nature and number of variations in substantive law but also articulate a plan for how those variations can be handled on an aggregate basis while respecting their differences in content, including as to pertinent defenses. In order to conduct such an inquiry, the court may need to accumulate and evaluate statutes, common-law decisions, and jury instructions from multiple jurisdictions. The court may reduce the burden on itself, however, by calling for submissions from the parties on these points.

f. Allocation of burdens. As Comment *a* underscores, the present Section contemplates no change in the court's selection or determination of choice-of-law principles. The relevant choice-of-law principles may speak, in particular, to who bears the burden of demonstrating that more than one body of substantive law applies to multiple claims—for example, by placing that burden on the party seeking the application of nonforum law. The proponent of aggregation thus is under no obligation to address hypothetical conflicts of law. Rather, the burden of demonstrating that multiple bodies of law are the same in functional content or arise in a manageable number of patterns such as to make aggregate treatment permissible, see subsections (b)(2)–(b)(3), arises only after an initial demonstration that multiple bodies of law apply to the claims for which aggregate treatment is sought. The burden to make that initial demonstration is a matter governed by applicable choice-of-law principles.

REPORTERS' NOTES

Comment a. This Section as a whole proceeds on the premise that choice of law is a dimension of the larger inquiry into the constraints imposed by substantive law on aggregation, not a matter of procedural choice akin to the decision to aggregate itself. See Larry Kramer, *Choice of Law in Complex Litigation*, 71 N.Y.U. L. Rev. 547, 549 (1996) ("Because choice of law is part of the process of defining the parties' rights, it should not change simply because, as a matter of administrative convenience and efficiency, we have combined many claims in one proceeding; whatever choice-of-law rules we use to define substantive rights should be the same for ordinary and complex cases."); Linda J. Silberman, *The Role of Choice of Law in National Class Actions*, 156 U. Pa. L. Rev. 2001, 2022 (2008) ("The reason for the class device is that a coherence of rights and claims *already exists* among potential class members, and it is the existence of those elements that makes the representative suit appropriate. To use the class action

as the justification for altering choice of law rules would be to put the cart before the horse and to misunderstand the role of both class actions and choice of law.").

The statement in subsection (a) of the court's obligation to undertake a choice-of-law analysis as a precondition to aggregate treatment builds on the status of that obligation in the class-action context as an aspect of constitutional due process. See Phillips Petroleum Co. v. Shutts, 472 U.S. 797, 821–822 (1985). See also In re St. Jude Medical, Inc., 425 F.3d 1116, 1120 (8th Cir. 2005) (citing *Shutts* to support reversal of class certification when "the district court did not conduct a thorough conflicts-of-law analysis with respect to each plaintiff class member before applying Minnesota law"). In this regard, subsection (a) counsels against the view of one outlier state court that has rejected the proposition that its state class-action rule—as distinct from Federal Rule 23—requires the trial court "to engage in a choice-of-law analysis prior to certifying a class" involving state-law claims asserted by a proposed nationwide class. Gen. Motors Corp. v. Bryant, 285 S.W.3d 634, 641 (Ark. 2008).

On the obligation of a federal court to use the choice-of-law rules of the state in which it sits when addressing claims based in state law, see Klaxon Co. v. Stentor Electric Mfg. Co., 313 U.S. 487 (1941). With respect to the further development of choice-of-law principles by appropriate institutions, this Section leaves open the possibility of a federal choice-of-law code. For one such proposal, see Complex Litigation: Statutory Recommendations and Analysis, Introductory Note to Chapter 6, 306 and Appendix A, 449–453. For criticism of *Klaxon* in the contemporary context of nationwide aggregate litigation, see Samuel Issacharoff, *Settled Expectations in a World of Unsettled Law: Choice of Law after the Class Action Fairness Act*, 106 Colum. L. Rev. 1839, 1842 (2006). For criticism of choice-of-law obstacles for small-stakes consumer class actions more generally, see Elizabeth J. Cabraser, *Just Choose: The Jurisprudential Necessity to Select a Single Governing Law for Mass Claims Arising from Nationally Marketed Consumer Goods and Services*, 14 Roger Williams L. Rev. 29 (2009).

Contests over the propriety of aggregation have intensified in recent years based on the widespread recognition that aggregate treatment will magnify the amount at stake in civil litigation. Much of this intensification has centered on choice-of-law questions, with defendants tending to raise all possible objections to aggregation, including choice-of-law questions that may properly be regarded as hypothetical. Illustration 1 is designed to clarify that the obligation of

the court to undertake a choice-of-law analysis under subsection (a) does not extend to hypothetical questions.

On the special treatment accorded to questions of foreign law in federal civil procedure generally, see Fed. R. Civ. P. 44.1 ("In determining foreign law, the court may consider any relevant material or source, including testimony, whether or not submitted by a party or admissible under the Federal Rules of Evidence."). "In some instances, the district judge may appoint a special master to aid in ascertaining the content of foreign law." 9A Charles Alan Wright & Arthur R. Miller, *Federal Practice and Procedure* § 2444, 533 (3d ed. 2005) (citing John G. Sprankling & George R. Lanyi, *Pleading and Proof of Foreign Law in American Courts*, 19 Stan. J. Int'l L. 3, 91–92 (1983)). Existing evidence law authorizes the use of court-appointed experts. See Fed. R. Evid. 706(a).

Comment b. As this Comment emphasizes, this Section "is designed to reflect the permissible approaches that exist in current doctrine rather than to set forth new choice-of-law principles for aggregate litigation." The latter enterprise is the subject of previous work by the Institute. See Complex Litigation: Statutory Recommendations and Analysis §§ 6.01–6.08.

For an illustration of the first approach to choice of law in class actions, calling for application of the laws of the respective jurisdictions in which class members are found, as understood in terms of the place of injury or place of domicile, for example, see In re Bridgestone/Firestone, Inc., 288 F.3d 1012, 1016 (7th Cir. 2002) (applying choice-of-law principle of lex loci delicti); In re Vioxx Prods. Liab. Litig., 239 F.R.D. 450

(E.D. La. 2006) (concluding that law of each proposed class member's home jurisdiction applied to their respective claims).

Examples of the second approach, involving the identification of a manageable number of patterns in substantive law include In re School Asbestos Litig., 789 F.2d 996, 1010 (3d Cir. 1986), and In re Prudential Ins. Co. Am. Sales Practices Litig., 148 F.3d 283, 315 (3d Cir. 1998). See also In re Telectronics Pacing Sys., Inc., 172 F.R.D. 271, 293–294 (S.D. Ohio 1997); In re LILCO Sec. Litig., 111 F.R.D. 663, 670 (E.D.N.Y. 1986). For commentary supporting judicial consideration of this second approach, see Manual for Complex Litigation (Fourth) § 22.317 (2004); Kramer, *Choice of Law*, 71 N.Y.U. L. Rev. at 584–587. The determination of manageability nonetheless remains with the court, which is under no obligation to accept assertions of manageability on the part of those advocating aggregation. Cole v. Gen. Motors Corp., 484 F.3d 717, 725–726 (5th Cir. 2007). For a similar emphasis on considerations of manageability when the proposed aggregation consisted of multiple subclasses, each for persons within a particular state, see In re Welding Fume Prods. Liability Litig., 245 F.R.D. 279, 294 (N.D. Ohio 2007) ("[A] court could manage the differences in medical monitoring law among the eight states chosen by the ... plaintiffs by holding separate trials for each state-wide subclass, or perhaps a combined trial for a few statewide subclasses, where the law in those states is similar enough to allow creation of jury instructions and a verdict form that is not too complex.").

The third approach, involving the nonarbitrary choice of law to govern a class action, is permitted by *Shutts*. See 472 U.S. at 823 (noting that "a state court may be free to apply one of several choices of law" as long as the choice made is not arbitrary). If anything, the Supreme Court's decisions since *Shutts* underscore even further the latitude available to courts in the making of a nonarbitrary choice of law. See Sun Oil Co. v. Wortman, 486 U.S. 717, 727 (1988) (recognizing that "it is frequently the case under the Full Faith and Credit Clause that a court can lawfully apply either the law of one State or the contrary law of another"). In Franchise Tax Board v. Hyatt, 538 U.S. 488 (2003), the Court upheld as constitutionally permissible the determination of a Nevada state court to subject a California tax-collection agency to litigation in Nevada, notwithstanding the immunity from suit that the agency would have enjoyed by California statute in a California court. The Court noted that the Nevada court was not constitutionally required to apply the California immunity statute in the face of its own conflicting public policy with regard to immunity for its own counterpart agencies. Id. at 499 (noting that Nevada had not exhibited a "policy of hostility" to California law but, rather, had "sensitively applied principles of comity with a healthy regard for California's sovereign status, relying on the contours of Nevada's own sovereign immunity from suit as a benchmark for its analysis").

The fourth approach was overturned in *Shutts* on grounds of constitutional due process. See 472 U.S. at 821–822 (holding that the forum "must have a 'significant contact or significant aggregation of contacts' to the claims asserted by each member of the plaintiff class, contacts 'creating state interests,' in order to ensure that the choice of [forum] law is not arbitrary or unfair") (quoting Allstate Ins. Co. v. Hague, 449 U.S. 302, 313 (1981)). A court may apply forum law to claims with no relationship to the forum aside from the location of the litigation, however, when the court determines that there is no conflict of laws. That determination nonetheless may not be based upon a misconstruction of another state's law "that is clearly established and that has been brought to the court's attention." *Sun Oil*, 486 U.S. at 731. The fifth approach is what the court in In re Rhone–Poulenc Rorer, Inc., 51 F.3d 1293, 1300 (7th Cir. 1995), appropriately criticizes as "a kind of Esperanto instruction" that corresponds to "no actual law of any jurisdiction." As the court observed in overturning class-wide treatment of the breach issue in nationwide negligence litigation: " 'The common law is not a brooding omnipresence in the sky, but the articulate voice of some sovereign or quasi sovereign that can be identified.' The voices of the quasi-sovereigns that are the states of the United States sing negligence with a different pitch." Id. at 1301 (quoting S. Pac. Co. v. Jensen, 244 U.S. 205, 222 (1917) (Holmes, J., dissenting)).

Comment c. In recent years, some cases have focused on the possibility of applying the substantive law of the defendant's principal place of business in the context of class actions involving consumers nationwide. Compare *Bridgestone/Firestone*, 288 F.3d at 1016 (observing that "[n]either Indiana nor any other state has applied a uniform place-of-the-defendant's-headquarters rule to products-liability cases" as the basis for decertification of a nationwide class action brought in federal court sitting in

Indiana), with Ysbrand v. Daimler-Chrysler Corp., 81 P.3d 618, 626 (Okla. 2003) (applying law of defendant's principal place of business to nationwide class alleging breach of warranty with regard to minivan airbags). The Oklahoma legislature subsequently amended the class-action rule of that state, such that class certification along the lines of *Ysbrand* is no longer available. See Okla. Stat. tit. 12, § 2023(D)(3) (2009) (restricting class membership to Oklahoma residents plus nonresidents with a pertinent nexus to the state, "unless otherwise agreed to by the defendant"). For the scholarly debate over the use of the defendant's principal place of business as the basis for choice of law, compare Samuel Issacharoff, *Getting Beyond Kansas*, 74 UMKC L. Rev. 613 (2006), with Richard A. Nagareda, *Bootstrapping in Choice of Law After the Class Action Fairness Act*, 74 UMKC L. Rev. 661 (2006); Allison M. Gruenwald, Note, *Rethinking Place of Business as Choice of Law in Class Action Lawsuits*, 58 Vand. L. Rev. 1925 (2005); see also Complex Litigation: Statutory Recommendations and Analysis § 6.03(c)(4), 372 (proposing that to determine "the governing law, . . . the court shall consider . . . the primary places of business or habitual residences of the plaintiffs and defendants").

Comment d. Efforts to harmonize state law through model statutes and model rules have existed for many years. On the work of the National Conference of Commissioners on Uniform State Laws, see Fred H. Miller, *The Significance of the Uniform Laws Process: Why Both Politics and Uniform Law Should be Local—Perspectives of a Former Executive Director*, 27 Okla. City U. L. Rev. 507

(2002). On the early Restatements of Law developed by The American Law Institute, see G. Edward White, *The American Law Institute and the Triumph of Modernist Jurisprudence*, 15 Law & Hist. Rev. 1 (1997); see also Complex Litigation: Statutory Recommendations and Analysis § 4.02 and Comments (proposing the creation of an Interstate Complex Litigation Compact or a Uniform Complex Litigation Act). These efforts have become increasingly important and energetic as economic and other activity has transcended state boundaries. Internet commerce and communication, in particular, have the potential to eclipse state boundaries.

In addition to efforts at harmonization of state law, a related development consists of efforts to seek aggregate treatment by casting claims sounding in state law as claims under uniform federal law, such as the Racketeer Influenced and Corrupt Organizations Act (RICO). See, e.g., Klay v. Humana, Inc., 382 F.3d 1241 (11th Cir. 2004) (upholding certification of nationwide class in managed-care litigation with respect to RICO claims but not state-law, breach-of-contract claims); McLaughlin v. Am. Tobacco Co., 522 F.3d 215 (2d Cir. 2008) (overturning certification of RICO class action concerning marketing of light cigarettes). In still another permutation, recent years have witnessed substantial attention by the Supreme Court to situations of possible federal preemption of state-law claims, particularly in product-liability litigation. See, e.g,, Wyeth v. Levine, 129 S.Ct. 1187 (2009); Altria Group, Inc. v. Good, 129 S.Ct. 538 (2008); Riegel v. Medtronic, Inc., 128 S.Ct. 999 (2008); Desiano v. Warner–Lambert & Co., 467 F.3d 85 (2d Cir. 2006), aff'd by an equally divided

Court sub nom. Warner–Lambert Co., LLC v. Kent, 128 S.Ct. 1168 (2008).

Comment f. Applying the constraints of the Full Faith and Credit Clause in the choice-of-law setting, the Supreme Court in *Sun Oil* rejected the proposition that, on appeal, class members "have some threshold burden of supporting" the forum court's determination there that forum law presented no conflict with the laws of various contending states. 486 U.S. at 732 n.4. As reflected in the Reporters' Note to Comment *b*, the onus rests on those who contend that there is a true conflict to bring to the court's attention "decisions plainly contradicting" its determination of a false conflict. Id. Hence, the indication in Comment *f* that "the burden of demonstrating that multiple bodies of law are the same in functional content or arise in a manageable number of patterns such as to make aggregate treatment permissible ... arises only after an initial demonstration that multiple bodies of law apply to the claims for which aggregate treatment is sought."

On the distinction between the burden to demonstrate the existence of a conflict of laws and the burden to demonstrate the appropriateness of aggregate treatment in the class-action setting, see Patrick Woolley, *Choice of Law and the Protection of Class Members in Class Suits Certified Under Federal Rule of Civil Procedure 23(b)(3)*, 2004 Mich. St. L. Rev. 799, 811 ("[I]f the laws of multiple jurisdictions must be applied under applicable state choice-of-law rules, the party seeking [class] certification bears the burden of demonstrating that certification of a class would nonetheless be appropriate despite the relevance of multiple bodies of law. But that obligation does not kick in until *after* the court has concluded [based upon applicable choice-of-law rules] that the law of more than one state will apply.").

Effect on current law. The approach of this Section is designed to be quite modest in its description of broadly recognized situations in which choice-of-law analysis does not counsel against aggregate treatment of common issues. Implementation of this Section may take place by way of judicial decisions, with no necessity for any manner of national choice-of-law statute.

§ 2.06   Legal or Factual Questions Relevant to Class–Action Treatment

(a) **If the suitability of multiple civil claims for class-action treatment depends upon the resolution of an underlying question concerning the content of applicable substantive law or the factual situation presented, then the court must decide that question as part of its determination whether to certify the class. The obligation recognized in this subsection provides no authorization for the court in the posture of a class-certification ruling to decide a question of law or fact or a mixed question of law and fact if determination of that question is not relevant to the suitability of class-action treatment.**

(b) **When deciding a question of fact pursuant to subsection (a), the court should apply a preponderance-of-the-evidence standard. The court's decision on a question of fact for purposes of a class-certification ruling, however, should not be binding in subsequent proceedings in the litigation.**

Comment:

a. Judicial obligation to decide. Subsection (a) of the present Section reflects the recognition in existing case law of two related dimensions of the class certification determination: first, that the court is obligated to decide all questions relevant to the suitability of class-action treatment; and, second, that the court should decide any such question whether it is characterized as one of law or fact or as a mixed question of law and fact.

The approach of subsection (a) is consonant with the emphasis in §§ 2.03–2.05 on the relationship between the content of applicable substantive law and the appropriateness of aggregate treatment. Applicable substantive law is not always clear in content. In applying §§ 2.03–2.05, the court may encounter gaps or ambiguities in applicable substantive law, whether in constitutional, statutory, or common-law form. Aggregation may be appropriate under one account of substantive law as to an issue of liability, for example, but inappropriate under another account. Open questions concerning the content of applicable substantive law may also arise in less direct ways. The appropriateness of aggregation might depend upon the applicability of substantive legal doctrine grounded in economic or statistical analysis, and the contending sides, in support of their respective positions, might present competing expert economic or statistical analyses of the situation presented in the litigation.

Subsection (a) proceeds from much the same insight that underlies the judicial obligation to ascertain, in the choice-of-law sense, the substantive law that properly governs the issues that the proposed class action would encompass. See § 2.05(a). When multiple bodies of substantive law would govern the issues involved—in the sense of law from multiple sovereigns—and those substantive laws would apply in different ways to the claimants in the case, aggregate treatment likely would not materially advance the resolution of multiple civil claims. But cf. § 2.05(b)(2)–(3) (noting the appropriateness of aggregation when multiple applicable laws are "the same in functional content" or "present a limited number of patterns" manageable on an aggregate basis). So, too, subsection (a) underscores the necessity of a judicial determination of the proper meaning of applicable substantive law—even when it is clear that the law of a single sovereign governs—if one interpretation of that law points toward satisfaction of pertinent aggregation principles but another interpretation points to the contrary.

The court should not proceed to aggregate on the premise that those advocating that path have identified a proper basis for that course predicated on one account of underlying substantive law, whereas their opponents have identified plausible reasons for a contrary conclusion on the class-certification question based on a competing account of substantive law. If the court's aggregation decision turns upon the resolution of an underlying question about the content of substantive law, then the court is obligated to decide that question before authorizing aggregate treatment.

Though likely to arise with less frequency than questions concerning the content of applicable substantive law, questions concerning the factual situation presented in the litigation also may be pertinent to class certification in a given instance. Subsection (a) treats those questions of fact in the same manner as questions of law pertinent to the suitability of class-action treatment. This view, again, is in keeping with the insight that the court is obligated to decide all questions relevant to satisfaction of a pertinent requirement for class-action treatment, irrespective of their characterization along the law-fact continuum. If class certification is appropriate under one view of the facts but inappropriate under another view, then the court must determine the facts as relevant to its ultimate decision on the class-certification question, just as it must determine the meaning of applicable law.

Illustrations:

    1. Multiple claimants, 1–100, who purchased shares in Defendant as part of an initial public offering allege that Defendant engaged in securities fraud in connection therewith. Applicable substantive law includes a reliance element for securities-fraud claims and, further, includes a rebuttable presumption of reliance upon a showing of fraud with respect to securities traded on efficient capital markets during the relevant time period. The parties agree that, absent such a presumption of reliance, the reliance element would pose individualized issues not susceptible to aggregate treatment. The court should determine whether the market for initial public offerings is properly regarded as an efficient capital market, such as to give rise to a presumption of reliance on the part of all claimants upon a showing of fraud. This judicial determination should encompass the evaluation of competing expert submissions, insofar as relevant to the characterization of the market for initial public offerings as one that exhibits the attributes of an efficient capital market. The reason for the court to engage competing expert submissions at the class-certification stage stems from the obligation recognized in subsection (a) to decide all questions that bear upon the satisfaction of applicable class-certification requirements. When the applicability of the presumption of reliance turns upon a proposition of economics and the parties debate the applicability of that presumption on such terms in the posture of a contested motion for class certification, the court likewise is obligated to engage the economic question in the course of deciding whether class certification is appropriate.

    2. In a contested motion for class certification, the determination whether class-action treatment would operate "in a manner superior to other realistic procedural alternatives" within the meaning of § 2.02(a)(1) depends on the estimated number of persons who are in the proposed class definition. Class counsel estimates that number to be such that all class members could not practicably be joined as conventional parties. Defendant estimates that number to be such that joinder would be a realistic procedural alternative that, in turn, would defeat the asserted superiority of class-action treatment. The court must resolve the question concerning the estimated number of persons within the proposed class as part of its class-certification ruling.

In discharging its obligation to decide, the court should approach questions of substantive law in the same manner that the court would approach any other question of law in the litigation. Thus, for example, a federal court confronted with an open question about the meaning of federal statutory law should address that question by using the ordinary tools of statutory interpretation. A state court facing an open question as to its own common law should answer that question through ordinary common-law reasoning. A federal court with diversity jurisdiction over litigation raising an open question of state law should seek to predict how the courts of the relevant state would answer that question.

The treatment of factual questions relevant to class certification gives rise to a need for the court to exercise considerable discretion to afford a process for development of facts, as needed to inform the court's determination. The need for controlled discovery into the facts relevant to class certification may, in a given instance, have the effect of delaying that stage of the litigation at which it may be prudent to resolve the motion for class certification.

b. Lack of authority to decide questions not pertinent to class certification. The obligation of the court to decide under subsection (a) nonetheless remains confined to pertinent questions about the content of substantive law or the factual situation presented. Consistent with § 2.05, Illustration 1, the court should not resolve hypothetical questions that do not bear on matters actually contested by the parties. Nor is the court authorized to reach out to decide in the posture of a class-certification ruling questions that do not bear upon satisfaction of the relevant principles for aggregation. Questions unrelated to the suitability of class-action treatment are appropriately engaged by the court through other procedural vehicles, such as summary judgment, or through pretrial rulings.

c. Preponderance standard for questions of fact. In deciding a factual question pertinent to its class-certification ruling, the court should apply the ordinary preponderance-of-the-evidence standard. The court's determination of such a factual question nonetheless should proceed with due regard for the role of the ultimate factfinder in a subsequent phase of the litigation, which might in a given instance consist of a jury rather than the court. The court's factual determination in the posture of class certification accordingly should not be binding upon the ultimate factfinder (whether a jury or the court itself). This approach to fact finding in the class-certification context accords broadly with the prevailing approach taken as to fact finding in connection with other pretrial rulings, such as with respect to a preliminary injunction pending trial.

REPORTERS' NOTES

Comment a. This Section builds on the class-certification analysis in In re IPO Securities Litig., 471 F.3d 24 (2d Cir. 2006). In *IPO*, class counsel conceded that the certifiability under Rule 23(b)(3) of a proposed securities-fraud class action depended upon application of the fraud-on-the-market doctrine in federal securities law. See id. at 42. If applicable, the doctrine considerably facilitates class certification by presuming that all investors who bought or sold the relevant shares on an efficient capital market during the time period that the fraud remained uncorrected did so in reliance upon the fraud.

In support of their respective positions on class certification, the parties in *IPO* presented competing evidence on whether the market for initial public offerings exhibits the attributes of an efficient capital market on which the fraud-on-the-market doctrine is based. The *IPO* court emphasized that:

> (1) a district judge may certify a class only after making determinations that each of the Rule 23 requirements has been met; (2) such determinations can be made only if the judge resolves factual disputes relevant to each Rule 23 requirement and finds that whatever underlying facts are relevant to a particular Rule 23 requirement have been established and is persuaded to rule, based on the relevant facts and the applicable legal standard, that the requirement is met; (3) the obligation to make such determinations is not lessened by overlap

between a Rule 23 requirement and a merits issue, even a merits issue that is identical with a Rule 23 requirement; [and] (4) in making such determinations, a district judge should not assess any aspect of the merits unrelated to a Rule 23 requirement....

Id. at 41. For the same view of the parameters for the class-certification determination, see In re Hydrogen Peroxide Antitrust Litig., 552 F.3d 305, 307 (3d Cir. 2008).

The *IPO* court ultimately concluded that the fraud-on-the-market doctrine, recognized by the Supreme Court in Basic Inc. v. Levinson, 485 U.S. 224 (1988), as a matter of federal securities law is inapplicable to the market for initial public offerings due to the lack of conformity between that market and the attributes of an efficient capital market. *IPO*, 471 F.3d at 42–43. Absent application of the doctrine, the need for individualized inquiry concerning the reliance element prevented the proposed class from materially advancing the resolution of the litigation. Illustration 1 reflects this holding in *IPO*.

Other courts have engaged similar questions at the class-certification stage concerning the applicability of the fraud-on-the-market doctrine when pertinent to the satisfaction of applicable certification requirements. See West v. Prudential Securities, Inc., 282 F.3d 935, 938 (7th Cir. 2002) (holding fraud-on-the-market doctrine inapplicable when alleged fraud involves nonpublic information); McLaughlin v. Am. Tobacco Co., 522

F.3d 215, 224 (2d Cir. 2008) (rejecting an effort to apply the equivalent of the fraud-on-the-market doctrine from the securities-fraud context to a proposed nationwide civil RICO class action involving fraud in the marketing of light cigarettes); In re Salomon Analyst Metromedia Litig., 544 F.3d 474, 482 (2d Cir. 2008) (holding fraud-on-the-market doctrine potentially applicable to misinformation transmitted by secondary actors, such as research analysts).

In *IPO*, the Second Circuit disavowed one of its own earlier decisions that had shied from the resolution of legal questions that bear on the satisfaction of class-certification requirements. Wal–Mart Stores, Inc. v. Visa U.S.A., Inc. (In re Visa Check/MasterMoney Antitrust Litig.), 280 F.3d 124 (2d Cir. 2001), involved an antitrust class action centered upon an alleged tying arrangement whereby the plaintiff retailers were required to honor both the credit cards and the debit cards issued by the respective defendant companies. On the question of class certification, the parties offered submissions from competing expert witnesses concerning the economic consequences they expected to flow from elimination of the alleged tie—specifically, whether the effect would be merely to reduce the price of the tied product (the fees charged by the defendants for debit-card transactions) or whether the effect also would be to increase the price of the tying product (the fees charged for credit-card transactions). The proposed plaintiff class consisted of retailers with different mixtures of credit- and debit-card transactions, a feature that raised the possibility that elimination of the alleged tie might affect class members in substantially different ways. See id. at 153 (Jacobs,

J., dissenting). The dispute between the competing expert witnesses was ultimately directed to how damages in a tying case should be determined under antitrust law: whether damages turn simply on the price of the tied product or on the price of the "package" consisting of the tied and tying products together. See 10 Phillip E. Areeda, Herbert Hovenkamp & Einer Elhauge, *Antitrust Law* ¶ 1769c, 413 (2d ed. 2004) ("Most plaintiff buyers base their damage claims on proof that a tie forced them to buy the tied product from the defendant at higher prices than prevail in the tied market generally.... This is quite wrong, for in most cases a premium price on the tied market must be accompanied by a reduction in the price of the tying product."). The court in *Visa Check* declined to resolve this question, certifying the proposed class of retailers based on the conclusion that each expert's opinion on the economics of the alleged tie was "not so flawed that it would be inadmissible as a matter of law." 280 F.3d at 135.

Like the Second Circuit subsequently held in *IPO*, the present Section finds the resolution of the admissibility question in *Visa Check* to be insufficient to discharge the court's obligation to resolve the underlying question concerning the proper method for damage calculation in a tying case as part of the decision whether to aggregate. The treatment suggested here is consistent with the *IPO* court's characterization of the class-certification decision as presenting a "mixed question of fact and law." 471 F.3d at 40. See also id. at 42 ("disavow[ing]" *Visa Check*).

Another circuit initially formulated its view of the proper scope for judicial inquiry on a motion for class certification in a manner similar to the pre-*IPO* decisions from the Second Circuit, such as *Visa Check*, but later revised its position in keeping with *IPO*. Dukes v. Wal–Mart, Inc., 474 F.3d 1214, 1229 (9th Cir.), withdrawn and superseded by 509 F.3d 1168, 1181 (9th Cir. 2007).

For further analysis of *IPO* and its implications for class certification, see Richard A. Nagareda, *Class Certification in the Age of Aggregate Proof*, 84 N.Y.U. L. Rev. 97 (2009).

The present Section speaks to the court's class-certification determination, not to the sequencing of judicial rulings on class-certification motions relative to rulings on a motion to dismiss or a motion for summary judgment, either of which directly concern the merits. Compare Fed. R. Civ. P. 23(c)(1), advisory committee's note (observing that "the party opposing the class may prefer to win dismissal or summary judgment as to the individual plaintiffs without certification and without binding the class that might have been certified"); Cowen v. Bank United, 70 F.3d 937, 941–942 (7th Cir. 1995) (Posner, J.) (describing similar considerations regarding sequencing of class-certification and summary-judgment rulings), with Fireside Bank v. Superior Court, 155 P.3d 268, 277 (Cal. 2007) (cautioning that courts "should not resolve the merits in a putative class action case before class certification and notice issues absent a compelling justification for doing so.").

Recognition of the judicial obligation to decide questions of law or fact pertinent to the suitability of class-action treatment accords with existing case law. In *Hydrogen Peroxide*, the Third Circuit explicitly noted that, "because each [pertinent] requirement of Rule 23 must be met, a

district court errs as a matter of law when it fails to resolve a genuine *legal or factual* dispute relevant to determining the requirements." 552 F.3d at 320. Illustration 2 is drawn from the Seventh Circuit's discussion in Szabo v. Bridgeport Machines, Inc., 249 F.3d 672, 676 (7th Cir. 2001):

> Before deciding whether to allow a case to proceed as a class action ... a judge should make whatever factual and legal inquiries are necessary under Rule 23. This would be plain enough if, for example, the plaintiff alleged that the class had 10,000 members, making it too numerous to allow joinder, see Rule 23(a)(1), while the defendant insisted that the class contained only 10 members. A judge would not and could not accept the plaintiff's assertion as conclusive; instead the judge would receive evidence (if only by affidavit) and resolve the disputes before deciding whether to certify the class.

On the need for judicial discretion as to development of facts relevant to class certification, see *IPO*, 471 F.3d at 41 ("To avoid the risk that a Rule 23 hearing will extend into a protracted mini-trial of substantial portions of the underlying litigation, a district judge must be accorded considerable discretion to limit both discovery and the extent of the hearing on Rule 23 requirements. But even with some limits on discovery and the extent of the hearing, the district judge must receive enough evidence, by affidavits, documents, or testimony, to be satisfied that each Rule 23 requirement has been met."). The exercise of such discretion is in keeping with existing rule language that situates the class certification "[a]t an early practicable time" within the litigation. See

Fed. R. Civ. P. 23(c)(1). See also Fed. R. Civ. P. 23, advisory committee's note (2003 amendments) (observing that "[t]ime may be needed to gather information necessary to make the certification decision," such as to warrant "controlled discovery into the 'merits,' limited to those aspects relevant to making the certification decision on an informed basis").

Comment b. The limitation that the court should engage questions of law or fact (or mixed questions thereof) only insofar as relevant to its class-certification determination stems from the recognition that other procedural mechanisms or pretrial rulings—such as summary judgment—appropriately regulate the relationship between the court and the factfinder generally. Well-established principles for summary judgment call for the moving party to show that "there is no genuine issue as to any material fact and that the movant is entitled to judgment as a matter of law." Fed. R. Civ. P. 56(c). Wholesale displacement of these principles by the lesser threshold of a mere preponderance of the evidence—the standard prescribed for the class-certification setting—threatens an unwarranted intrusion by the court upon the role of the factfinder at trial. See Nagareda, *Class Certification in the Age of Aggregate Proof*, 84 N.Y.U. L. Rev. at 140, 149. The authority of the court to engage questions relevant to class certification under a preponderance standard proceeds from the recognition that the certification question—as distinct from the merits—is a matter exclusively for judicial determination at the pretrial stage. See Fed. R. Civ. P. 23(c)(1)(A) (specifying that "the court must determine by order whether to certify the action as a class action").

Comment c. Existing case law establishes that "the preponderance of the evidence standard applies to evidence proffered to establish Rule 23's requirements." Teamsters Local 445 Freight Div. Pension Fund v. Bombardier, Inc., 546 F.3d 196, 202 (2d Cir. 2008); accord *Hydrogen Peroxide*, 552 F.3d at 307 (same). Case law also recognizes that the court's decision on a question of fact for purposes of class certification is not binding on the ultimate factfinder. See *IPO*, 471 F.3d at 41 ("[T]he determination as to a Rule 23 requirement is made only for purposes of class certification and is not binding on the trier of facts, even if that trier is the class certification judge."). On the broadly similar treatment of fact finding for purposes of a request for a preliminary injunction, see 11A Charles Alan Wright, Arthur R. Miller, & Mary Kay Kane, *Federal Practice and Procedure* § 2950 (3d ed. 2005).

The proper relationship between the preponderance-of-the-evidence standard for factual questions concerning class certification and the standard for admissibility of expert testimony at trial remains a point for further development in case law in the aftermath of *IPO* and other similar decisions. For divergent views in commentary, compare Alan B. Morrison, *Determining Class Certification: What Should the Courts Have to Decide?*, 8 Class Action Litig. Rep. (BNA) 541, 543 (July 27, 2007) (arguing that class-certification disputes involving expert submissions should be guided by the evidentiary standard of Daubert v. Merrell Dow Pharmaceuticals, Inc., 509 U.S. 579 (1993)), with Heather P. Scribner, *Rigorous Analysis of the Class Certification Expert: The Roles of* Daubert *and the Defendant's Proof*, 28 Rev. Litig. 71, 111 (2008) (deeming *Daubert* analysis of expert testimony "necessary, but not sufficient" for class certification).

Effect on current law. This Section reflects the consensus of the federal courts of appeals on the appropriate scope for the class-certification inquiry. No rule change at the federal level would be needed for implementation of this Section. There is nonetheless case law in some states indicating that courts at the class-certification stage should not scrutinize expert submissions said to demonstrate compliance with a pertinent certification requirement. See, e.g., Howe v. Microsoft Corp., 656 N.W.2d 285, 295 (N.D. 2003) (explaining, in the antitrust context, that the "certification hearing [is not] the appropriate time to engage in a full-blown examination of the validity of an expert's analysis, opinions, and methodology"); Comes v. Microsoft Corp., 696 N.W.2d 318, 324–325 (Iowa 2005) (accepting plaintiffs' expert affidavit supporting commonality among class members, over opposition by defendant).

TOPIC 3

SCOPE OF PRECLUSION AS A CONSTRAINT ON AGGREGATION

§ 2.07 Individual Rights in Aggregation of Related Claims

(a) **As necessary conditions to the aggregate treatment of related claims by way of a class action, the court shall**

(1) **determine that there are no structural conflicts of interest**

(A) **between the named parties or other claimants and the lawyers who would represent claimants on an aggregate basis, which may include deficiencies specific to the lawyers seeking aggregate treatment or**

(B) **among the claimants themselves that would present a significant risk that the lawyers for claimants might skew systematically the conduct of the litigation so as to favor some claimants over others on grounds aside from reasoned evaluation of their respective claims or to disfavor claimants generally vis-à-vis the lawyers themselves,**

(2) **provide claimants the opportunity to avoid the preclusive effect of any determination made on an aggregate basis, absent the exception recognized in subsection (c); and**

(3) **provide claimants appropriate notice of the opportunity to participate in the aggregate proceeding and, if**

applicable, to avoid its preclusive effect under subsection (a)(2).

(b) Claimants who exercise their opportunity to avoid the preclusive effect of the aggregate proceeding, as provided in subsection (a)(2), should be treated as nonparties to that proceeding.

(c) If the court finds that the aggregate proceeding should be mandatory in order to manage indivisible relief fairly and efficiently as to the related claims, then aggregate treatment by way of a class action need not afford claimants an opportunity to avoid the preclusive effect of any determination of those claims.

(d) In accordance with §§ 2.02(a)(3) and 2.12, the court shall ensure that aggregate treatment of related claims does not compromise the ability of any person opposing the aggregate group in the litigation to dispute the allegations made by claimants or to raise pertinent substantive defenses.

Comment:

a. *Distinguishing aggregation of related claims from aggregation of common issues.* This Section sets forth individual rights applicable when a court pursues a class action as the vehicle for aggregate treatment of related claims, as understood in § 2.01, Comment *d*. Section 2.08 takes up the related topic of preclusion when aggregate treatment by way of a class action encompasses only a common issue raised by multiple civil claims, with other issues to be addressed in other proceedings.

b. *Relationship of due process to finality.* This Section carries forward the general principle of § 1.03(c) by enabling the determination of related claims in the aggregate to have preclusive effect as to all claimants. Strictures of constitutional due process comprise the most significant constraints on the preclusive effect of the aggregate proceeding. Constitutional due process also underlies the need to protect the interests of participants in aggregate proceedings. Section 2.11 discusses separately the preclusive effect of the aggregation decision itself.

c. *Due-process rights.* Subsection (a) as a whole organizes the due-process rights of claimants in aggregate proceedings on related claims. The sequencing of the three rights within subsection (a) is not designed to suggest a hierarchy of importance among them. Rather, the reference at the outset to the protection of claimants against structural conflicts of interest in the class representation stems simply from the practical recognition that such conflicts might exist from the

148

inception of the aggregate proceeding, prior in time to the provision to claimants of notice or any required opportunity to avoid the preclusive effect of the proceeding.

For convenience of reference, the Comments in this Section speak of these various due-process rights in terms of the typology of exit, voice, and loyalty rights often used to describe the array of ways that individuals might advance their interests within a variety of arrangements that are collective or aggregative in nature. Within corporations, for example, shareholders may sell their shares (an exit right), participate in corporate governance (a voice right), or leave the management of the corporation to various agents obliged to advance corporate interests rather than their own (a loyalty right). As elaborated in the Comments that follow, aggregate litigation by way of a class action calls for an analogous array of rights.

d. Loyalty as protection against structural conflicts of interest. Subsection (a)(1) casts the right of loyalty as the absence of structural conflicts of interest in the representation of claimants on an aggregate basis. In operational terms, the vehicle for implementation of the loyalty right in the class-action setting consists of judicial scrutiny throughout the aggregate proceeding—in particular, as part of the determination whether to aggregate. The practical need for judicial scrutiny of loyalty stems from the reality that the representational arrangements for absent class members generally are not matters of contract between lawyers and individual clients but, instead, are the legal consequence of the aggregation decision itself. Further, the limited ability of class members as a practical matter to participate in the actual conduct of a case that proceeds as a class action underscores the importance of judicial oversight of class-action procedures. Similarly, in many class actions—notably those involving small individual claims—the ability to exit as a formal matter may not be of great practical significance, thereby underscoring again the importance of oversight.

The present Section speaks to aggregate treatment "by way of a class action," but the reference in subsection (a) is not intended to imply that the loyalty right is of concern only in the class-action setting. To the contrary, loyalty concerns also might arise in other forms of aggregate proceedings, such as administrative aggregations within the meaning of § 1.02(b). In that setting, however, loyalty usually may be addressed more easily due to the existence of contractual, lawyer–client relationships with respect to each claimant that administrative aggregation would encompass. To determine which lawyers will take the lead in such a proceeding, there may be a need for negotiation among the lawyers representing individual claimants. But, again, any arrangement for representation reached among those lawyers involved would be the appropriate subject of individual client consent.

The casting of loyalty in terms of structural conflicts of interest proceeds from the premise that no procedural regime can align completely the various interests involved, whether they consist of the interests of claimants and their lawyers in the aggregate proceeding or the interests of claimants themselves. The objective, instead, is for the court to determine whether conflicts of interest are such as "would present a significant risk that the lawyers for claimants might skew systematically the conduct of the litigation so as to favor some claimants over others on grounds aside from reasoned evaluation of their respective claims or to disfavor claimants generally vis-à-vis the lawyers themselves." In making this determination, the court should remain mindful of the practical reality that the decision to aggregate often gives rise to dynamics that lead to settlement on an aggregate basis. The inquiry into the existence of structural conflicts of interest, accordingly, should take place with particular attention to conflicts with a significant potential to skew the conduct of settlement negotiations. The court should accord no deference in this inquiry, however, based upon the existence of a contractual relationship between the lawyers and those who would serve as class representatives in the proceeding for which judicial authorization is sought.

Structural conflicts of interest might arise between named parties or other claimants and the lawyers who would represent claimants in the aggregate—for instance, when those lawyers also represent other persons whose claims would not be subject to aggregate treatment. See subsection (a)(1)(A). As part of its inquiry, the court should consider the alignment between the economic interests of claimants and their lawyers—for example, as reflected in the anticipated fee arrangement for representation in the aggregate proceeding. Structural conflicts also might arise from easily identifiable differences in the claims to be aggregated, such that a common lawyer could not reasonably advance the interests of all claimants. See subsection (a)(1)(B).

In framing the conflicts that compromise the adequacy of representation for claimants in terms of conflicts that are "structural" in nature, subsection (a)(1) encompasses both conflicts arising from the nature of the aggregation sought and conflicts arising from the particular lawyers involved. Subsection (a)(1), in other words, speaks both to conflicts that would disable any lawyer from representing claimants on the aggregate basis for which judicial authorization is sought and to conflicts that would disable only the particular lawyers before the court from undertaking that representation. The term "structural" underscores, nevertheless, that the judicial inquiry in subsection (a)(1) focuses on conflict, whatever its genesis, that is such as to present a significant risk that the conduct of the litigation will be skewed systematically—that is, in some direction predictable before the determination of related claims on an aggregate basis.

The focus on structural conflicts, again, is consistent with the premise that no aggregate proceeding can eliminate all conceivable conflicts of interest. In practice, judicial attention to structural conflicts of interest is likely to result in somewhat greater tolerance for conflicts arising from within the proposed aggregate unit than for those arising from the particular lawyers involved. The expectation is that the latter sorts of conflicts have a greater tendency, generally speaking, to give rise to a systematic skewing of the representation. This differentiation in practical application stems from the difficulty of applying to aggregate litigation existing rules for conflicts of interest crafted with conventional, individual lawsuits in mind.

Subsection (a)(1), moreover, casts judicial scrutiny as to structural conflicts of interest as a precondition to aggregate treatment by way of a class action. This approach has two implications. First, structural conflicts of interest necessarily consist of those in existence at the time of the aggregation decision or, at least, that emerge in the course of the aggregate litigation before the determination of the related claims therein. Differences among claimants that do not preexist aggregate treatment but, instead, are simply the product of the judgment that concludes the aggregate proceeding—for example, differences among claimants created by the terms of a class settlement agreement—cannot form the basis for a structural conflict of interest within the meaning of subsection (a)(1). The fairness of settlements in aggregate litigation and the framework for their review are significant topics, but they remain distinct from the loyalty right safeguarded in subsection (a)(1). Chapter 3 separately addresses the topic of settlements in aggregate litigation, an approach consistent with the treatment of adequate representation as a requirement for class certification that remains distinct in procedural law from the requirement of judicial review for class settlements.

Second, subsection (a)(1) consciously implies that a judicial finding of loyalty as part of the decision to aggregate—like a determination made on the merits in the aggregate proceeding—should have preclusive effect, unless challenged on direct appeal. This approach is consistent with the framework for postjudgment challenges to the aggregate proceeding, as further elaborated in § 3.14.

e. Presumptive opportunity to exit. Subsection (a)(2) frames the right of exit as a presumptive right in the sense of calling for an affirmative determination under subsection (c) in order to make membership in a class action mandatory. The presumptive quality of the right of exit reflects two considerations. First, an individual's ability to control the manner of adjudicating that individual's claim is important and should not lightly be curtailed. It is reasonable to infer that a person who exercises the exit right recognized in subsection (a)(2) places a premium on claim control. Second, the exit right enables claimants to protect themselves from inadequate representation and, in so doing, generates pressure for the representative parties and their lawyers to act faithfully on behalf of the represented claimants. The opportunity to exit under subsection (a)(2) thus reinforces judicial review for loyalty under subsection (a)(1).

Considerations of constitutional due process may call for an opportunity to exit but, nonetheless, leave open the precise mechanics of that opportunity. Questions surrounding the mechanics of exit may take many forms. Current law, for example, does not insist on affirmative consent of class members to be bound by the judgment in an opt-out class action, but instead infers consent from the failure of a given class member to exit. Recent amendments to the federal class-action rule address the further possibility of a second opportunity for exit in the event of a class settlement. Subsection (a)(2) leaves open these and other questions of exit mechanics for development on terms that are appropriately pragmatic, not constitutional, in nature. In addition, as subsection (c) and Comments *h–i* elaborate, the right of exit does not extend to aggregate proceedings confined to claims for indivisible remedies. See § 2.04.

f. Notice and the opportunity to participate. Subsection (a)(3) casts the right of voice in terms of the opportunity to appear in the aggregate proceeding and, as its precondition, the provision of appropriate notice to claimants concerning that proceeding and any opportunity to avoid its preclusive effect. As to non-class forms of aggregate treatment, notice is easily provided, as the lawsuits to be consolidated are already on file. As to class actions, however, notice poses more nuanced questions, and the reference to "appropriate" notice in subsection (a)(3) is designed to accommodate those nuances.

Current law on class actions presumes that appropriate notice for claims seeking divisible relief consists of individualized notice to persons whose names and addresses are known and who can be contacted directly by mail or other means with reasonable effort. This presumption stems from underlying due-process notions of notice in the class-action context in terms of the best notice that is practicable under the circumstances. Early case law on class notice understandably reflects the circumstances of its time—in particular, the available means for notice as a practical or technological matter. As the methods for diffusion of information become more advanced with the development of Internet-based and other avenues for communication, however, individualized notice as conventionally understood may not necessarily be the best notice that is practicable in all situations. The reference to "appropriate" notice in subsection (a)(3) is designed to accommodate these changes in the means available to provide notice.

Subsection (a)(3), moreover, does not mandate individualized notice when the cost of notice to all known class members would be grossly disproportionate to its value. As experience with aggregate litigation has grown, it has become increasingly clear that notice may have limited value in some contexts. In referring to "appropriate" notice, subsection (a)(3) invites reflection in light of the concerns of viability and variation discussed in § 2.02, Comment *b*. The value of notice is likely to be low, for example, when claimants have small stakes and when they have little information of value to contribute to the aggregate proceeding. Subsection (a)(3) affords the court discretion to tailor notice to the practicalities of the litigation, an approach in keeping with procedural rules that have emerged in some states since the inception of the federal class-action rule.

Subsection (a)(3) also draws no strict, categorical distinction between aggregation of divisible claims and aggregation of indivisible claims. Rather, notice under subsection (a)(3) is "appropriate" whenever it would be valuable. The point of notice is to afford claimants a meaningful opportunity to participate in the aggregate proceeding, to inform them of any opportunity to exit, and to enable them to monitor the conduct of the litigation on their behalf. Notice may be especially valuable, and thus especially appropriate, with respect to some claims for indivisible relief. For example, in aggregate proceedings seeking to enjoin employment discrimination or other civil-rights violations, claimants may possess important information and have considerable stakes in the outcome. They also might have conflicting interests in the outcome, particularly as it may encompass not only a prohibitory injunction but also injunctive relief to prescribe affirmatively a course of future conduct on the defendant's part. In speaking of appropriate notice, subsection (a)(3) again recognizes judicial discretion to tailor notice to those instances of indivisible relief in which individual notice would be valuable.

Matters of notice aside, subsection (a)(3) describes the right of voice in terms of an opportunity to appear in the aggregate proceeding. By this, subsection (a)(3) includes the opportunity to appear through one's lawyer and, subject to general principles concerning intervention, to acquire all the participatory rights extended to conventional parties—particularly with respect to class settlements. The opportunity to appear in the aggregate proceeding stands as an application of the general principle that individuals must have an opportunity to be heard in proceedings that stand to alter their rights, a principle well established in the due-process treatment of administrative proceedings, for example.

As with the right of exit, subsection (a)(3) casts the right of voice in general terms, leaving subconstitutional questions about the precise operation of that right for judicial treatment on pragmatic terms. Thus, for example, considerations of due process do not determine whether the court should afford an individual claimant, upon the exercise of the voice right, access to the information assembled in the course of earlier discovery in the litigation by the lawyers now seeking aggregate treatment, much less the terms on which any such access may be granted.

g. Consequences of exit. Subsection (b) reinforces the implication of subsection (a)(2) that individual claimants who exit are nonparties vis-à-vis the aggregate proceeding. The most familiar and straightforward consequence of this nonparty status is that individual claimants who exit receive neither the benefit nor the detriment of the preclusive effect exerted by the judgment in the class action. Subsection (b) nonetheless speaks more broadly, in terms of nonparty status, rather than exclusively to the scope of preclusion. The nonparty status of claimants who exit also bears upon their prospects to benefit from aspects of the class action in other regards, such as with respect to discovery obtained by the class.

Subsection (b) does not prescribe a single, undifferentiated approach to situations in which claimants who exit nonetheless seek to benefit from the class proceedings in some regard other than preclusion. Rather, the recognition in subsection (b) of such claimants' nonparty status is designed to afford the latitude already present for arrangements—whether the products of discussion among the relevant counsel or the results of judicial oversight by the class-action court or by the court handling the relevant claimant's case—to manage the availability of discovery obtained in one case for use in another case that involves different parties. Recognition of exiting claimants' nonparty status vis-à-vis the class action reflects that such claimants—like nonparties to a conventional, individual lawsuit—enjoy no presumptive right of access to the discovery so obtained. The absence of such a presumptive right of access stems from the practical recognition that development of the claims advanced in the class litigation often involves considerable effort and expense on the part of class counsel. A presumptive right of access would generate the potential for exiting claimants to free-ride on these efforts, a benefit inconsistent with their status as nonparties to the class action.

Though not required to do so, the parties to the class action nonetheless may find it advantageous to agree to afford such access in a given instance, such as when one of the parties thereby would avoid the practical need to respond to duplicative discovery across both the class action and the individual exiting claimant's case. Such use should be accompanied by financial arrangements to account for the benefit obtained by the exiting claimant from the discovery efforts of class counsel—in the first instance, through contractual negotiation among the parties to the class action and the exiting claimant and, if necessary, by order of the class-action court to sequester a portion of any recovery obtained by the exiting claimant to account for the benefit obtained from the class discovery. Use at trial of evidence so obtained—for instance, prior testimony—remains subject to the applicable rules of evidence.

Coordination of the class-action proceeding with proceedings for those claimants who exit therefrom is likely to be easier insofar as the same court stands to handle both. Cf. § 2.02, Comment b (analogously recognizing the greater ease of coordination when the same court stands to handle both an issue class action and nonclass proceedings on remaining issues in the same litigation). Even when the two sorts of proceedings take place across different courts, however, judicial discretion might be exercised to stay opt-out cases pending the disposition of the class litigation.

h. *Mandatory aggregation to manage indivisible remedies.* Subsection (c) recognizes that a court may mandate the litigation of claims on a class-wide basis to manage indivisible remedies fairly and efficiently when multiple lawsuits are proceeding or threatened. When multiple claims exist for an indivisible remedy as against a generally applicable course of conduct on the defendant's part, unitary adjudication is desirable to avoid inconsistent results and to facilitate judicial management of the remedy. Section 2.04 recognizes the desirability of aggregate treatment with regard to indivisible remedies, and the present Section elaborates on that observation by permitting aggregate treatment to proceed on a mandatory basis. Mandatory aggregation with respect to claims for an indivisible remedy simply recognizes the preexisting interdependence of such claims. Even without an aggregate proceeding, a successful lawsuit brought by an individual claimant would affect all persons subject to the generally applicable course of conduct. A declaratory judgment that a particular employment practice is unlawful, for example, would likely cause the defendant to alter its practices across the board, to the benefit or detriment of all subjected to the practice in question. When a lawsuit seeks to prohibit a given practice or policy, the fates of all affected persons are already intertwined. Subsection (c) recognizes this reality by permitting the court to mandate inclusion in the aggregate proceeding.

The mandatory nature of the proceeding advances due process in several ways. First, it creates a forum in which all interested persons may voice their views concerning the practice or policy. Second, it enables the court to craft an indivisible remedy that burdens the defendant and any dissenting claimants to the minimum extent needed to vindicate the rights asserted in the complaint. Third, it avoids the risk of inconsistent adjudications and relief. See also § 2.04, Comment *a*. Fourth, it affords complete resolution of the dispute concerning indivisible relief in the event of judgment on the merits in favor of the party opposing the aggregated claimants.

By authorizing mandatory aggregation, this Section does not presuppose that claimants' interests align more closely with respect to indivisible remedies than for divisible ones, such as damages. Disagreements and conflicts of interest can arise whenever multiple claims are aggregated. Inclusion in the aggregate proceeding nonetheless may be mandated for practical reasons. When potential claimants' fates intertwine because all are subject to the same challenged policy or practice, an individual claimant's decision to exit would not insulate that claimant from the consequences of the litigation as a practical matter.

i. Mandatory aggregation to allocate equitably a preexisting limited fund. As reflected in § 2.04, Comment *a*, the situation of a limited fund against which claims might be made presents a further example of a case involving an indivisible remedy. Here, the interdependence of claims stems from the practical reality that a victory by one claimant necessarily reduces the sum available to satisfy other claimants. The point of mandatory aggregation in the limited-fund scenario is to avoid a disorderly rush of individual claimants upon the fund. The court, as a practical matter, must decide whether to proceed with mandatory aggregation at a time when depletion of the fund is merely a prediction about what the future holds rather than an observation of present conditions.

The court should call for proof of the limited nature of the fund, drawing on appropriate financial and other expertise as presented by those seeking and opposing mandatory aggregation. In contemplating the presentation of such proof, this Comment uses the concept of a limited fund in the same sense reflected in current class-action law. There, a limited fund consists of one as to which the totals of the claims against the fund and the fund available for satisfying them, each set at its realistic maximum, demonstrate the insufficiency of the fund to pay all claims. This understanding is consistent with the operation of mandatory class treatment in the limited-fund scenario as similar to an interpleader action initiated by class plaintiffs rather than the defendant stakeholder. The interpleader device currently enables a plaintiff to join all persons having claims against the plaintiff when those claims create a risk of multiple liability with respect to an ascertained fund or asset.

In keeping with existing law, the limited nature of the fund must preexist aggregate treatment itself. It must not be the creation or consequence of the decision to aggregate. This principle stems from the need to avoid intrusion of mandatory, limited-fund class actions upon the framework legislated by Congress for reorganization proceedings in bankruptcy. As preconditions to the use of reorganization proceedings, for example, the law of bankruptcy does not require a showing of insolvency or a demonstration of the limited nature of the debtor's funds along the lines required for limited-fund class actions. But bankruptcy law contains a variety of other constraints that bear on the treatment of claimants—for example, voting procedures for the confirmation of a reorganization plan and the "absolute priority" rule, which prioritizes for payment the holders of debt claims over holders of equity.

j. Due process for defendants. Subsection (d) underscores that considerations of due process in aggregation also extend to persons opposing the aggregate group litigating related claims on an aggregate basis. Subsection (d) casts the process due for such persons—typically, aligned as defendants in the litigation—in terms that parallel those used in § 2.02(a)(3). Replication in subsection (d) of the present Section avoids the negative implication that might otherwise arise from omission of discussion focused on the due-process rights of those opposing the aggregated claimants. This Section consists of an admonition to the court to design its adjudication plan under § 2.12 so as not to compromise the ability of such persons to dispute the allegations made by claimants or to litigate pertinent substantive defenses. Aggregation should not proceed if the court is unable to formulate an adjudication plan that ensures due process for a defendant in these regards.

REPORTERS' NOTES

Comment b. On the relationship between the preclusive effect of aggregate proceedings and constitutional due process, see Samuel Issacharoff, *Preclusion, Due Process, and the Right to Opt Out of Class Actions,* 77 Notre Dame L. Rev. 1057 (2002). On the ways in which courts may limit the preclusive effect of their judgments, see Tobias Barrington Wolff, *Preclusion in Class Action Litiga-*

tion, 105 Colum. L. Rev. 717, 768–776 (2005).

Comment c. The listing in subsection (a) of exit, voice, and loyalty rights stems from the Supreme Court's discussion of due process in class actions seeking divisible remedies. Phillips Petroleum Co. v. Shutts, 472 U.S. 797, 811 (1985). The *Shutts* Court famously stated:

> If the forum ... wishes to bind an absent plaintiff concerning a claim for money damages or similar relief at law, it must provide minimal procedural due process protection. The plaintiff must receive notice plus an opportunity to be heard and participate in the litigation, whether in person or through counsel.... Additionally, we hold that due process requires at a minimum that an absent plaintiff be provided with an opportunity to remove himself from the class by executing and returning an "opt out" or "request for exclusion" form to the court. Finally, the Due Process Clause [of the Fourteenth Amendment] of course requires that the named plaintiff at all times adequately represent the interests of the absent class members.

472 U.S. at 811–812. The shorthand labels "exit," "voice," and "loyalty" stem from academic commentary. See John C. Coffee, Jr., *Class Action Accountability: Reconciling Exit, Voice, and Loyalty in Representative Litigation*, 100 Colum. L. Rev. 370, 376–377 (2000) (drawing on the typology of Albert O. Hirschman, *Exit, Voice, and Loyalty: Responses to Decline in Firms, Organizations, and States* (1970)); Samuel Issacharoff, *Governance and Legitimacy in the Law of Class Actions*, 1999 Sup. Ct. Rev. 337,

366 (same). For an argument to ground the constitutional status of the right to opt out more in due-process case law concerning deprivations of property than in the related line of cases focused upon personal jurisdiction, see Brian Wolfman & Alan B. Morrison, *What the* Shutts *Opt–Out Right Is and What It Ought to Be*, 74 UMKC L. Rev. 729, 733 (2006).

Comment d. Commentary on conflicts of interest in class representation recognizes that any insistence on loyalty must stop short of the " 'Balkanization' of the class action: namely, its fragmentation into a loose-knit coalition of potentially feuding enclaves that could seldom litigate effectively as an organization." Coffee, *Class Action Accountability*, 100 Colum. L. Rev. at 374. See also Charles Silver & Lynn Baker, *I Cut, You Choose: The Role of Plaintiffs' Counsel in Allocating Settlement Proceeds*, 84 Va. L. Rev. 1465, 1496–1497 (1998) ("If the Due Process Clause absolutely prohibits counsel for a group from resolving conflicts among claimants, each class member must be separately represented on the matter of settlement allocation. To us, this conclusion is a *reductio ad absurdum* of the 'no tradeoffs' approach. Embracing the conclusion denies plaintiffs the benefits that make group litigation attractive.").

For commentary conceptualizing adequate representation in class actions in terms of structural conflicts of interest, whether between class counsel and class members or among class members themselves, see Samuel Issacharoff & Richard A. Nagareda, *Class Settlements under Attack*, 156 U. Pa. L. Rev. 1649, 1677–1697 (2008); Issacharoff, *Governance and Legitimacy*, 1999 Sup. Ct. Rev. at

385. See also Geoffrey P. Miller, *Conflicts of Interest in Class Action Litigation: An Inquiry into the Appropriate Standard*, 2003 U. Chi. Legal F. 581. For illustrations in class-action case law, see, e.g., Amchem Prods., Inc. v. Windsor, 521 U.S. 591, 626–627 (1997) (pointing to structural conflict between class members with present disease and those merely at risk of future disease); Ortiz v. Fibreboard Corp., 527 U.S. 815, 854–856 (1999) (pointing to similar conflict between present and future claimants as well as to conflict between class counsel's interest in settling the class action and class counsel's interest in settling their "inventory" cases excluded from the class definition).

The foregoing case law and commentary have elaborated on the meaning of adequate representation beyond that extant at the time of the Restatement Second of Judgments § 42(1)(d), and the present Section accordingly seeks to account for those developments in the law. The language of § 42(1)(d) nonetheless is prescient in its call for judicial inquiry into whether "there was such a substantial divergence of interest between [the representative of the class] and the members of the class, or a group within the class, that he could not fairly represent them with respect to the matters as to which the judgment is subsequently invoked." The focus on the existence of a "substantial divergence of interest" is consistent with the recognition here of the impossibility of eliminating all conflicts of interest.

Commentary also has noted the difficulty of applying conventional conflict-of-interest rules to class representation. See Nancy J. Moore, *"Who Should Regulate Class Action Lawyers,"* 2003 U. Ill. L. Rev. 1477.

Conventional conflict-of-interest rules may well apply more readily to conflicts arising from a lawyer's duties to other current clients and to former clients than to intra-class conflicts. See id. at 1482. On the conceptual connection between consent by multiple clients to conflicts of interest on the part of a common lawyer in ordinary litigation and the appropriate standard for adequate representation in class actions, see Silver & Baker, *I Cut, You Choose*, 84 Va. L. Rev. at 1506–1515. On conflicts of interest in non-class aggregate litigation, see Howard M. Erichson, *Beyond the Class Action: Lawyer Loyalty and Client Autonomy in Non–Class Collective Representation*, 2003 U. Chi. Legal F. 519. On the need to develop second-best checks on legal representation in aggregate litigation due to the inadequacy of checks arising from the market for such representation, see Jill E. Fisch, *Lawyers on the Auction Block: Evaluating the Selection of Class Counsel by Auction*, 102 Colum. L. Rev. 650, 670–671 (2002).

On the distinction drawn by existing class-action law between application of the requirements for class certification—including adequate class representation—and judicial review of the fairness of a proposed class settlement, see *Amchem*, 521 U.S. at 621 (noting that the Rule 23(e) requirement of judicial review for class settlements "was designed to function as an additional requirement, not a superseding direction, for the 'class action' to which Rule 23(e) refers is one qualified for certification under Rule 23(a) and (b)"). See also Restatement Second, Judgments § 42, Reporter's Note to Comment *f* (recognizing that "collusion and inadequate diligence or vigor by a representative are logically distinct from conflict of interest on his part," but also noting "as a practical matter the two will often coalesce.").

On the importance of evaluating loyalty at the time of the class-certification determination and of according that evaluation preclusive effect, see Issacharoff & Nagareda, *Class Settlements under Attack*, 156 U. Pa. L. Rev. at 1685–1691; Richard A. Nagareda, *Administering Adequacy in Class Representation*, 82 Tex. L. Rev. 287, 318–324 (2003); Marcel Kahan & Linda Silberman, *The Inadequate Search for "Adequacy" in Class Actions: A Critique of* Epstein v. MCA, Inc., 73 N.Y.U. L. Rev. 765, 776–783 (1998). For contrary views, see Henry Paul Monaghan, *Antisuit Injunctions and Preclusion Against Absent Nonresident Class Members*, 98 Colum. L. Rev. 1148, 1195–1199 (1998); Patrick Woolley, *The Availability of Collateral Attack for Inadequate Representation in Class Suits*, 79 Tex. L. Rev. 383, 388 (2000); Susan P. Koniak, *How Like a Winter? The Plight of Absent Class Members Denied Adequate Representation*, 79 Notre Dame L. Rev. 1787, 1790–1791 (2004).

The treatment of loyalty as a precondition to aggregate treatment in subsection (a)(1) disapproves of the analysis of adequate class representation in Stephenson v. Dow Chemical Co., 273 F.3d 249 (2d Cir. 2001), aff'd by equally divided Court, 539 U.S. 111 (2003). In *Stephenson*, the Second Circuit denied claim-preclusive effect to a settlement in class-action litigation concerning the alleged health effects of the defoliant Agent Orange upon military personnel during the Vietnam War. In relevant part, the class settlement provided cash benefits to class members who manifested disease within a specified time period but denied cash benefits to those who

manifested disease thereafter. The court concluded that the judgment approving the class settlement could not be accorded claim-preclusive effect on the ground that the class proceedings violated class members' due-process right to adequate representation. In the court's view, the due-process violation lay in the conflict between veterans who manifested disease before the cutoff for cash benefits specified by the class settlement and those who manifested disease thereafter—a distinction that did not exist at the time of class certification but, rather, was the creation of the class settlement itself. For discussion of whether the representational arrangements in the Agent Orange class might have involved a structural conflict of interest on other grounds discernible at the time of class certification, see Issacharoff & Nagareda, *Class Settlements under Attack*, 156 U. Pa. L. Rev. at 1688–1689; Nagareda, *Administering Adequacy*, 82 Tex. L. Rev. at 324–330.

By and large, *Stephenson* has not garnered much following in subsequent case law. Even courts purporting to follow its reasoning have not sought to permit absent class members such broad escape from the preclusive effects of judgments. See, e.g., Wilkes ex rel. Mason v. Phoenix Home Life Mutual Ins. Co., 902 A.2d 366, 382 (Pa. 2006) (citing *Stephenson* to support collateral review, but characterizing the question for such review as concerning the plaintiffs' contention that they were "wrongfully included in the class," not as pertaining to differences in treatment under the class settlement of the sort considered problematic in *Stephenson* itself). For its part, the Second Circuit itself has cabined the reach of *Stephenson* in a subsequent decision:

> [I]f, in the class action, a defendant opposing class certification or an objector to the settlement had made a serious argument that [the representation of class interests had been inadequate], and that argument had been considered and rejected by the class action court, it would not be unfair to preclude collateral review of that ruling and relegate [the plaintiff] to her direct review remedies. It would not be a denial of due process to give full faith and credit to the class action court's ruling on adequacy of representation unless that ruling was made in the absence of an adversarial presentation. . . .

Wolfert v. Transamerica Home First, Inc., 439 F.3d 165, 172 (2d Cir. 2006). This statement concerning the availability of collateral review places the Second Circuit in line with an emerging consensus among the federal courts of appeals. See In re Diet Drugs Prods. Liab. Litig., 431 F.3d 141 (3d Cir. 2005); Nottingham Partners v. Trans–Lux Corp., 925 F.2d 29 (1st Cir. 1991). The position reflected here on the availability of collateral review into the adequate-representation question—a view introduced in Comment *d* and further elaborated in § 3.14—accords with this emerging consensus.

The casting of subsection (a)(1) in terms of "structural conflicts of interests" is designed to lend greater precision to the loyalty inquiry in connection with class actions, an inquiry historically phrased in terms of adequate representation. As reflected in the foregoing citations, case law

on class actions in recent years increasingly reflects that the concept of adequate representation has been overloaded with multiple, varying meanings, not all of which carry the same significance for postjudgment challenges to a class judgment. One meaning—that of "structural conflicts of interest" discernible as part of the determination to aggregate or that emerge as part of that proceeding—speaks to the legitimacy of the class judgment from its inception and irrespective of its outcome. Another meaning—that of adequate representation in the sense of an adequate class settlement—is quite different, for it is inextricably linked to outcome. Put less formally, a legitimately constituted class nonetheless might yield a mediocre or even unfair class settlement; and, conversely, a class settlement might be sensible in content but nevertheless might stem from an improperly constituted class. See *Amchem*, 521 U.S. at 622–623 ("The benefits asbestos-exposed persons might gain from the establishment of a grand-scale compensation scheme . . . is not pertinent to the predominance inquiry" designed to police the composition of the class.). Existing law has a tendency to confuse matters still further by casting adequate representation—without clear differentiation between structure and outcome—as an aspect of personal jurisdiction, at least when class members otherwise lack "minimum contacts" with the rendering forum. See *Shutts*, 472 U.S. at 812 ("[T]he Due Process Clause of course requires that the named plaintiff at all times adequately represent the interests of the absent class members."). For criticism of the lumping together of these varying meanings under the common rubric of adequate representation, see Issacharoff

& Nagareda, *Class Settlements under Attack*, 156 U. Pa. L. Rev. at 1656–1658.

Comment e. For discussion of how the opportunity to opt out may reinforce the adequacy of class representation by bringing competitive pressure to bear upon class counsel, see Richard A. Nagareda, *The Preexistence Principle and the Structure of the Class Action*, 103 Colum. L. Rev. 149, 168–174 (2003). On the choice between exit rights structured in terms of an opportunity to opt out of the class and exit rights cast as an opportunity to opt in, compare *Shutts*, 472 U.S. at 812 (rejecting the "contention that the Due Process Clause of the Fourteenth Amendment requires that absent plaintiffs affirmatively 'opt in' to the class, rather than be deemed members of the class if they do not 'opt out' "), with John Bronsteen & Owen Fiss, *The Class Action Rule*, 78 Notre Dame L. Rev. 1419, 1446–1447 (2003) (arguing for class settlements to bind only those claimants who opt in). See § 2.10 (discussing the possibility of aggregation by actual consent of claimants in exceptional situations).

On the possibility of an additional opportunity to opt out of a class action in the event of settlement, compare Fed. R. Civ. P. 23(e)(4) ("If the class action was previously certified under Rule 23(b)(3), the court may refuse to approve a settlement unless it affords a new opportunity to request exclusion to individual class members who had an earlier opportunity to request exclusion but did not do so."), with David Rosenberg, *Adding a Second Opt–Out to Rule 23(b)(3) Class Actions: Cost Without Benefit*, 2003 U. Chi. Legal F. 19 (criticizing second opt-out on pragmatic grounds).

Comment f. The reference to "appropriate notice" stems from the locution now used in the law of class actions to recognize the possibility of notice to class members seeking indivisible remedies. See Fed. R. Civ. P. 23(c)(2)(A) ("For any class certified under Rule 23(b)(1) or (b)(2), the court may direct appropriate notice to the class."). The casting of notice for claims seeking divisible remedies in terms of the "best notice that is practicable" stems from Fed. R. Civ. P. 23(c)(2)(B) (notice in class actions certified under Rule 23(b)(3)), which itself draws from the phrasing used by the Supreme Court for due-process purposes in a case that predates the modern Rule 23: Mullane v. Central Hanover Bank & Trust Co., 339 U.S. 306, 317 (1950). The *Mullane* Court understood the best notice that is practicable to consist of notice "reasonably calculated, under all the circumstances, to apprise interested parties of the pendency of the action and afford them an opportunity to present their objections." 339 U.S. at 314–315.

For the presumption that individualized notice is the best notice practicable with regard to claims for divisible remedies, see Fed. R. Civ. P. 23(c)(2)(B) (requiring "individual notice to all members who can be identified through reasonable effort"); Eisen v. Carlisle & Jacquelin, 417 U.S. 156, 176 (1974) ("[I]ndividual notice to identifiable class members is not a discretionary consideration to be waived in a particular case. It is, rather, an unambiguous requirement of Rule 23."). For commentary questioning this aspect of *Eisen*, see Wolfman & Morrison, Shutts *Opt–Out Right*, 74 UMKC L. Rev. at 751.

In existing doctrine, "one finds the single largest number of variations from federal [class-action] practice" in state rules concerning notice to class members. Thomas D. Rowe, Jr., *State and Foreign Class–Action Rules and Statutes: Differences from—and Lessons for?—Federal Rule 23*, 35 W. St. U. L. Rev. 147, 162 (2007). "All [such variations] are in the direction of less stringent requirements, which seems to reflect a fairly widespread sense that the Federal Rule's text—despite due-process concerns in the background—does not coincide with a constitutional mandate." Id. For examples of state class-action rules that contemplate greater flexibility as to notice, see Cal. R. Ct. 3.766(f) ("If personal notification is unreasonably expensive or the stake of individual class members is insubstantial, or if it appears that all members of the class cannot be notified personally, the court may order a means of notice reasonably calculated to apprise the class members of the pendency of the action—for example, publication in a newspaper or magazine; broadcasting on television, radio, or the Internet; or posting or distribution through a trade or professional association, union, or public interest group."); 735 Ill. Comp. Stat. 5/2–803 (2003) ("[T]he court in its discretion may order such notice that it deems necessary to protect the interests of the class and the parties"); Iowa R. Civ. P. 1.266(3) ("In determining the manner and form of the notice to be given, the court shall consider the interests of the class, the relief requested, the cost of notifying the members of the class, and the possible prejudice to members who do not receive notice."); Md. R. Civ. P. 2–231(e) ("In a class action maintained under subsection (b)(3), notice shall be given to members of the class in the manner the court directs."); N.Y. C.P.L.R.

§ 904(c) (McKinney 2006) ("In determining the method by which notice is to be given, the court shall consider ... the cost of giving notice by each method considered ... the resources of the parties and ... the stake of each represented member of the class, and the likelihood that significant numbers of represented members would desire to exclude themselves from the class or to appear individually, which may be determined, in the court's discretion, by sending notice to a random sample of the class."); Pa. R. Civ. P. 1712(a) ("In determining the type and content of notice to be used and the members to be notified, the court shall consider the extent and nature of the class, the relief requested, the cost of notifying the members and the possible prejudice to be suffered by members of the class or by other parties if notice is not received."); S.C. R. Civ. P. 23(d)(2) ("The court ... may order that notice be given in such a manner as it may direct of the pendency of the action by the party seeking to maintain the action on behalf of the class."). The flexibility recognized in these state class-action rules is in keeping with the approach in Canada. See Rowe, *State and Foreign Class–Action Rules*, 35 W. St. U. L. Rev. at 164 ("Canadian class proceedings legislation is remarkably flexible on the question of notice. While setting out the factors which the court must consider when determining what notice is required in the circumstances, Ontario and [British Columbia] also allow that the court 'may dispense with notice if ... the court considers it appropriate to do so.'") (citing Craig Jones, *Theory of Class Actions* 126 (2003)); see also Parsons v. McDonald's Restaurants of Canada Ltd., C41264, [2005] O.J.

506 QUICKLAW (O.A.C. Feb. 16, 2005).

On the importance of absent class members' opportunity to be heard with regard to the disposition of their claims, see Patrick Woolley, *Rethinking the Adequacy of Adequate Representation*, 75 Tex. L. Rev. 571 (1997). On the opportunity to be heard as a component of due process in adjudicatory proceedings by administrative agencies, see Londoner v. City and County of Denver, 210 U.S. 373, 385–386 (1908).

Comment g. Denial of both the preclusive benefit and the preclusive detriment of the class judgment is consistent with the longstanding goal to prevent one-way intervention in class actions when absent class members have the opportunity to opt out. See Fed. R. Civ. P. 23(b)(3), advisory committee's note. But see § 2.10 (discussing exceptional situations that may warrant use of opt-in aggregation). For an example of a class-action court ordering sequestration of a portion of any recovery obtained by opt-out claimants to account for benefits they obtained from class discovery and development of the merits by class counsel, see In re Linerboard Antitrust Litig., 292 F.Supp.2d 644 (E.D. Pa. 2003).

Comment h. Subsection (c) seeks to streamline the treatment of mandatory aggregation by gathering together concepts currently dispersed in multiple rule provisions for class actions. Like § 2.04, subsection (c) of the present Section abandons the distinction nominally drawn between mandatory class treatment when the prosecution of "separate actions by . . . individual class members would create a risk of inconsistent or varying adjudications with respect to individual class members that would es-tablish incompatible standards of conduct for the party opposing the class" (Fed. R. Civ. P. 23(b)(1)(A)) and mandatory class treatment when "the party opposing the class has acted or refused to act on grounds that apply generally to the class, so that final injunctive relief or corresponding declaratory relief is appropriate respecting the class as a whole" (Fed. R. Civ. P. 23(b)(2)). See § 2.04, Reporters' Notes (discussing the lack of functional difference between Rule 23(b)(1)(A) and Rule 23(b)(2) classes).

The analysis of the practical benefits of mandatory aggregation with regard to claims for indivisible relief stems from Allen v. Int'l Truck & Engine Corp., 358 F.3d 469 (7th Cir. 2004). There, the Seventh Circuit noted that "class certification obliges counsel (and the representative plaintiffs) to proceed as fiduciaries for all [affected] employees, rather than try to maximize the outcome for the[] 27 [employees with individual lawsuits on file] at the potential expense of the other 323." Id. at 471. In addition, the court noted that class certification "will entitle counsel to attorneys' fees representing the gains (if any) achieved by all employees, and not just the named plaintiffs." Id.

The focusing of mandatory aggregation on claims for indivisible remedies has the further benefit of ensuring the finality of the aggregate proceeding—in particular, of avoiding the barriers to finality identified in Johnson v. General Motors Corp., 598 F.2d 432 (5th Cir. 1979), and Brown v. Ticor Title Ins. Co., 982 F.2d 386 (9th Cir. 1992). In *Johnson*, the court held that a member of a Rule 23(b)(2) mandatory class action for employment discrimination could not be precluded from seeking the divisible remedy of back pay in an individual lawsuit, because the plaintiff employee had not received notice of the class action. 598 F.2d at 436. The court in *Ticor Title* went further, holding that the members of an ostensibly mandatory class in securities litigation could not be precluded thereafter from bringing individual lawsuits for the divisible remedy of damages based upon a class settlement that purported to resolve in their entirety claims for both indivisible and divisible remedies. 982 F.2d at 392. To give the mandatory class settlement preclusive effect as to the distribution of the damage remedy, the *Ticor Title* court reasoned, would violate class members' due-process rights, for the mandatory class had afforded them no opportunity to opt out. Id.

One may best understand the insistence upon notice in *Johnson* and upon the opportunity to opt out in *Ticor Title* as stemming from an underlying suspicion about the suitability of mandatory class treatment to adjudicate in their entirety claims seeking divisible remedies, at least outside the scenario of a limited fund. The problem in both cases stemmed not so much from the effect of the class settlements upon subsequent litigation as from the inappropriateness of mandatory class treatment in the first place. Subsection (c) acts on the well-taken concerns of the *Johnson* and *Ticor Title* courts by confining mandatory aggregation to situations in which the mandatory nature of the proceeding is needed to manage fairly and efficiently claims for indivisible remedies. As § 2.04 reflects, claims for divisible remedies should be analyzed separately, both as to the appropriateness of aggregate treatment and as to the presumptive opportunity to exit any such aggregate proceeding, per subsection (a)(1) of the present Section.

Comment i. Ortiz v. Fibreboard Corp., 527 U.S. 815 (1999), speaks to the need for proof of a limited fund and for its limited nature to stem from conditions that preexist aggregate treatment. In *Ortiz*, the Court struck down a mandatory class settlement as inconsistent with Rule 23(b)(1)(B). Drawing heavily on early equity precedents that it regarded as setting the bounds of the current Rule 23(b)(1)(B), the Court held that "the first and most distinctive characteristic [of a limited fund] is that the totals of the aggregated liquidated claims and the fund available for satisfying them, set definitely at their maximums, demonstrate the inadequacy of the fund to pay all the claims." Id. at 838. The Court went on to emphasize that the purported limited fund in *Ortiz*—in essence, the sum provided by Fibreboard's insurers in settlement of related litigation concerning their coverage obligations for asbestos-related tort claims—was simply the creation of the class settlement negotiations themselves and fell well short of the maximum sum that Fibreboard might have committed to the settlement. See id. at 859.

For commentary conceptualizing mandatory class treatment in the limited-fund scenario as a procedure similar to an interpleader action, see, e.g., Samuel Issacharoff, *Class Action Conflicts*, 30 U.C. Davis L. Rev. 805, 820–821 (1997). On this view, the ability of plaintiffs to seek mandatory common resolution of the division of a fixed pot serves the same function as interpleader, but places the authority to invoke the procedure in the hands of the claimants rather than the stakeholder. The interpleader device itself is well established in procedural law. See Fed. R. Civ. P. 22.

The most significant question to arise under Rule 23(b)(1)(B) in the aftermath of *Ortiz* concerns the availability of mandatory class treatment when the limited nature of the fund arises not from the net worth of the defendant but, instead, from limitations of constitutional due process upon the maximum punitive damages that the defendant may be compelled to pay for a single course of conduct. Compare In re Simon II Litig., 407 F.3d 125, 127 (2d Cir. 2005) (overturning certification of mandatory punitive-damages class for lack of "evidence by which the district court could ascertain the limits of either the fund or the aggregate value of punitive claims against it, such that the postulated fund could be deemed inadequate to pay all legitimate claims"), with In re Exxon Valdez, 229 F.3d 790, 795 (9th Cir. 2000) (noting that "courts have encouraged the use of mandatory class actions to handle punitive damages claims in mass tort cases"). The present Section frames the inquiry into the availability of mandatory class treatment for punitive-damages claims in terms of whether the constitutional limit for such relief is such as to give rise to a preexisting interdependence among punitive-damages claims, as distinct from a merely theoretical limit that, as a practical matter, would not make for interdependence of those claims absent aggregate treatment. Cf. Philip Morris USA v. Williams, 549 U.S. 346, 355 (2007) (distinguishing between constitutionally permissible consideration of defendant's conduct vis-à-vis similarly situated persons other than plaintiff in order to evaluate the reprehensibility of that conduct as to plaintiff and con-

stitutionally impermissible punishment of defendant for its conduct as to such other persons); State Farm Mut. Auto. Ins. Co. v. Campbell, 538 U.S. 408, 419–424 (2003) (striking down a punitive-damages award in individual litigation as unconstitutionally excessive due, in part, to the trial court's error in permitting the plaintiffs to invoke the defendant's course of conduct in other states). The significance of the Court's analysis of punitive damages in *Williams* for the certifiability of mandatory punitive-damages class actions remains a subject of debate in the scholarly literature. Compare, e.g., Byron G. Stier, *Now It's Personal: Punishment and Mass Tort Litigation after* Philip Morris v. Williams, 2 Charleston L. Rev. 433 (2008) (contending that the logic of *Williams* forecloses certification of mandatory punitive-damages class actions), with Elizabeth J. Cabraser & Robert J. Nelson, *Class Action Treatment of Punitive Damages Issues after* Philip Morris v. Williams: *We Can Get There from Here*, 2 Charleston L. Rev. 407 (2008) (finding latitude for mandatory punitive-damages class actions after *Williams*).

It is "well established" that a showing of insolvency is not a precondition to a petition for reorganization under Chapter 11 of the Bankruptcy Code. See, e.g., In re SGL Carbon Corp., 200 F.3d 154, 163 (3d Cir. 1999). But bankruptcy law does contain an implicit requirement that such a petition must be filed in "good faith" in the sense of arising from a "serious threat" to the continued successful operations of the debtor. See id. at 160–162. For the voting requirements for confirmation of a reorganization plan, see 11 U.S.C. § 1126. For the "absolute priority" rule, see id.

§ 1129(b)(2). On the importance of policing the boundary between the limited-fund class action and bankruptcy in light of the additional protections afforded to claimants in the latter proceedings, see John C. Coffee, Jr., *Class Wars: The Dilemma of the Mass Tort Class Action*, 95 Colum. L. Rev. 1343, 1457–1461 (1995).

Comment j. Subsection (d) speaks to due process for defendants in the class-action context, but in a manner informed by the considerable controversy that has arisen over the mass consolidation of widely disparate claims in state-court proceedings in asbestos litigation. See State ex rel. Mobil Corp. v. Gaughan, 565 S.E.2d 793, 794 (W. Va. 2002) (Maynard, J., concurring) (discussing due-process questions presented by consolidation of "thousands of dissimilar and unrelated asbestos claimants into a single trial"). Existing case law notes that the constitutional due-process rights of defendants impose outer limits on the permissible scope of consolidation. See, e.g., In re Chevron U.S.A., Inc., 109 F.3d 1016, 1020 (5th Cir. 1997) (reversing the consolidation of

over 3000 asbestos claims when trial plan lacked "safeguards designed to ensure that the claims against [the defendant] of the non-represented plaintiffs" would be "determined in a proceeding that is reasonably calculated to reflect the results that would be obtained if those claims were actually tried"); Todd–Stenberg v. Dalkon Shield Claimants Trust, 56 Cal. Rptr.2d 16, 18 (Cal. Ct. App. 1996) (upholding consolidation of product-liability claims but cautioning that "dire" situations might exist in which the "confusion and prejudice" created by consolidation would violate the due-process rights of defendants).

Effect on current law. The approach of this Section, in large part, is to describe the emerging understanding of due process in the context of aggregate litigation. The reference to "appropriate notice" in subsection (a)(3), however, would require amendment of the existing Rule 23(c)(2)(B), insofar as it categorically requires "individual notice to all members who can be identified through reasonable effort."

§ 2.08   Class–Action Treatment of Common Issues

The court may authorize aggregate treatment of a common issue by way of a class action if the court

    (a) provides the protections described in § 2.07(a) and (d);

    (b) enforces the constraint of § 2.07(b); and

    (c) authorizes interlocutory appeals as provided in § 2.09(a)(2).

Comment:

    a. Preclusion in issue class actions. This Section carries forward the implications of the authority recognized in §§ 2.02–2.04 for courts to treat common issues on an aggregate basis. As such, the authority described in this Section remains subject to the limitations provided in §§ 2.02–2.04.

This Section recognizes judicial discretion to provide for aggregate litigation of a common issue by way of a class action and underscores three limits on the preclusive effect of that proceeding. Subsection (a) limits the court's power to authorize aggregate treatment in accordance with § 2.07(a)—that is, upon affording claimants exit, voice, and loyalty rights. As provided in § 2.07(a)(2), however, exit rights need not be conferred in aggregate proceedings described in § 2.07(c). In practical effect, the kinds of aggregate proceedings as to common issues that would trigger the application of § 2.07(c) consist of those that concern indivisible remedies. By its nature, the limited-fund scenario for mandatory aggregation (§ 2.07(c), Comment *i*) would necessarily encompass all claims against the fund, not just common issues raised by those claims. The additional reference in subsection (a) to § 2.07(d) serves as a reminder that due-process protections also apply to those opposing the aggregate group in an issue class proceeding. Subsection (b), in turn, carries forward to this Section the constraint of § 2.07(b) that claimants who exit from the issue class action thus are nonparties to that proceeding.

REPORTERS' NOTES

Comment a. By providing for class-action treatment of common issues in accordance with § 2.07(a), subsection (a) of this Section brings constitutional due process for such proceedings into accord with the process due in more familiar aggregations involving related claims. On the latter subject, see § 2.07(a), Reporters' Notes.

§ 2.09   Interlocutory Appeals

(a) An opportunity for interlocutory appeal should be available with respect to

(1) the class-certification determination under § 2.07 or § 2.08; and

(2) any class-wide determination of a common issue on the merits that the court authorizes pursuant to § 2.08.

(b) Consideration of an interlocutory appeal under subsection (a) should be discretionary on the part of the relevant appellate court.

Comment:

a. Interlocutory appeal as to class certification. Subsections (a)(1) and (b), together, reflect the existing recognition in federal class-action procedure of an opportunity for interlocutory appellate review of class-certification determinations—whether granting or denying certification, in whole or in part—at the discretion of the relevant appellate court, but without the need for authorization on the part of the trial-level court that has made that determination. Procedures in some state systems afford a similar opportunity for appellate review of class-certification determinations, though the precise procedural vehicles for such review range from specification within the relevant state class-action rule itself (on the federal model) to various writs. Some states do not provide for appeals from denials of class certification.

The cross-reference to both § 2.07 and § 2.08 makes clear that the interlocutory appeal described in subsection (a)(1) applies to both the certification of class actions with respect to related claims and the certification of class actions limited to particular issues, as the case may be in a given instance. This, too, works no change in existing federal law on such interlocutory review.

The reference in subsection (b) to discretion on the part of the relevant appellate court as to whether to grant the appeal, moreover, affords due recognition to the possibility that a denial of class certification in a given instance might leave class counsel in a position to reframe the class-certification motion, such as would counsel against appellate consideration pending such revision. In order to facilitate appellate consideration of this point, the trial-level court should make clear the existence of such latitude for the reframing of the class-certification motion.

b. Interlocutory appeal as the determination of a common issue on the merits. Subsection (a)(2) effectively conditions the court's discretion to authorize an issue class action by specifying that any such authorization must be accompanied by the opportunity for interlocutory appeal as to any class-wide determination of the common issue on the merits. The availability of such an appeal from any merits determination of the common issue operates in addition to the interlocutory appeal available under subsection (a)(1) with respect to the determination to certify an issue class action in the first place.

Determination of a common issue in a class action would not necessarily qualify as a final judgment, because that determination would leave other issues to be addressed in other proceedings. The specification in subsection (a)(2) that an opportunity for interlocutory appeal on the merits must be made available nonetheless builds on existing practice in the federal system, whereby a final—and, hence, appealable—judgment may be entered with respect to "one or more but fewer than all of the claims" in a given action upon the court's "express determination that there is no just reason for delay and upon an express direction for the entry of judgment." The court's "express determination" effectively identifies the time at which appeal may be taken.

The merits determination of the certified common issue or issues on a class-wide basis would exhaust all of the matters that define the domain of the issue class action. Put less formally, determination of the certified common issue on the merits would do all that the issue class action stands able to do. Determination of the common issue on the merits accordingly should be regarded as being of sufficient definiteness to permit interlocutory appeal, especially given the practical significance of that determination for subsequent proceedings. A central objective of the issue class action is to yield issue preclusion with respect to the common issue encompassed.

In practical terms, unitary appellate review of a merits determination of the common issue prevents the waste of judicial resources that would occur if subsequent proceedings were to go forward but only thereafter to reveal some defect in the merits determination of the common issue. Unitary merits review also avoids the possibility of multiple appeals—potentially, to multiple courts—concerning the common issue in the aftermath of other proceedings that do, ultimately, yield final judgments. Authorization of an aggregate interlocutory appeal thereby preserves the efficiency and equity gains to be realized through the treatment of the common issue in a single proceeding.

The conditioning of aggregate treatment on the availability of an interlocutory appeal on the merits serves an additional purpose. The expectation is that such an appeal will serve as an added backstop against efforts to seek aggregate treatment as to trivial or insignificant issues that nonetheless are common in a given litigation. Part of this backstop effect already comes from the specification in § 2.02(a)(1) that the court should determine whether aggregate treatment of a common issue by way of a class action will "materially advance the resolution of multiple civil claims by addressing the core of the dispute in a manner superior to other realistic procedural alternatives, so as to generate significant judicial efficiencies." The constraints found elsewhere in this Chapter add to this backstop effect. Subsection (a)(2) of the present Section nonetheless proceeds from a recognition that the brake on aggregate treatment of trivial or insignificant common issues need not consist exclusively of a verbal formulation for courts to apply. Subsection (a)(2) speaks as much to the incentives of those who might seek aggregate treatment of a common issue as that subsection does to appellate review on the merits.

The practical effect of subsection (a)(2) is that those seeking aggregate treatment of a common issue should be prepared to face the possibility of an aggregate interlocutory appeal on the merits of that issue in addition to the possibility of an interlocutory appeal with respect to the initial decision whether to aggregate. The disposition of both appeals should precede the disposition of the remaining issues raised by the underlying claims—for example, the obtaining of damage awards for particular claimants. In so specifying, this Section remains cognizant of the delay sometimes associated under current law with interlocutory appeals in the class-action setting. To be sure, the application of subsection (a)(2) as to interlocutory appeal on the merits is also likely to result in delay. Such delay, however, reinforces the practical brake on efforts to seek aggregate treatment as to issues that would not materially advance the resolution of multiple claims.

In casting interlocutory appeal as pertaining to the "determination" of a common issue on the merits, subsection (a)(2) nonetheless provides no authority for such appeal with respect to rulings on the merits that do not determine the common issue. A denial of summary judgment with respect to the common issue accordingly would not trigger the opportunity to seek interlocutory review under subsection (a)(2).

Taken together, subsections (a)(2) and (b), respectively, require the availability of an interlocutory appeal on the merits as part of the judicial determination to proceed by way of an issue class action but leave discretion in the relevant appellate court to grant or deny such an appeal. In both respects, these subsections chart new ground in procedural law, but in a way that builds on existing statutory authority for interlocutory appeals in federal civil litigation generally. Statutory authority presently exists for a federal district judge to authorize interlocutory appeal from a nonfinal order in any civil action if the judge is "of the opinion that such order involves a controlling question of law" and that "an immediate appeal from the order may materially advance the ultimate termination of the litigation." By requiring that the opportunity for an interlocutory appeal be made available with respect to the merits determination of a common issue resolved on a class-wide basis, subsection (a)(2) effectively treats such a merits determination as being of sufficient centrality to proceedings on other issues—again, due to issue preclusion—as to be tantamount, as a categorical matter, to the sort of "controlling question of law" to which existing statutory law refers. Section 2.02(a)(1) concerning the identification of common issues suitable for class treatment uses the same "materially advance" locution, so as to lend congruity to the determination to afford issue-class treatment and the framework for interlocutory appeal as to the merits of that issue.

In the event that the relevant court of appeals exercises discretion to decline an appeal as to the initial class-certification determination under subsection (a)(1), then the appeal on the merits determination of the common issue under subsection (a)(2) may encompass both the merits and—if challenged—the underlying determination to aggregate.

When the same trial court stands to handle both the issue class proceeding and non-class proceedings on the remaining issues in the litigation, the relevant appellate court might choose to exercise its discretion to decline an appeal on the initial class-certification determination and, instead, await the generation of final judgments with respect to particular claimants within the class.

Similarly, failure to pursue an appeal as to the initial class-certification determination under subsection (a)(1) should not operate as a waiver in the context of an interlocutory appeal under subsection (a)(2) as to either the merits or the underlying class-certification determination.

c. Related judicial orders concerning attorneys' fees. Aggregate treatment of a common issue by way of a class action has consequences that are related to those for appellate review. As noted in Comment *b*, the point of such treatment is to generate a determination of the common issue that, in turn, has issue-preclusive effect in proceedings on the remaining issues in the litigation. The lawyers in the aggregate proceeding will have conferred a substantial benefit on claimants insofar as that preclusive effect, in a given instance, inures to their advantage in other proceedings. In practice, however, the lawyers for the aggregate proceeding as to a common issue may differ from the lawyers who handle the remaining issues—for example, by representing claimants on an individual basis with respect to the determination of damages after liability has been found on an aggregate basis.

Lawyers for the aggregate proceeding and lawyers who anticipate representation of individual claimants on the remaining issues in the litigation might enter into contractual arrangements that provide for the allocation of attorneys' fees as between the two, in recognition of the joint benefit that the former lawyers effectively confer upon the latter. In the absence of such contractual arrangements, courts in consolidated multidistrict litigation in the federal system have begun to articulate—with some ambiguity—the concept of a "quasi-class action" and, on that basis, have issued orders concerning the allocation of fees as between the two types of lawyers—orders that, in practical effect, tax the fees for lawyers who represent claimants on the remaining issues in the litigation to account for the benefit provided by the lawyers in the aggregate proceeding. Cf. § 2.02, Comment *a* (preferring the terminology of these Principles over the emerging notion of a "quasi-class action").

REPORTERS' NOTES

Comment a. Existing authority for interlocutory appellate review of class-certification determinations appears in Fed. R. Civ. P. 23(f). On the development of Rule 23(f), see Michael E. Solimine & Christine Oliver Hines, *Deciding to Decide: Class Action Certification and Interlocutory Review by the United States Courts of Appeals under Rule 23(f)*, 41 Wm. & Mary L. Rev. 1531 (2000).

Some, but not all, state systems have counterpart rules or processes. See Richard D. Freer, *Interlocutory Review of Class Action Certification Decisions: A Preliminary Empirical Study of Federal and State Experience*, 35 W. St. U. L. Rev. 13, 22–26 (2007) (analyzing state experience with interlocutory review of class-certification decisions, both with and without state counterpart rules to Fed. R. Civ. P. 23(f)). In some instances, the vocabulary used in state law differs in phrasing, if not in function, from Rule 23(f). E.g., La. Code Civ. Pro. Ann., art. 592(A)(3)(b) (2009) (providing for "suspensive or devolutive appeal" from class-certification orders); Hewlett–Packard Co. v. Superior Court, 83 Cal.Rptr.3d 836, 837 (Cal. Ct. App. 2008) (undertaking review of class-certification decision via "peremptory writ of mandate"). In some states, the opportunity for appeal does not extend to denials of class certification. See, e.g., Garza v. Swift Transp. Co., 213 P.3d 1008 (Ariz. 2009) (overruling prior precedent permitting appeal from the denial of class certification because "an order denying class certification does not, as a legal matter, 'in effect determine[] the action and prevent[] judgment from which an appeal [may] be taken.'" (quoting Ariz. Rev. Stat. Ann. § 12–2101(d)), while leaving open the possibility of interlocutory review in "an extraordinary case" under Arizona's special-action rules); Palmer v. Friendly Ice Cream Corp., 940 A.2d 742, 746–747 (Conn. 2008) (deeming denial of class certification unappealable because such denial does not "terminate[] a separate and distinct proceeding, or . . . so conclude the rights of the parties that further proceedings cannot affect them." (internal quotation marks omitted)). Other states provide for interlocutory appellate review of the denial of class certification. Pennsylvania, for example, deems the denial of class certification a collateral order, appealable as a matter of right. See Keppley v. Sch. Dist. of Twin Valley, 866 A.2d 1165, 1168 n.1 (Pa. Commw. Ct. 2005).

Comment b. Existing law recognizes the possibility of treating a judicial decision as a final judgment for issue-preclusion purposes even though it is confined to a particular part of a larger claim. See, e.g., Zdanok v. Glidden Co., 327 F.2d 944, 955 (2d Cir. 1964) (Friendly, J.). For commentary anticipating the possibility of the same approach with respect to claim preclusion, see 18A Charles Alan Wright, Arthur R. Miller & Edward H. Cooper, *Federal Practice and Procedure* § 4434 (3d ed. 2005).

The suggestion to treat a judgment as to a common issue as functionally equivalent to a final judgment also builds on the recognition in current law that courts may enter a final judgment as to a particular claim among multiple claims advanced in a single action. See Fed. R. Civ. P. 54(b) (conditioning entry of final judgment with respect to "one or more, but fewer than all, claims" involved in a given action upon an express determination "that there is no just reason for delay").

On the practical need for interlocutory appellate review on the merits of a determination of a common liability issue, see Complex Litigation: Statutory Recommendations and Analysis § 3.07(c), Comment *d*, 139 ("Providing for one review of the liability decision avoids the possibility of multiple appeals of the same matter following the various damage judgments....").

Existing statutory authority for district-court authorization of an interlocutory appeal, subject to the discretion of the relevant court of appeals, appears in 28 U.S.C. § 1292(b)—the source for the quoted language in Comment *b*. The further indication that an interlocutory appeal on the merits of a common issue may encompass the initial determination to certify the class—if that determination was not itself the subject of a Rule 23(f) appeal—also draws on existing practice under § 1292(b). See Yamaha Motor Corp., U.S.A. v. Calhoun, 516 U.S. 199, 205 (1996) (noting that "appellate jurisdiction [under § 1292(b)] applies to the *order* certified to the court of appeals, and is not tied to the particular question formulated by the district court"); 16 Wright, Miller & Cooper, *Federal Practice and Procedure* § 3929 at 388 ("The court [of appeals] may ... consider any question reasonably bound up with the certified order, whether it is antecedent to, broader or narrower than, or different from the question specified by the district court.").

Even before § 1292(b), interlocutory appellate review of liability determinations was a longstanding feature of admiralty law under 28 U.S.C. § 1292(a)(3), which permits appeals from "[i]nterlocutory decrees ... determining the rights and liabilities of the parties to admiralty cases in which appeals from final decrees are allowed." As one court explains, "this provision was originally designed to cover situations distinctive to admiralty where it was not uncommon for the district court to enter an order finally resolving the liability issues and then to refer the case to a special master for a determination of damages.... In such cases, an immediate appeal was permitted from the order resolving the liability issues." Central State Transit & Leasing Corp. v. Jones Boat Yard, Inc., 77 F.3d 376, 377–378 (11th Cir. 1996). On the difficulties presented by § 1292(a)(3) in light of the subsequent authorization in Rule 54(b) and § 1292(b) for interlocutory appeals, see 16 Wright, Miller & Cooper, *Federal Practice and Procedure* § 3927, 344–345 ("[A]rguments for expansive interpretation of § 1292(a)(3) are offset by the availability of Rule 54(b) and the more recent adoption of § 1292(b), which allows interlocutory appeals on permission of the trial court and appellate court in admiralty cases as well as in other cases. Only Congress can decide whether these alternative means of appeal, not available in 1926 when § 1292(a)(3) was adopted, justify repeal of § 1292(a)(3).").

Comment c. For a thoughtful account of the need for careful judicial oversight of fees as between counsel for claimants in consolidated federal proceedings and counsel in subsequent individual proceedings, see In re Zyprexa Prods. Liab. Litig., 424 F.Supp.2d 488 (E.D.N.Y. 2006). The court observed:

While the settlement in the instant action is in the nature of a private agreement between individual plaintiffs and the defendant, it has many of the characteristics of a class action and may be properly characterized as a quasi-class action subject to general equitable powers of the court.... The large number of plaintiffs subject to the same settlement matrix approved by the court; the utilization of special masters appointed by the court to control discovery and to assist in reaching and administering a settlement; the court's order for a huge escrow fund; and other interventions by the court, reflect a degree of court control supporting its imposition of fiduciary standards to ensure fair treatment to all parties and counsel regarding fees and expenses.

Id. at 491. In the same litigation, the court went on to explain:

Should any amount be recovered by federal plaintiffs from defendant by settlement or judgment, a percentage of those plaintiffs' attorneys' fees will be held back in an escrow account.... Any lawyer who has worked for the common benefit of all federal Zyprexa plaintiffs ... may apply for compensation from the common benefit account.

In re Zyprexa Prods. Liab. Litig., 467 F.Supp.2d 256, 266 (E.D.N.Y. 2006). The court, however, described this approach as amounting to "a holdback, not a levy." Id. For additional recognition of the taxing power of the transferee court in cases consolidated for pretrial proceedings by the Judicial Panel on Multidistrict Litigation (MDL), see In re Vioxx Prods. Liab. Litig., 574 F.Supp.2d 606 (E.D. La. 2008); In re Guidant Corp. Implantable Defibrillators

Prods. Liab. Litig., MDL No. 1708, 2008 WL 682174 (D. Minn. Mar. 7, 2008). In these cases, the MDL transferee court asserted authority to override the fee terms set by contract between claimants and the lawyers they retained to represent them on an individual basis in order to account for the benefit provided by other lawyers in the MDL-consolidated proceedings. For that matter, in some earlier mass-disaster cases, courts recognized the existence of authority for common-benefit assessments of various sorts in litigation not judicially identified or characterized as a quasi-class action. See In re Air Crash Disaster at Florida Everglades on Dec. 29, 1972, 549 F.2d 1006, 1019 (5th Cir. 1977) (recognizing authority for eight percent assessment to account for common work of court-designated counsel). See also In re MGM Grand Hotel Fire Litig., 570 F.Supp. 913, 916–917 (D. Nev. 1983) (noting use of similar assessment to spread costs of MDL common discovery work).

The concept of a "quasi-class action" in *Zyprexa*, *Vioxx*, and *Guidant* remains at an early developmental stage in doctrine, one that admits of further refinement in the future. For scholarly criticism of the concept as a basis for judicial fee oversight, see Charles Silver & Geoffrey P. Miller, *The Quasi–Class Action Method of Managing Multi–District Litigations: Problems and a Proposal*, 63 Vand. L. Rev. 107 (2010). Restitutionary principles do not support allocation orders that tax the fees of lawyers for individual claimants in order to pay the lawyers in the aggregate proceeding. The fee arrangements for the former sorts of lawyers typically are set by contractual lawyer–client retention agreements, such that there generally is no basis for judicial intervention on restitutionary grounds. See Restatement Third, Restitution and Unjust Enrichment § 30, Comment *b*, 77 (Tentative Draft No. 3, 2004) ("By comparison with class actions, court-imposed fees to appointed counsel in consolidated litigation frequently appear inconsistent with restitution principles, since litigants may have no choice but to accept and pay for certain legal services as directed by the court. The fact that such fees may not be authorized by this Section is probably irrelevant, however, since their predominant rationale is not unjust enrichment but administrative convenience."). As a result, orders concerning the allocation of fees between the two sets of lawyers have sought to ground their authority in general equitable principles, other than restitution.

By contrast, orders that would directly tax the ultimate recoveries of claimants themselves, insofar as they choose to make use of benefits from the aggregate proceeding—rather than tax the fees of the lawyers who represent them on the remaining issues in the litigation—would more closely approximate restitutionary principles. As to many claimants, the work done by lawyers for the aggregate proceeding is not the subject of a previous contractual retention agreement but, rather, is the kind of uncontracted-for benefit roughly analogous to the work of class counsel on behalf of absent class members. In class actions that generate a "common fund," a restitutionary fee award to class counsel comes from the fund itself—that is, from class members' recovery—absent negotiation otherwise by way of a duly approved class settlement. See id. at 72–74; Charles Silver, *A Restitutionary Theory of Attorneys' Fees in Class Actions*, 76 Cornell L. Rev. 656 (1991).

Emerging judicial doctrine aside, the relevant legislature might, over time, seek to set forth by way of statute a set of best practices concerning fee allocation. At this early stage in the development of the "quasi-class action" concept, these best practices have yet to crystallize in real-world practice.

Effect on current law. Subsection (a)(1) of the present Section reflects the existing Fed. R. Civ. P. 23(f). Subsection (a)(2) explicates the emerging judicial treatment of common issues when the aggregate proceeding does not encompass all issues in a given litigation. Statutory amendment would be necessary to authorize the kind of interlocutory appeal on the merits of the common issue described in subsection (a)(2), albeit modeled closely on the existing authority in 28 U.S.C. § 1292(b) for interlocutory appeals from orders on controlling issues of law.

§ 2.10 Aggregation by Consent

When justice so requires, a court may authorize aggregate treatment of related claims or of a common issue by affirmative consent of each affected claimant.

Comment:

a. Discretion to aggregate by consent. This Section recognizes that justice may require the court to afford aggregate treatment of a common issue by affirmative consent of the persons who would comprise the aggregate group. Aggregation by consent is distinct from the process for class certification, whereby claimants may be brought before the court based upon appropriate notice and failure to exclude themselves from the class action. See § 2.07(a). The authorization recognized in this Section nonetheless does not afford a vehicle for evasion or sidestepping of the principles stated elsewhere in this Chapter but, rather, must respect those principles that are pertinent under the circumstances.

Without limiting the courts in their identification of appropriate situations, this Section proceeds on the expectation that aggregation by consent will remain exceptional. Such a situation might arise, for example, when litigation takes place in the United States but primarily involves claimants located in foreign countries. A judicial order enabling claimants to consent to be bound by an aggregate proceeding in the United States operates, in practical effect, as an invitation to joinder or, in the parlance of class-action law, an "opt-in" proceeding. The authority recognized in this Section is intended to have no effect on the relatively rare substantive regimes in existing law that explicitly provide for aggregation on an opt-in basis. Aggregation by consent under this Section, moreover, cannot confer subject-matter jurisdiction on the court when none otherwise would exist.

The reference to the "affirmative consent of each affected claimant" is phrased to underscore that the requisite consent to the binding effect of the proceeding need not come from the persons opposing the aggregate group. As to those persons, the aggregate treatment recognized by this Section would remain nonconsensual, in the same manner as the proceedings described in §§ 2.07–2.08. As reflected in § 2.07(d), however, even aggregation under this Section should not compromise the ability of persons opposing the aggregate group to dispute the underlying claims and to raise pertinent substantive defenses.

REPORTERS' NOTES

Comment a. This Section breaks from existing law regarding class actions by recognizing the desirability, in exceptional instances, of judicial orders that effectively create an opt-in class. The district court sought to do so with respect to liability issues raised by a ski-train accident in Austria that resulted in the death of 155 passengers and crew members, the vast majority of whom were not United States citizens. In re Ski Train Fire in Kaprun, Austria on Nov. 11, 2000, 220 F.R.D. 195 (S.D.N.Y. 2003). The district court's certification of an opt-in class met with reversal, however, with the appellate court finding a lack of authorization for classes of that sort in the current Rule 23. Kern v. Siemens Corp., 393 F.3d 120 (2d Cir. 2004).

Existing statutes authorize representative actions on an opt-in basis in particular substantive areas. See, e.g., 29 U.S.C. §§ 216(b) (authorizing actions under the Fair Labor Standards Act (FLSA) "by any one or more employees for and in behalf of himself or themselves and other employees similarly situated" but also providing that "[n]o employee shall be a party plaintiff to any such action unless he gives his consent in writing to become such a party") & 626(b) (providing for enforcement of the Age Discrimination in Employment Act "in accordance with the ... procedures provided in" 28 U.S.C. § 216). See also 15 U.S.C. § 77p(d)(2)(A) (Securities Litigation Uniform Standards Act, preserving existing authority of state pension plans to sue "as a member of a class comprised solely of other States, political subdivisions, or State pension plans that are named plaintiffs, and that have authorized participation, in such action."). For detailed discussion of the FLSA framework, see 7B Charles Alan Wright, Arthur R. Miller & Mary Kay Kane, *Federal Practice and Procedure* § 1807 (3d ed. 2005).

Effect on current law. This Section rejects the result in *Kern* that an opt-in class is per se impermissible under the current Rule 23 and, instead, would provide courts with authority to create opt-in mechanisms for voluntary aggregation of claimants by their affirmative consent. On the assumption that the *Kern* court properly read the current Rule 23, rule amendment would suffice for this purpose.

§ 2.11 Preclusive Effect of the Aggregation Decision Itself

A judicial decision to deny aggregate treatment for a common issue or for related claims by way of a class action should raise a rebuttable presumption against the same aggregate treatment in other courts as a matter of comity.

Comment:

a. *Potential for multiple attempts at class certification.* This Section addresses situations in which the denial of class certification by one court precedes efforts to obtain the same or a similar treatment from another court. The potential for relitigation of the same or a similar class-certification question stems from structural divisions within the judicial system. The potential for relitigation of the aggregation question across multiple federal courts is reduced by the authority of the Judicial Panel on Multidistrict Litigation ("MDL Panel") to consolidate for pretrial proceedings related lawsuits pending within the federal system, whether on the basis of initial filing there or proper removal from state court. As yet, there is no comparable institution for the coordination of civil litigation across the various states or between the federal courts and the various state courts. As a result, the denial of class certification by one court may leave proponents of aggregation free to seek the same or similar treatment from a court in a different judicial system. At its extreme, this process has the potential to turn into a search for one anomalous court willing to certify a class action previously rejected by multiple other courts—a particular problem when the challenged conduct is both nationwide in scope and gives rise to causes of action under state law.

b. Comity in lieu of preclusion. This Section provides that a denial of class certification should raise a rebuttable presumption against the same aggregate treatment in another court. The basis for this presumption is not preclusion but, rather, comity: the authority of the subsequent court to exercise discretion in its aggregation decision so as to avoid, insofar as is possible, unnecessary friction between judicial systems. Such friction arises with greatest force when the party opposing certification raises in a subsequent forum the same alleged defect that defeated class certification in the initial forum.

The choice of comity rather than preclusion as the focus of this Section stems from the difficulties associated with the latter with respect to a denial of class certification. The major difficulty arises from the recognition that, as to such a denial, the prospective absent class members have become neither parties to the proposed class action nor persons with any attributes of party status (such as the capacity to be bound thereby, as in a duly certified class action). Nor is there any guarantee that prospective absent class members even would be aware of the court's determination of their ability to assert claims as a class action. The notion that absent class members could be bound in an issue-preclusion sense with respect to the seeking of certification in another court, even for the same proposed class action, runs afoul of existing precedents that confine to certain narrowly defined categories the situations in which preclusion can be extended to reach nonparties. Issue preclusion arising from a denial of class certification as to would-be absent class members would approach the kind of "virtual representation" disallowed under current law.

Apart from the further due-process limitations, issue preclusion itself requires that the same issue must have been litigated and determined in the proceeding that produced the adjudication now said to have preclusive effect. The same-issue requirement is relatively strict, calling for litigation and determination in the initial proceeding not simply of the same kind of issue concerning the appropriateness of aggregation but, rather, the identical issue. Same-issue status is not present when the aggregation question in the first proceeding arose under a procedural rule of the rendering court and the aggregation question in the subsequent proceeding arises under a procedural rule—albeit, perhaps, an identically phrased rule—that need not be interpreted or applied in identical fashion. Issue preclusion is generally not appropriate in such a situation, for the court in the subsequent proceeding must have the opportunity, if it chooses, to construe its procedural rule differently on the aggregation question, within the ambit afforded by federal constitutional due process. Similar obstacles to issue preclusion also may arise when the basis for the denial of class certification stems from choice-of-law problems with respect to state-law claims but the court in the subsequent proceeding stands to apply materially different choice-of-law principles in its certification analysis.

Short of issue preclusion, however, the court in the subsequent proceeding should generally exercise its discretion to avoid unnecessary friction with the court that initially denied class certification. Accordingly, that denial should be a relevant consideration for the court in the subsequent proceeding both when the two courts' respective class-action rules are identically phrased and when those rules exhibit overlapping concerns (even in the absence of identical phrasing) such that certification in the subsequent proceeding would have the harmful forum-shopping consequences described in Comment *a*. Under existing law, it is already commonplace for state courts to look to federal class-action precedents to inform their interpretation and application of their own state class-action requirements.

c. Rebutting the presumption. Like presumptions in the law generally, the presumption stated in this Section remains rebuttable. The expectation of this Section is that situations for rebuttal of the presumption stated here may arise more frequently than situations with respect to some other presumptions used in the law, as to which successful rebuttal is relatively rare.

One important basis for rebuttal of the presumption consists of the affirmative demonstration of inadequate representation in connection with an earlier denial of class certification. The subsequent court should guard against the possibility of strategic jockeying by defendants to obtain a favorable determination of the aggregation question in a proceeding in which the lawyers for claimants operate under structural conflicts of interest with a significant potential to skew systematically their incentive to press vigorously the use of aggregation. See § 2.07(a)(1) (discussing loyalty rights in aggregation in terms of structural conflicts of interest). In addition, when the basis for the earlier denial (such as inadequacy of the particular class counsel to represent the proposed class) is no longer present in a subsequent proceeding (due to a change of counsel to one who would adequately represent the proposed class), the presumption stated in this Section would be rebutted.

REPORTERS' NOTES

Comment a. In re Bridgestone/Firestone, Inc., Tires Products Liability Litigation, 333 F.3d 763 (7th Cir. 2003), speaks to the practical problems associated with repeated efforts to seek certification of the same nationwide class action in multiple fora. The court observed: "Even if just one judge in ten believes that a nationwide class is lawful, then if the plaintiffs file in ten different states the probability that at least one will certify a nationwide class is 65% . . . . Filing in 20 states produces an 88% probability of national class certification." Id. at 767. In short, "[a] single positive [ruling on class certification] trumps all the negatives." Id. at 766–767. For further discussion of the problems generated by the search for the anomalous certifying court, see Samuel Issacharoff & Richard A. Nagareda, *Class Settlements under Attack*, 156 U. Pa. L. Rev. 1649, 1660–1666 (2008).

The Class Action Fairness Act of 2005 substantially expands the domain both for initial filing in the federal courts of proposed nationwide class actions for state-law claims and for removal of such actions from state court at the behest of defendants. 28 U.S.C. § 1332(d)(2) (expanding diversity jurisdiction to reach class actions involving more than $5 million in controversy and minimal diversity of citizenship). For an early assessment of the impact of CAFA on class-action practice, see Richard L. Marcus, *Assessing CAFA's Stated Jurisdictional Policy*, 156 U. Pa. L. Rev. 1765 (2008). Once in federal court, duplicative or overlapping proposed class actions are subject to the general authority of the MDL Panel to coordinate for pretrial purposes "civil actions involving one or more common questions of fact." 28 U.S.C. § 1407(a). For a state procedural counterpart, see Tex. R. Jud. Admin. 13.

Comment b. In the law of federal courts, the courts of one judicial system often seek to avoid unnecessary friction with determinations made by courts of another judicial system, not as a result of preclusion or legal compulsion but, rather, due to considerations of comity. For overviews of these comity doctrines, see generally Richard H. Fallon, John F. Manning, Daniel J. Meltzer & David L. Shapiro, *Hart and Wechsler's The Federal Courts and the Federal System* 1049–1140 (6th ed. 2009); 17A Charles Alan Wright, Arthur R. Miller & Edward H. Cooper, *Federal Practice and Procedure* §§ 4244–4247 (3d ed. 2005).

On the rejection of "virtual representation" as a basis for preclusion of nonparties, see Taylor v. Sturgell, 128 S.Ct. 2161 (2008). There, the Supreme Court observed that "the rule against nonparty preclusion is subject to exceptions." Id. at 2172. The Court hastened to underscore, however, that those exceptions "delineate discrete" situations that "apply in 'limited circumstances,'" id. at 2175 (quoting Martin v. Wilks, 490 U.S. 755, 762 n.2 (1989)), none of which extend generally to the situation of a would-be absent class member with respect to a denial of class certification.

Informed by the *Taylor* Court's analysis of the outer bounds for nonparty preclusion, this Section rejects the *Bridgestone/Firestone* court's pre-*Taylor* view of the issue-preclusive effect that may properly flow from a denial of class certification. Even in the pre-*Taylor* period, moreover, the approach to issue preclusion in *Bridgestone/Firestone* represented the minority view within the federal circuits, with other courts emphasizing the stringency of the same-issue requirement for issue preclusion. See

J.R. Clearwater Inc. v. Ashland Chem. Co., 93 F.3d 176, 180 (5th Cir. 1996); accord In re Gen. Motors Corp. Pick–Up Truck Fuel Tank Prods. Liab. Litig., 134 F.3d 133, 146 (3d Cir. 1998) (citing with approval *Clearwater*). On the content of the same-issue requirement for issue preclusion, see Restatement Second, Judgments § 27, Comment *c*; 18 Wright, Miller & Cooper, *Federal Practice and Procedure* § 4417. For a pre-*Taylor* argument in favor of the injunctive power asserted in *Bridgestone/Firestone*, see Tobias Barrington Wolff, *Federal Jurisdiction and Due Process in the Era of the Nationwide Class Action*, 156 U. Pa. L. Rev. 2035, 2109–2117 (2008).

For the proposition that procedural rules track judicial systems, see generally Baker v. General Motors Corp., 522 U.S. 222, 239–241 (1998). In *Baker*, the Court held that an injunction barring a former employee from testifying against General Motors, entered in the employee's wrongful-discharge action against that firm in Michigan state court, did not prevent the employee from testifying in a separate product-liability action brought against General Motors in Missouri state court. The Supreme Court noted that the Michigan injunction could not "command obedience elsewhere on a matter [concerning the admissibility of evidence under Missouri law that] the Michigan court lacks authority to resolve." Id. at 241.

Effect on current law. The approach of this Section could be implemented by judicial interpretation, without a need for rule change.

TOPIC 4
JUDICIAL MANAGEMENT OF AGGREGATION

§ 2.12 Adjudication Plan for Aggregation

(a) **When authorizing the aggregate treatment of a common issue or of related claims by way of a class action, the court should adopt an adjudication plan that explains**

(1) **the justification for aggregate treatment based on the principles in this Chapter;**

(2) **the procedures to be used in the aggregate proceeding to determine the common issue, insofar as aggregate treatment is so confined; and**

(3) **the anticipated effect that a determination of the common issue will have in the class proceeding and with respect to any other proceedings on the remaining issues.**

(b) **In developing the adjudication plan described in subsection (a), the court should resolve any pertinent disputes concerning the feasibility of aggregate treatment.**

(c) **In the event that the court's authorization of aggregate treatment applies only for purposes of settlement as** provided in § 3.06, an adjudication plan under subsection (a) is not required.

Comment:

a. *Functions of an adjudication plan.* This Section underscores that courts should not lightly undertake aggregate treatment of a common issue or of related claims. The courts, instead, should do so only upon careful consideration of the procedural alternatives to such treatment (see § 2.02(a)(1)), articulation of the procedures for the aggregate proceeding, and analysis of the anticipated effect of the proceeding on the treatment of individual issues. Insistence on an adjudication plan that addresses these matters operates, in practice, as a significant threshold requirement by disallowing any approach that would "aggregate first and ask questions later." This Section casts the obligation on the part of the court in terms of the formulation of an adjudication plan coincident with the authorization of class-action treatment that, in turn, provides a focal point for appellate review as provided in § 2.09.

The choice of the phrasing "adjudication plan" rather than the more familiar formulation "trial plan" is designed to avoid the descriptively inaccurate implication that aggregate proceedings usually proceed through full-fledged trial. At the same time, however, the shift from the formulation "trial plan" is not intended to suggest that the framework by which the common issue could be tried is somehow unimportant to the determination whether to authorize aggregate treatment. To the contrary, trial—along with dispositive pretrial motions, to be sure—is the principal vehicle available to be "used in the aggregate proceeding to determine the common issue" within the meaning of subsection (a)(2).

In describing the adjudication plan as an obligation on the court's part, the present Section does not leave the plan design solely to judicial creation. Rather, the objective is to focus the attention of litigants on the design and consequences of aggregation, with the expectation that the litigants' submissions will enhance the information available to the court on those subjects. The adjudication plan also critically informs the scope of both preclusion and interlocutory appellate review of issues for aggregate resolution.

b. *Issue identification and preclusion.* In operation, subsections (a)(2) and (a)(3) work in support of one another. Clear and precise identification of the common issues to be addressed in the aggregate proceeding—insofar as only common issues are to be addressed, see § 2.08—is important so as to enable the determination of those issues to have preclusive effect in other proceedings on the remaining individual issues.

When a common issue is to be tried by a jury on an aggregate basis, one approach would be for the court, with the assistance of counsel, to craft as part of the adjudication plan a special verdict form to be used in the determination of the common issue. In the aggregate proceeding itself, the special verdict form would serve its usual function of lending structure to the jury's consideration of the common issue. Formulation of the special verdict form can also assist the court to minimize the practical need for reconsideration in subsequent proceedings of the evidence presented in the aggregate proceeding. See § 2.06(b).

In addition, for purposes of subsection (a)(3), the special verdict form would facilitate the identification in other proceedings of precisely what issues were litigated and determined in the aggregate proceeding. In fact, courts already use special verdict forms in this way outside of aggregate litigation. A special verdict form can be especially useful when claimants advance multiple factual theories with regard to a particular common issue—say, alternative sets of facts, each alleged to support a finding of negligence on the defendant's part. A special verdict form can assist the courts in subsequent proceedings to ascertain which of the alternative factual theories, if any, were used in the aggregate proceeding as the basis for any findings on the common issue. Even when the common issue in the aggregate proceeding is not one for jury determination, the development of a special verdict form or similar framework as part of the adjudication plan encourages the careful consideration of preclusive effect as part of the decision to aggregate. Lack of precision and specificity in the special verdict form has a considerable potential to undercut the capacity of the aggregate proceeding on a common issue to yield issue-preclusive effect in subsequent proceedings.

By stating that the court should consider the anticipated effect that a determination of the common issue in the aggregate proceeding will have on other proceedings, subsection (a)(3) does not suggest that the court may predetermine the preclusive effect of its own proceedings. Subsection (a)(3) instead reinforces the principle of § 1.03(c) that aggregation should be undertaken so as to have preclusive effect, and, conversely, that a lack of preclusive effect should serve as a significant signal that aggregate treatment is not appropriate. In order to apply the principle of § 1.03(c) as part of its aggregation decision, the court necessarily must think in terms of the anticipated preclusive effect of the determinations envisioned to be made in the aggregate proceeding. The obligation under this Section for the court to develop an adjudication plan for the aggregate proceeding thus stands to serve a disciplining function with regard to whether the aggregation will, in fact, yield the desired preclusive effect.

    c. Judicial obligation to decide feasibility questions. Subsection (b) stands as the counterpart in the area of judicial feasibility to § 2.06 for questions concerning the content of applicable substantive law. In keeping with the approach in § 2.06, subsection (b) obliges the court to resolve any pertinent disputes concerning the feasibility of aggregate treatment as part of its decision to aggregate. Just as a court should not undertake aggregation based simply on the existence of a disagreement among the parties concerning the content of applicable substantive law, the court likewise should not aggregate based simply upon the existence of a genuine issue concerning the feasibility of aggregation. Rather, the court should resolve any such issue, a job that may entail the resolution of disputes among competing expert witnesses over the techniques realistically available for aggregate treatment.

REPORTERS' NOTES

    Comment a. The notion of a trial plan is already a well-established feature of the law of aggregate litigation, see, e.g., Manual for Complex Litigation (Fourth) § 22.756 (2004), and, indeed, of civil procedure for ordinary trials, see generally Fed. R. Civ. P. 16(e). The adjudication plan contemplated in the present Section should consist not simply of a "how-to" manual for the aggregate proceeding but also of an explanation of why the court regards that procedural path as appropriate. See § 2.02(a)(1). Although the burden of justification in an adjudication plan is not a high one, courts should give guidance as to why the procedures chosen would materially advance the resolution of the dispute. In this regard, a court may choose from a long list of experimental procedures that have been tested in complex proceedings. In keeping with § 2.02(b), those techniques include bellwether trials, bifurcation of claims or of liabilities and remedies, phased trials, and the use of claims procedures to streamline the actual

litigation. For a helpful discussion of these approaches, see Edward F. Sherman, *Segmenting Aggregate Litigation: Initiatives and Impediments for Reshaping the Trial Process*, 25 Rev. Litig. 691 (2006).

    Comment b. Consistent with the general approach throughout these Principles, the main objective is to provide litigants with a clear and equitable final resolution of the claims on a basis that will allow preclusion to lie. The use of special verdicts is one technique that allows a verdict to have clear estoppel value in subsequent litigation, and one whose use has long-standing authority in civil litigation. See, e.g., Fed. R. Civ. P. 49(a)(1) ("The court may require a jury to return only a special verdict in the form of a special written finding on each issue of fact."). Indeed, procedural law affords the court considerable discretion over the implementation of special verdicts. See Fed. R. Civ. P. 49(a)(2) ("The court must give the instructions and explanations necessary to enable the jury to make its findings on each submitted issue."). Courts look to special verdicts to clarify what the jury in an earlier proceeding actually determined for purposes of issue preclusion in a subsequent proceeding. See, e.g, Recoveredge L.P. v. Pentecost, 44 F.3d 1284, 1291 (5th Cir. 1995); In re McNallen, 62 F.3d 619, 626 (4th Cir. 1995). When the special verdict form lacks precision and specificity, determination of a common issue on an aggregate basis may be challenged as unlikely to yield issue preclusion in subsequent proceedings. See Brown v. R.J. Reynolds Tobacco Co., 576 F.Supp.2d 1328 (M.D. Fla. 2008), appeal docketed, No. 08–90023–J (11th Cir. Nov. 3, 2008) (holding that determination of common issues in tobacco class action did not yield issue preclusion in postdecertification individual actions by smokers).

Effect on current law. The approach of this Section describes broadly accepted judicial practice with regard to trial plans under current law.

Chapter 3

AGGREGATE SETTLEMENTS

TOPIC 1

PRINCIPLES COMMON TO CLASS AND NON–CLASS AGGREGATE SETTLEMENTS

§ 3.01 General Settlement Principles

(a) **Claimants and respondents may settle aggregate proceedings on terms that may not be available as remedies in contested lawsuits, provided that any such settlement affords equitable treatment among claimants.**

(b) **Class actions may also be settled on terms that may include remedies not available in contested lawsuits so long as**

187

the settlement is fair, reasonable, and adequate, and so long as class counsel adequately represent all claimants that will be subject to it. The fairness of the settlement must also be addressed by the court as part of the settlement approval process.

(c) Postjudgment challenges to aggregate settlements are disfavored unless no proper procedure for contemporaneous challenge was available and, accordingly, should be limited as set forth in this Chapter.

Comment:

a. Scope. While there are certain common features to all aggregate proceedings in terms of limitations on parties' control of the proceedings, the considerations relating to class actions differ significantly from those relating to non-class aggregate proceedings. Class actions are representative actions; unnamed class members normally do not select either the class representatives or class counsel and typically do not have a contractual relationship to class counsel. (Some variations of the class-action model exist by statute. Under the Private Securities Litigation Reform Act, for example, the "lead plaintiff" designates class counsel, subject to court approval.) No class settlement can be effectuated without a court certifying the class, and all class settlements are subject to court review and approval. Non-class aggregate settlements, by contrast, involve attorneys who have been hired by the individual claimants and whose relation to claimants is subject to contract. Non-class settlements do not normally require court approval, and the approval mechanism is governed by the retainer agreement, subject to rules of professional responsibility. Although judges sometimes review these settlements because of potential conflicts or the presence of minors, this remains the exception. Indeed, many non-class settlements take place without the filing of lawsuits on behalf of many of the affected parties.

As a result, apart from this Section, which sets forth principles applicable to both class and non-class aggregate settlements, class and non-class settlements are treated separately. Principles applicable to class settlements are discussed in §§ 3.02–3.14. Principles applicable to non-class settlements are discussed in §§ 3.15–3.18. As with Chapters 1 and 2, the present Chapter does not address the use of bankruptcy proceedings to resolve civil claims, nor does this Chapter address parens patriae settlements.

b. Settlement is a normal feature of litigation, including aggregate litigation. The goal of this Chapter is to ensure that settlements are not unduly impeded while, at the same time, requiring protections that facilitate the underlying fairness to the class of any settlement reached. Litigation of claims that the parties wish to settle imposes needless costs on the judicial system and the parties.

　　c.　Settlement on terms not permissible in contested litigation. In the context of a contested case, fundamental principles of due process, remedy, and other law impose substantial limitations on the relief that may be imposed. For instance, a jury must ordinarily liquidate the recovery due to a particular claimant, taking note of all factors bearing on the recovery. In the context of a settlement, however, these same limitations may not apply. As discussed in § 3.07, for instance, a cy pres award might well be a feasible way to settle aggregate litigation even if, in a contested case, the same claimants might not be compelled to accept a cy pres award in lieu of individualized damages. As another example, aggregate settlements sometimes ignore factors that might influence the size of jury verdicts, for example, by treating all persons in particular disease categories the same without detailed proof of individual circumstances.

　　d.　Timing of challenges to settlements. For both class and non-class aggregate settlements, the approach of this Chapter is to require that, with limited exceptions, any challenges to a settlement be made at the time the settlement is reached (and, if applicable, approved by the court). This approach enables the trial court and the parties to address potential problems before the settlement becomes final, as opposed to waiting and raising issues on collateral attack. In the class-action settlement context, this process is facilitated by allowing for early appellate review of class-settlement issues. See § 3.12.

　　It should be noted that the goal of achieving finality of settlement and requiring challenges to the settlement at the time the settlement is reached does not foreclose postsettlement challenges by claimants against their counsel for grievances relating to the settlement. See § 3.14(b).

REPORTERS' NOTES

Comment a. For authorities recognizing the strong policy favoring settlement of aggregate litigation, see, e.g., In re Warfarin Sodium Antitrust Litig., 391 F.3d 516, 534 (3d Cir. 2004); In re Gen. Motors Corp. Pick-Up Truck Fuel Tank Prods. Liab. Litig., 55 F.3d 768, 784 (3d Cir. 1995); Edward H. Cooper, *Aggregation and Settlement of Mass Torts*, 148 U. Pa. L. Rev. 1943, 1979–1980 (2000). For a discussion of parens patriae, see § 1.02, Reporters' Notes, supra.

Comment b. The concept of cy pres settlements is discussed in § 3.07. For authorities supporting the position that settlement recoveries need not comport with the requirements for awards in contested cases, see, e.g., Manual for Complex Litigation

(Fourth) § 21.662, at 333 n.1001 (2004).

Comment c. Restrictions on collateral challenges to class settlements are discussed in § 3.14.

Comment d. Few commentators have addressed non-class aggregate settlements. For notable exceptions, see, e.g., Elizabeth Chamblee Burch, *Procedural Justice in Nonclass Aggregation*, 44 Wake Forest L. Rev. 1 (2009); Howard M. Erichson, *A Typology of Aggregate Settlements*, 80 Notre Dame L. Rev. 1769 (2005); Howard M. Erichson, *Beyond the Class Action: Lawyer Loyalty and Client Autonomy in Non–Class Collective Representation*, 2003 U. Chi. Legal F. 519; Charles Silver & Lynn A. Baker, *Mass Lawsuits and the*

Aggregate Settlement Rule, 32 Wake Forest L. Rev. 733 (1997); Nancy J. Moore, *The Case Against Changing the Aggregate Settlement Rule in Mass Tort Lawsuits*, 41 S. Tex. L. Rev. 149 (1999). For some of the many discussions of class-action settlements, see, e.g., Roger C. Cramton, *Individualized Justice, Mass Torts, and "Settlement Class Actions": An Introduction*, 80 Cornell L. Rev. 811 (1995); Richard A. Nagareda, *Closure in Damage Class Settlements:* The Godfather *Guide to Opt–Out Rights*, 2003 U. Chi. Legal F. 141.

Effect on current law. Implementation of these principles will change current law as explained in §§ 3.02–3.18.

TOPIC 2
CLASS SETTLEMENTS

§ 3.02 Court Approval of a Class–Action Settlement

(a) **A certified class action may be settled, compromised, or dismissed only after appropriate notice to the class and approval by the court.**

(b) **Before a class action is certified, a settlement or voluntary dismissal on behalf of only the named class representatives may be consummated only if it is approved by the court. When a proposed settlement or dismissal does not involve any payment or other special consideration to class counsel or the named representative, a court should presume the propriety of the decision not to prosecute the claim and should rarely withhold approval or require notice to the class.**

Comment:

a. Treatment of classwide settlements. This Section, which requires judicial approval of any settlement of a certified class, is consistent with federal practice and the practice in every state that permits class actions, i.e., all states but Mississippi. Because a class action is a representative action, the rights of unnamed class members will be adjudicated even though such individuals are not present in court and may not even be monitoring the proceedings. Indeed, in the vast majority of situations, the unnamed class members will have played no role in selecting either the class representative or class counsel. See § 1.05, Reporters' Notes (discussing separation of ownership and control in aggregate proceedings). Because of these unique features of class actions, it is critical that certain protections be imposed. Among these is the requirement that any resolution that would bind the class be subject to class notice and judicial approval. In addition, for actions seeking divisible relief, the right to opt out must be afforded to all class members at the time the class is notified of the certification decision. See § 2.07(a)(2).

In class actions seeking divisible relief, the requirements of notice and judicial approval recognize the potential for conflict between class members (who seek to maximize their own recoveries net of fees) and class counsel (who may have an economic incentive to maximize their fees, even if the result is that less money is available for the class).

In a broad array of class actions, especially those organized to overcome the low value of individual claims, class representatives alone cannot be relied upon to ensure adequate and conflict-free representation by class counsel. In many cases, class representatives are little more than placeholders (assuring that the minimum requirements of a case or controversy are met), with the litigation being controlled entirely or mainly by class counsel. While settlements are an appropriate way to resolve class litigation, there is the risk that in some cases defendants may attempt to "buy off" representatives and class counsel by offering special incentives that maximize the recovery of a subset of the class or of class counsel at the expense of the class as a whole. Ideally, class counsel's ethical and fiduciary obligations to the class, as well as their reputational interests, should provide incentives to class counsel to maximize the recovery for the class. Nonetheless, judicial review and approval of class settlements are critical. Other measures that may be available to ensure fairness to class members are the appointment of a special master, special officer, or other court adjuncts (see § 3.09) and the encouragement of meritorious objections (see § 3.08).

One troublesome form of collusion involves the so-called "reverse auction," in which various plaintiff lawyers compete to reach a classwide settlement with a defendant. The defendant benefits by being able to select the plaintiff lawyer offering the best terms (from the defendant's standpoint). Such settlements raise potentially serious concerns, including inadequate representation by class counsel and class representatives.

Subsection (a) addresses settlements reached after a class is certified. A separate category of classwide settlements involves the situation in which the parties simultaneously seek certification and approval of the settlement. That category is addressed in § 3.06.

b. Treatment of settlements by class representatives before certification. Considerable controversy has surrounded the treatment of precertification settlements by class representatives. Some courts and commentators have recognized that class representatives may sometimes use their leverage as representatives to negotiate large personal settlements. In effect, class representatives may often stand as gatekeepers to aggregate litigation. Defendants are often willing to pay this premium in the hope that, when the class representatives dismiss their individual claims, no new plaintiffs will come forward as class representatives, thus eliminating the threat of a class-action judgment. Other courts have expressed concern that class members who have relied on the pendency of the putative class action as a reason not to file individual lawsuits may inadvertently allow the statute of limitations to run if the putative class-action suit is dismissed without warning. These concerns have led some courts and commentators to argue for the necessity of judicial review of precertification settlements or voluntary dismissals with class representatives. Other courts and commentators, however, do not believe that courts should supervise precertification resolutions or dismissals, given that such dispositions do not bind anyone in the putative class except for the particular representatives who settle or dismiss their cases. The 2003 amendments to Rule 23 opt for the latter approach and permit precertification settlements without the need for court approval.

This Section favors the approach of requiring limited judicial oversight. The potential risks of precertification settlements or voluntary dismissals that occur without judicial scrutiny warrant a rule requiring that such settlements take effect only with prior judicial approval, after the court has had the opportunity to review the terms of the settlement, including fees paid to counsel. Indeed, the very requirement of court approval may deter parties from entering into problematic precertification settlements.

In many and perhaps most instances, court approval will be virtually automatic. For instance, as reflected in § 3.02(b), when the proposal is for a voluntary dismissal in which neither putative class counsel nor the client receives any monetary benefit, there is little or no reason for concern that the settlement is an effort to utilize the threat of a class action to receive a settlement that would not be justified had the case been brought as an individual action. The same may be true if there is indeed a monetary benefit to class counsel or the class under the settlement but such payment is nominal or otherwise not substantial in light of the individual claims that are being settled.

    c. Necessity of court notice. Although this Section requires court approval for dismissals or compromises before certification, only in rare circumstances would the court need to order notice of the dismissal or compromise to members of the putative class. The exceptional circumstance requiring notice would be one in which the lawsuit, even before the certification, had received such extensive publicity that the court might reasonably be concerned that putative class members were relying on the lawsuit as a reason not to file individual lawsuits. In such cases, there is a risk that without some form of notice, such putative class members might unwittingly allow the statute of limitations to expire, given that whatever tolling effect there might be on the limitations period would cease upon the dismissal of the putative class action.

    Even if the court decides that the case is a rare one in which notice of precertification settlement or dismissal is required, the court should not be restricted in its approach to notice. Individual notice is an expensive and time-consuming process. The court might well decide, for example, that news coverage of such a high-profile case, or other publication, or Internet notice is sufficient to alert putative class members of the dismissal or compromise.

    d. Options if the court finds that representatives and counsel are not adequate. If the court refuses to permit a representative and class counsel to go forward with a precertification settlement or voluntary dismissal, the court may be faced with a dilemma if the proposed settlement reflected an attempt by class counsel or the representative to extract a large payment by leveraging the threat of a class action. The court may conclude, as a result of the proposed settlement, that the putative class counsel and representative are not adequate to represent the class. The court's options at that point would be to (1) dismiss the class-action allegations on grounds of inadequacy of representation, or (2) leave the case open for a short period of time to allow an opportunity for other putative class representatives and class counsel to come forward and assume representation of the class. In implementing the latter alternative, the court may wish to consider conditioning dismissal on the defendant's extension of the statute of limitations to permit new counsel and representatives to come forward.

REPORTERS' NOTES

Comment a. For authorities discussing the potential conflicts between class members and class counsel, see, e.g., John C. Coffee, Jr., *Class Wars: The Dilemma of the Mass Tort Class Action*, 95 Colum. L. Rev. 1343, 1367–1384 (1995); Susan P. Koniak, *Feasting While the Widow Weeps: Georgine v. Amchem Products, Inc.*, 80 Cornell L. Rev. 1045, 1048 (1995). For authorities discussing the need for court review and approval of class settlements, see, e.g., Knisley v. Network Assocs., Inc., 312 F.3d 1123, 1125 (9th Cir. 2002) (Kozinski, J.) (noting need for judicial review of settlements because of possibility that "class counsel may collude with the defendants, tacitly reducing the overall settlement in return for a higher attorney's fee"); L. Elizabeth Chamblee, *Unsettling Efficiency: When Non–Class Aggregation of Mass Torts Creates Second–Class Settlements*, 65 La. L. Rev. 157, 159 (2004); Sylvia R. Lazos, Note, *Abuse in Plaintiff Class Action Settlements: The Need for a Guardian During Pretrial Settlement Negotiations*, 84 Mich. L. Rev. 308, 316–325 (1985).

For authorities discussing "reverse auctions," see, e.g., Reynolds v. Beneficial Nat'l Bank, 288 F.3d 277, 282 (7th Cir. 2002) (Posner, J.) (collecting authorities); John C. Coffee, Jr., *Class Wars: The Dilemma of the Mass Tort Class Action*, 95 Colum. L. Rev. 1343, 1370–1373 (1995); Charles Silver, *We're Scared to Death: Class Certification and Blackmail*, 78 N.Y.U. L. Rev. 1357, 1404 (2003).

Comment b. For cases requiring court approval of precertification settlements, see, e.g., Shelton v. Pargo, Inc., 582 F.2d 1298, 1306 (4th Cir.

1978) (noting that "the District Court should have both the power and the duty, in view of its supervisory power over and its special responsibility in actions brought as class actions, as set forth in 23(d), to see that the representative party does nothing . . . which will prejudice unfairly the members of the class") (footnote omitted); Roper v. Consurve, Inc., 578 F.2d 1106, 1110–1111 (5th Cir. 1978), aff'd, 445 U.S. 326 (1980); Diaz v. Trust Territory of Pac. Islands, 876 F.2d 1401, 1408 (9th Cir. 1989). The approach taken in this Section is consistent with current practice in California under Cal. R. Ct. 3.770(a), which requires that in all class actions, putative or certified, "[a] dismissal of an entire class action, or of any party or cause of action in a class action requires court approval." The California rule does not necessarily require precertification notice to all class members if the court determines that there will be no prejudice to their interests. Cal. R. Ct. 3.770(c). See also Or. R. Civ. P. 32(D) (requiring court approval and notice "to some or all members of the class in such manner as the court directs," except that dismissal without notice "may be ordered . . . if there is a showing that no compensation in any form has passed directly or indirectly from the party opposing the class to the class representative or to the class representative's attorney and that no promise of such compensation has been made").

In light of the 2003 amendments to Rule 23, several courts now recognize the absolute right of class representatives, precertification, to settle their own claims without the need for court approval. See, e.g., Eckert v. Equitable Life Assurance Soc'y, 227 F.R.D.

60, 62 (E.D.N.Y. 2005) ("because [the putative class representative's] acceptance of the settlement was only on behalf of his claims rather than the certified class, [he] need not obtain the Court's permission prior to withdrawing from the action"); Aikens v. Deluxe Fin. Servs., No. 01–2427–CM, 2005 WL 1041351, at *6 (D. Kan. Mar. 2, 2005); Daniels v. Bursey, No. 03 C 1550, 2004 WL 2358291, at *1–2 (N.D. Ill. Oct. 21, 2004). Significantly, however, some courts even after 2003 have found that review of precertification settlements is required. See, e.g., Doe v. Lexington–Fayette Urban County Gov't, 407 F.3d 755, 761–764 (6th Cir. 2005) (finding that district court erred in refusing to notify putative class of precertification settlement because "the putative class members were likely lulled into believing that their claims continued to be preserved"); Griffith v. Javitch, Block & Rathbone, LLP, 358 B.R. 338, 342 (S.D. Ohio 2007) ("[E]ven under the current version of the Rule, the Court has a duty to the putative class members, and must examine whether prejudice could result from the dismissal of [a] claim [before certification]"); Ramirez v. Cintas Corp., No. C 04–00281 JSW, 2007 WL 4410414, at *1 (N.D. Cal. Dec. 14, 2007) ("Assuming without deciding that Rule 23 applies in this instance" court permitted class representative to dismiss her claim without notice); Cramblit v. City of Columbus, Ohio, No. 2:05–CV–301, 2006 WL 1735329, at *1 & n.1 (S.D. Ohio June 21, 2006) (reviewing and approving joint motion to dismiss class claims; court acknowledges 2003 amendment but relies on preamendment rule and case law in exercising review); accord, Manual for Complex Litigation

(Fourth) § 21.61, at 309 n.948 (2004) (noting that, despite 2003 amendments to Rule 23, "in certain situations in which a voluntary dismissal might represent an abuse of the class action process, the court should inquire into the circumstances behind the dismissal").

The California rule requires that parties seeking precertification dismissal "clearly state [in a declaration] whether consideration, direct or indirect, is being given for the dismissal" and "describe the consideration in detail." Cal. R. Ct. 3.770(a). See also Or. R. Civ. P. 32(D) (quoted above) (notice not required where no consideration has changed hands). For an example of a decision summarily approving a precertification dismissal where plaintiff received no consideration under the proposed dismissal, see Zavala v. Takata Corp., No. BC 277327, 2006 WL 4511430, at *1 (Cal. Super. Ct. Dec. 22, 2006) (dismissing one of several defendants).

Comment c. One court, in discussing precertification settlements, has identified three purposes for notice of a settlement or dismissal: (1) "protect[ing] a *defendant* by preventing a plaintiff from appending class allegations to her complaint in order to extract a more favorable settlement"; (2) "protect[ing] the class from objectionable structural relief, trade-offs between compensatory and structural relief, or depletion of limited funds available to pay the class claims"; and (3) "protect[ing] the class from prejudice it would otherwise suffer if class members have refrained from filing suit because of knowledge of the pending class action." *Diaz*, 876 F.2d at 1409 (emphasis in original).

For cases discussing tolling of the statute of limitations in the class-action context, see, e.g., Crown, Cork & Seal Co. v. Parker, 462 U.S. 345, 354 (1983) (filing of a putative class-action suit tolls the statute of limitations for members of the putative class "until class certification is denied"); Armstrong v. Martin Marietta Corp., 138 F.3d 1374 (11th Cir. 1998) (en banc) (tolling ceases upon trial court's denial of class certification, even if an appeal of the denial of certification is attempted); Culver v. City of Milwaukee, 277 F.3d 908, 914 (7th Cir. 2002) (Posner, J.) (noting that tolling of a putative class action ceases "when the suit is dismissed without prejudice"). For cases raising concerns about prejudice to class members after tolling of the statute of limitations ceases, see, e.g., *Culver*, 277 F.3d at 914 (ordering notice of decertification out of concern that "when [a class-action] suit is dismissed without prejudice or when class certification is denied the statute [of limitations] resumes running for the class members"; "[u]nless they are notified that the suit is dismissed, they may fail to file their own suits and thus fail to 're-arrest' the statute of limitations, and as a result they may find themselves time barred without knowing it"). For a case holding that notice of a dismissal or decertification of a class action is not required where the case has attracted little publicity, see, e.g., Clarke v. Ford Motor Co., 228 F.R.D. 631, 637 (E.D. Wis. 2005) (notice of decertification of Rule 23(b)(2) class not required because no notice to class had been given at time of certification).

Comment d. Although a court rejecting a precertification settlement with class representatives should have the option to leave a case open for a brief period to allow adequate representatives and class counsel to come forward, this device is used primarily when the parties have already made substantial progress towards trial or when there are indications that other representatives would come forward. Compare, e.g., Birmingham Steel Corp. v. Tenn. Valley Auth., 353 F.3d 1331 (11th Cir. 2003) (district court abused its discretion in ordering decertification without affording opportunity for new class representative to be substituted; case was in advanced stage, postdiscovery, and ready for trial), with *Culver*, 277 F.3d 908 (upholding decertification without first holding case open for new representative because there was no indication that volunteers would be forthcoming).

Effect on current law. The requirement of appropriate notice and approval by the court for class actions is consistent with current law. The requirement of court approval for precertification settlements with class representatives would require a change to the federal system and to any jurisdiction that has an approach similar to Rule 23(e)(1)(A). For authority in current law consistent with the approach advocated here with regard to precertification settlements, see Cal. R. Ct. 3.770(a).

§ 3.03 Hearing and Review Procedure for Class Settlements

In reviewing a proposed class-action settlement, the court must engage in a two-step process:

(a) Before approving notice, the court must conduct a preliminary review of the proposed settlement. The purpose of the preliminary review is to determine whether any defects in the proposed notice or other formal or substantive irregularities exist that warrant withholding notice. The preliminary review is not, however, a substitute for a thorough and careful review of the settlement at the time of the actual fairness hearing pursuant to subsection (b). In any order following preliminary review, the court must establish a schedule for the submission of papers supporting the motion to approve the settlement and the motion for attorneys' fees. Absent special circumstances, the schedule should provide a reasonable time for class members and objectors to respond after the submission of the moving papers.

(b) After notice and an opportunity for objections (and, when required, opt-outs), the court must conduct a full review of the settlement, including an in-court hearing, with an opportunity for the parties and objectors to offer evidence and present arguments. Whether the court approves or disapproves the settlement, it must make on-the-record findings and conclusions in support of its decision.

Comment:

a. Preliminary review. Many courts, at the preliminary-review stage, view the issue as whether to grant preliminary *approval* of the settlement. This Section rejects that approach. Even a preliminary decision in favor of the settlement may, as a practical matter, give an unwarranted presumption of correctness to a proposal that the court has not carefully considered. A "preliminary approval"—described as such to the class—may make a court reluctant at the fairness hearing to reject the settlement, having already given an initial endorsement to the settlement at the preliminary-approval stage.

Nonetheless, although the preliminary-review process is not for the purpose of approval, the court should confer with counsel to identify any obvious flaws in the notice or any other defects (formal or substantive) that might jeopardize the settlement. The court should articulate any misgivings that it identifies. If problems with the proposed settlement are apparent to the court, it is in the interest of the court and the parties to address those issues promptly, before significant time and resources are invested in notifying the class of the proposed settlement. In many cases, the court will have had an active role in the case before the proposed settlement and will be in a position to offer the parties meaningful guidance concerning potential pitfalls in the proposal.

The crucial point, however, is that when a court renders a decision in favor of permitting class notice of the proposed settlement, the ruling should not be characterized as a preliminary "approval." Rather, the court must engage in its definitive review at the time of the fairness hearing under § 3.03(b). By refraining from using the term "approve" to describe the preliminary review under § 3.03(a), the court can avoid having the preliminary-review stage interpreted as an implicit guarantee regarding how the court will rule, after a full hearing, at the approval stage. Of course, as a practical matter, the court should give more weight to its preliminary analysis and assessment if the presentation at the preliminary stage is extensive—for example, involving evidence and submissions by objectors—and less weight if the presentation is brief or superficial.

If feasible, the court should endeavor to notify interested persons, such as counsel with similar cases, that a preliminary-review proceeding has been scheduled. If the case is mature and potentially objecting parties are known, notice of the preliminary-review hearing may permit the court to expand the preliminary-review hearing stage into a fuller examination of the merits of the settlement. Absent an informed examination of the terms, however, there should be no implication that the court has "approved" the underlying merits of the proposed settlement.

An important determinant in whether objectors are able to make meaningful submissions regarding the fairness of a class settlement and a request for attorneys' fees is the schedule. The last sentence of § 3.03(a) would make clear that a motion to approve a class settlement and a request for attorneys' fees should be treated in the customary fashion for all motions. Thus, absent exceptional circumstances, class members and objectors should not be required to make their submissions until after the moving record is complete. Unless special circumstances dictate otherwise, objectors should have a reasonable period of time to make submissions after the settling parties have filed their supporting papers, and then the settling parties should have a reasonable period of time to respond to any objections.

b. Approval. The approval-hearing process should be conducted with great care to ensure that the court has reviewed and analyzed all potential flaws in the proposed settlement. The court should normally permit the parties to offer live evidence before it makes findings regarding the fairness of the settlement.

The court should also be receptive to active participation by objectors. Discovery requests in the context of settlement objections require a careful exercise of the court's discretion to balance the interests among the objectors' need for information to support a good-faith objection, the cost and delay involved, the potential for strategic abuse of discovery, and any work-product considerations involved.

In some instances, particularly in cases involving relatively small or simple class actions, courts have made findings from the bench without memorializing those findings in separate orders. To underscore the importance of these findings and ensure proper appellate review, this Section takes the position that a court that chooses to reveal its findings from the bench should memorialize those findings in an on-the-record order. Ideally, the court should draft its own findings and should not simply repeat verbatim the proposed findings submitted by the parties.

REPORTERS' NOTES

Comment a. For a discussion of the "cursory" nature of the preliminary-review stage, see 5 James Wm. Moore et al., Moore's Federal Practice ¶ 23.165[2] (3d ed. 2009). For a discussion of criteria and procedures the court should consider in reviewing settlements, see Manual for Complex Litigation (Fourth) § 21.632, at 320–321 (2004) ("In some cases, this initial evaluation can be made on the basis of information already known, supplemented as necessary by briefs, motions, or informal presentations. . . . The judge must make a preliminary determination on the fairness, reasonableness, and adequacy of the settlement terms and must direct the preparation of notice. . . . [T]he judge can have a court-appointed expert or special master review the proposed settlement terms. . . . The judge should raise questions at the preliminary hearing and perhaps seek an independent review if there are reservations about the settlement. . . . The parties then have an opportunity to resume negotiations in an effort to remove potential obstacles to court approval."); see also Cal. R. Ct. 3.769(c). For a case demonstrating the process for settlement approval under the California rule,

see Chavez v. Netflix, Inc., No. CGC–04–434884, 2006 WL 2613144 (Cal. Sup. Ct. Apr. 28, 2006).

For examples of courts that, despite the cursory nature of the review, give preliminary *approval* as a result of such review, see, e.g., New England Health Care Employees Pension Fund v. Fruit of the Loom, Inc., 234 F.R.D. 627, 631 (W.D. Ky. 2006) (" 'Preliminary approval gives rise to a presumption that the settlement is fair, reasonable and adequate. Objectors, therefore, have the burden of persuading this Court that the proposed settlement is unreasonable.' ") (citation omitted); Bennett v. Behring Corp., 737 F.2d 982 (11th Cir. 1984) (upholding district court's preliminary approval); Hickerson v. Velsicol Chem. Corp., 121 F.R.D. 67, 69 (N.D. Ill. 1988) (giving preliminary approval before requiring notification of settlement to absent class members).

Comment b. For a decision noting the general need for a hearing before approval of a settlement, see Gen. Motors Corp. v. Bloyed, 916 S.W.2d 949, 958 (Tex. 1996) ("Given the heightened responsibility of the trial court in approving class action settlements ... we think that a plenary hearing, with the opportunity for questioning by the court and vigorous cross-examination by counsel representing objecting class members, should be the general rule."). See also Fed. R. Civ. P. 23(e)(2) ("If the proposal would bind class members, the court may approve it only after a hearing and on finding that it is fair, reasonable, and adequate.").

Rule 23(e)(2) requires a finding in support of the fairness of the settlement, and the Advisory Committee Notes state that "[t]he findings must be set out in sufficient detail to explain to class members and the appellate court the factors that bear on applying the standard." Unlike the Federal Rules, many states do not require specific findings in support of a settlement's fairness. See, e.g., Ala.

R. Civ. P. 23(e); Colo. R. Civ. P. 23(e); Ohio Rev. Code Ann. § 23(e) (West 1970). Moreover, neither the Federal Rules nor any state rules require specific findings in support of the conclusion that a settlement should be rejected as unfair. See § 3.12 (discretionary appeal from finding that settlement is unfair).

Effect on current law. The approach here would change existing practice in those jurisdictions that, by rule or case law, require preliminary "approval" before notice of a proposed settlement is sent out. The requirement of on-the-record findings of fact and conclusions of law in the event of either approval or rejection of a settlement would also require a change in existing practice and goes beyond case-law requirements in many jurisdictions.

§ 3.04 Notice of Class Settlement

(a) **The purpose of a notice of a proposed class settlement is to set forth the major contours of the proposal and to inform class members of their right to attend the fairness hearing and to lodge written objections by a prescribed date should they so desire.**

(b) **At the preliminary-review stage, the court should determine the appropriate form and content of the notice. In fashioning notice of a class settlement, the court should consider the cost of notice and the likely recovery involved under the proposed settlement to ascertain whether individual notice is required, or whether some other form of notice would suffice. Individual notice should be presumptively viewed by a court as less important when the claims are likely too small to be pursued individually in the absence of a class action.**

(c) **The notice of a class settlement, when required, should be written in plain language and should contain, at a minimum: (i) a definition of the class, (ii) the specific material terms and conditions of the settlement (including the precise relief to be given to class members), (iii) the proposed fees sought by class counsel, (iv) how the class member can** obtain additional information about the case, (v) whether opt-out rights are provided, and (vi) details about the court hearing on approval of the settlement and the submission of objections.

Comment:

a. Reason for departure from current law. The conventional rule is that individual notice is required in all suits under Rule 23(b)(3) for all individuals who can be identified through reasonable effort. This approach is based on Rule 23(c)(2)(B). Under the Due Process Clause, however, it is important to balance the benefit of notice against the cost of providing notice.

In many cases, personal notice may not make economic sense. The value of the claim may be so small that litigation outside of the class context would not be viable, and the likelihood of opting out or objecting may be so low that individual notice would simply consume resources from the settlement without generating any real benefit for the class. This Section supports an approach that dispenses with direct, individual notice in this circumstance.

This Section seeks to give greater protection to settling parties by eliminating technical objections to the form of notice in the original settlement. The approach taken is consistent with the due-process requirement of reasonable and practicable notice to affected parties, as well as pragmatic considerations of cost effectiveness in light of the overall stakes in the litigation. This approach would eliminate the individual-notice requirement in certain contexts, contrary to the current federal practice based on judicial interpretation of Rule 23(c)(2)(B), which provides that "the court must direct to class members the best notice that is practicable. . . ." The court and the parties should explore low-cost options for direct-mail notice before dispensing with that obligation. For instance, if class members are utility customers, the utility company may be able to effect notice at a very low cost by including the notice in the customers' monthly billing statements. The object is to make notice both effective and reasonable in terms of cost. In the case of inserts as a substitute for direct notice, the court and the parties must recognize the possibility that customers may discard such inserts without reading them.

Illustrations:

1. Plaintiff sues on behalf of a class of consumers who purchased defective computer keyboards. The parties propose a settlement whereby class members receive $3 for each qualifying

keyboard purchased. The cost of notifying each class member by U.S. mail (postage, printing, envelopes, claims-administration charges) is about $5 per class member. Individual notice by U.S. mail is not required, given the high cost of notice relative to the value of each class member's recovery. Publication notice (and possibly notice via the Internet or electronic mail) will suffice.

2. Plaintiff sues on behalf of purchasers who overpaid for vacation packages. Each class member seeks to recover more than $5000. Defendant has current addresses for all class members, and the cost of notifying each class member by U.S. mail is about $5 per class member. Individual notice is required.

b. Content of notice. This Section, consistent with the prevailing view of commentators, takes the position that the notice of settlement, when required, should be written in clear, understandable language and should contain the material terms of the settlement and the amount of attorneys' fees requested, along with information about opt-out rights (if any), the fairness hearing, and lodging objections.

REPORTERS' NOTES

Comment a. The origin of the rule requiring individual notice in all Rule 23(b)(3) class actions for all class members who can be reasonably identified is Eisen v. Carlisle & Jacquelin, 417 U.S. 156, 173 (1974). The *Eisen* Court based its decision on the wording of then-Rule 23(c)(2) (now Rule 23(c)(2)(B)). See also Advisory Committee Notes to 2003 Amendments to Rule 23 ("Reasonable settlement notice may require individual notice in the manner required by Rule 23(c)(2)(B) for certification notice to a Rule 23(b)(3) class."); id. (noting that individual notice is "appropriate" if, for example, "class members are required to take action—such as filing claims—to participate in the judgment, or if the court orders a settlement opt-out opportunity under Rule 23(e)(3)"). Although the Advisory Committee Notes to the 1966 version of then-Rule 23(c)(2) relied on the due-process standard of

Mullane v. Central Hanover Bank & Trust Co., 339 U.S. 306 (1950), *Mullane* itself states that "within the limits of practicability notice must be such as is reasonably calculated to reach interested parties." Id. at 318. In small-claims cases, claimants may have little interest in receiving individual notice. Moreover, in 1950, U.S. mail was the only reasonable method of individual notice. Today, electronic mail and the Internet provide alternative vehicles for achieving reasonable notice. Thus, notice by U.S. mail should not be viewed as a necessary element of all Rule 23(b)(3) cases in which class members can be identified.

For criticism of *Eisen*'s requirement of individual notice, even in small-claim cases, see Kenneth W. Dam, *Class Action Notice: Who Needs It?*, 1974 Sup. Ct. Rev. 97, 107–109; Brian Wolfman & Alan B.

Morrison, *What the* Shutts *Opt–Out Right Is and What It Ought to Be,* 74 UMKC L. Rev. 729, 751 (2006). For the proposition that due process requires a balancing of costs and benefits in light of the interests at stake, see, e.g., Van Harken v. City of Chicago, 103 F.3d 1346, 1351 (7th Cir. 1997) (Posner, J.) (due process "requires a comparison of the costs and benefits of whatever procedure the plaintiff contends is required"). See also Jones v. Flowers, 547 U.S. 220, 229 (2006) (noting that due process requires "balancing the 'interest of the State' against 'the individual interest sought to be protected by the Fourteenth Amendment'" (quoting *Mullane*, 339 U.S. at 314)); Dam, supra at 115 (noting that Court in *Mullane* "was not oblivious to the desirability of weighing costs against benefits").

For a discussion of the purposes of settlement notice, see, e.g., Manual for Complex Litigation (Fourth) § 21.633 (2004). A useful example of a flexible approach to notice is found in Cal. R. Ct. 3.766(e) and (f). Subsection (f) instructs:

> If personal notification is unreasonably expensive or the stake of individual class members is insubstantial, or if it appears that all members of the class cannot be notified personally, the court may order a means of notice reasonably calculated to apprise the class members of the pendency of the action—for example, publication in a newspaper or magazine; broadcasting on television, radio, or the Internet; or posting or distribution through a trade or professional association, union, or public interest group.

Because defendants typically pay for the cost of notice as part of a class settlement, this change would, in certain circumstances, reduce the overall cost of settlement administration. Not spending money on mailed individual notice when individual class members are unlikely to take action on their own behalf should make available additional funds to the class for relief under the terms of the settlement.

Comment b. Examples of notices of class settlements written in plain language are contained on the website of the Federal Judicial Center. See www.fjc.gov (last visited Jan. 27, 2010), under the "Class Action Notices Page." Helpful examples of the information necessary for informed class-member response to class notice may be found in Cal. R. Ct. 3.766(d).

For discussions of information that should be included in class-settlement notices, see, e.g., *National Association of Consumer Advocates' Standards and Guidelines for Litigating and Settling Consumer Class Actions,* 48–51 (2006), available at http://www.naca.net/_assets/media/Revised Guidelines.pdf (last visited Jan. 28, 2010); Darren Carter, Note, *Notice and the Protection of Class Members' Interests,* 69 S. Cal. L. Rev. 1121, 1135–1137 (1996). See also Howard M. Downs, *Federal Class Actions: Diminished Protection for the Class and the Case for Reform,* 73 Neb. L. Rev. 646, 693–696 (1994) (urging that notices contain information about objections by class representatives and the precise distribution scheme for the settlement fund, i.e., "details on how and to whom the settlement fund will be paid").

Effect on current law. Subsection (a) would require no change in procedural rules. Subsection (b) would require a change in procedural rules to the extent that a jurisdiction's rules mandate individual notice regardless of the size of the individual class member's potential recovery. Subsection (c) describes best practices that a court can implement without a rule change.

§ 3.05 Judicial Review of the Fairness of a Class Settlement

(a) Before approving or rejecting any classwide settlement, a court must conduct a fairness hearing. A court reviewing the fairness of a proposed class-action settlement must address, in on-the-record findings and conclusions, whether:

(1) the class representatives and class counsel have been and currently are adequately representing the class;

(2) the relief afforded to the class (taking into account any ancillary agreement that may be part of the settlement) is fair and reasonable given the costs, risks, probability of success, and delays of trial and appeal;

(3) class members are treated equitably (relative to each other) based on their facts and circumstances and are not disadvantaged by the settlement considered as a whole; and

(4) the settlement was negotiated at arm's length and was not the product of collusion.

(b) The court may approve a settlement only if it finds, based on the criteria in subsection (a), that the settlement would be fair to the class and to every substantial segment of the class. A negative finding on any of the criteria specified in subsections (a)(1)–(a)(4) renders the settlement unfair. A settlement may also be found to be unfair for any other significant reason that may arise from the facts and circumstances of the particular case.

(c) The burden is on the proponents of a settlement to establish that the settlement is fair and reasonable to the absent class members who are to be bound by that settlement. In reviewing a proposed settlement, a court should not apply any presumption that the settlement is fair and reasonable.

(d) A court may approve or disapprove a class settlement but may not of its own accord amend the settlement to add, delete, or modify any term. The court may, however, inform the parties that it will not approve a settlement unless the parties amend the agreement in a manner specified by the court. This subsection does not limit the court's authority to set fair and reasonable attorneys' fees.

(e) If, before or as a result of a fairness hearing, the parties agree to modify the terms of a settlement in any material way, new notice must be provided to any class members who may be substantially adversely affected by the change. In particular:

(1) For opt-out classes, a new opportunity for class members to opt out must be granted to all class members substantially adversely affected by the changes to the settlement.

(2) When a settlement is modified to increase significantly the benefits to the class, class members who opted out before such modifications must be given notice and a reasonable opportunity to opt back into the class.

(f) For class members who did not opt out of the class, new notice and opt-out rights are not required when, as a result of a fairness hearing, a settlement is revised and the new terms would entitle such class members to benefits not substantially less than those proposed in the original settlement.

Comment:

a. Settlement criteria. The current case law on the criteria for evaluating settlements is in disarray. Courts articulate a wide range of factors to consider, but rarely discuss the significance to be given to each factor, let alone why a particular factor is probative. Factors mentioned in the cases include, among others, the risks of establishing liability; the risks of establishing damages; the likelihood of recovery at trial; the likely amount recoverable at trial; the public interest served by the settlement; whether the negotiations were at arm's length; the experience of counsel; the views of counsel; the expense, complexity, and likely duration of further litigation; the risk of not maintaining class-certification status throughout trial; the ability of the defendant to withstand a larger judgment at trial; whether a governmental entity participated in the negotiations or approved the settlement; the nature and extent of objections to the settlement; the reasonableness of the proposed attorneys' fees; the extent of discovery completed; the stage of proceedings; the extent of opt-outs; the vigor with which the case was prosecuted; evidence of coercion or collusion that may have marred the negotiations; and the strength of plaintiffs' case.

Many of these criteria may have questionable probative value in various circumstances. For instance, although a court might give weight to the fact that counsel for the class or the defendant favors the settlement, the court should keep in mind that the lawyers who negotiated the settlement will rarely offer anything less than a strong, favorable endorsement. For that reason, in determining whether to give weight to the fact that counsel for the class and for defendant favor the settlement, the court should consider the presence or absence of an incentive for class counsel to recommend an inadequate settlement. When class counsel shares class members' interest in maximizing claim values, counsel's willingness to propose a settlement may be entitled to some weight.

A court, in reviewing a settlement, should not give any predetermined weight either to the fact that the case was pending for a substantial period of time before a settlement was reached or to the fact that a settlement was reached early in the case. The timing of a settlement may or may not be probative on the issue of fairness. For instance, an early settlement may simply reflect a realistic appraisal of a case rather than a settlement negotiated without an adequate knowledge of the facts or merits of the case.

Similarly, the mere fact that a settlement occurred many months (or even many years) after the case was originally filed does not in itself ensure that the agreement is fair and reasonable. Likewise, whether a settlement is proposed following an adversarial hearing on class certification may or may not be probative of whether the negotiations were conducted at arm's length. And the resolution of a case before certification does not necessarily reflect collusiveness or a lack of arm's-length negotiations.

By the same token, the number of objectors may or may not be probative of the settlement's fairness. Class members are sometimes urged to object by lawyers with similar lawsuits who are unhappy that they did not achieve the settlement themselves, thus missing out on attorneys' fees, or by lawyers who may seek private gain from interposing strategically motivated objections. In such instances, lawyer-driven objections have little merit. Likewise, the absence of a significant number of objections does not necessarily reflect tacit approval of class members to the fairness of the settlement. For instance, a settlement may raise serious fairness issues, but the amounts involved per class member may be so small that no class member has a sufficient incentive to object. The court, therefore, should focus on the substance of the objections, not on a mechanical head count.

As another example, the extent of opt-outs may or may not be probative of the settlement's fairness. In most class-action settlements, the number of opt-outs is small. In some cases with large numbers of opt-outs, the large number is simply the result of orchestrated efforts by lawyers, hoping to have a chair at settlement negotiations or hoping to bring further litigation on behalf of the opt-outs. Thus, the number of opt-outs may in fact tell the court little about the actual fairness of the settlement.

Apart from the fact that many of the criteria have questionable probative value, the sheer number of these criteria has led to confusion. Some of these criteria, such as whether the settlement is in the "public interest," are amorphous and seem poorly directed to the protection of the class. Courts have ended up picking and choosing from among these factors, with little or no discussion of why some criteria are selected and others are not. Moreover, with so many potential factors, courts are unable to provide any guidance as to the relative importance of each factor. In many cases, certain factors appear to be highlighted merely because they support a predetermined outcome.

Finally, the sheer number of factors—and the confusion about their relative merit—make it difficult for class counsel, counsel for the defendant, and counsel for the objectors to address the pertinent considerations in a meaningful way.

b. *Proposed changes regarding settlement criteria.* This Section articulates four simple but important factors that courts should consider in reviewing any settlement. Moreover, as noted in subsection (b), these four factors do not preclude the court from considering other facts relevant to a particular settlement. All four factors, and any additional fact-specific considerations, should be addressed in on-the-record findings and conclusions. Because each of the (a)(1)–(a)(4) criteria is so critical, failure to satisfy any of them renders the settlement unfair. Subsection (b) recognizes that facts specific to a settlement may render the settlement unfair, even if the settlement satisfies (a)(1)–(a)(4).

With respect to the first factor, the court should assess the adequacy of representation provided to the class, as described in § 2.07(a)(1). In "settlement classes," in which the request for class certification and approval of the settlement are made at the same time, the adequacy of representation is considered as part of the approval process. In cases that have already been certified before settlement, however, a decision will already have been made on the adequacy of representation. Yet, that decision may be cast in doubt by the lawyer's subsequent handling of the litigation and the proposed settlement, and a court that considers only fairness and not adequacy at the time of settlement may overlook important concerns bearing on the fairness of the settlement. Indeed, a fresh examination of adequacy may be the most productive way to assess the ultimate fairness of the settlement.

Because, in the settlement context, neither the class nor the defense will have any interest in raising adequacy concerns with the court, the court may need to take an active role in investigating the adequacy of representation, especially when no helpful objections have been filed. As contemplated by Rule 23(g), for example, the court may need to request specific, detailed information from the parties to address the adequacy of class counsel. In some cases, the court may also consider the need to appoint a special master or special officer to scrutinize the adequacy of representation. See § 3.09. Although such a new appointee will face some of the same obstacles as a court in reviewing a completed settlement, a special master or special officer may have more time and resources to devote to the task. The court may also need to study with care any objections to the settlement that are lodged.

Second, the court should address the relief afforded by the settlement in light of the relief sought by the class and ascertain whether that relief is meaningful and sufficient, given the strength and risks of the case and the potential recovery in the event of a favorable verdict. Also, a proposed settlement in which the class receives an insubstantial payment while the fees requested by counsel are substantial could raise fairness concerns. As with the issue of adequacy, both class counsel and defense counsel will have every incentive to highlight the strengths of the settlement and to downplay its weaknesses. Thus, the court may need to assume greater responsibility, again possibly including the appointment of a special master or special officer.

Third, the court should look at whether class members are treated equitably among themselves and whether the settlement accounts for material differences among class members. For instance, an agreement that gives the same monetary remedy to all members of the class, despite significant differences in the nature of their claims or injuries, may not be fair and reasonable. In addition, the court should consider whether class members might be disadvantaged by the settlement. For example, a broad release going beyond the claims that are the subject of the litigation may be inappropriate in light of the nature of the recovery under the proposed settlement.

Fourth, the court should ensure that the settlement was the product of arm's-length negotiations and was not the result of collusion.

c. Burdens of proof. Some courts have adopted a presumption that a settlement is fair and reasonable if the attorneys offering the settlement are experienced class-action lawyers, the negotiations were conducted at arm's length, and relatively few class members object.

These presumptions may not be warranted. As noted above, for example, the presence or absence of objectors may or may not be probative. Likewise, the experience of the lawyers should not normally lighten the parties' burden of demonstrating fairness based on the specific facts of the settlement. Finally, as reflected in § 3.05(a)(4), the existence of arm's-length negotiations should be a feature of every fair class settlement.

As set forth in this Section, the burden of proof rests with the proponents of the settlement. The purpose of the court's inquiry is to ensure that the interests of the absent class members are adequately protected so that they may fairly be bound by the outcome of the case. As such, the responsibility for ensuring the fairness of the settlement rests with the class representatives, class counsel, and the court.

  d. No option to impose different or additional terms. Subsection (d) follows existing law in giving courts only two options when faced with a proposed settlement: approval or disapproval. Of course, the court can identify terms that, if added or deleted, would cause the court to approve the settlement, but the decision whether to incorporate the changes or additions suggested by the court rests solely with the parties. The court may not unilaterally modify the settlement or force terms upon the parties. The court does, however, have authority to set attorneys' fees, despite the fees requested by plaintiffs' counsel.

  e. Modifications during the fairness process. Under subsection (e), material changes to a settlement may necessitate (1) new notice to all adversely affected class members, including any who previously opted out, and (2) new opt-out rights for members of opt-out classes. When changes adversely affect only a subpart of the class, new notice and opt-out rights should be limited to that subpart. Permitting material changes in the absence of such procedural protections would be unfair to those who relied upon the earlier terms in deciding whether to remain in the class or whether to object. For instance, a class member may have opted out because of a concern that the recovery was too low. That person should have a chance to reconsider that opt-out decision if the recovery has been substantially increased. Similarly, a class member may have decided not to opt out because the settlement afforded a certain type of important remedy. If that remedy is eliminated after the opt-out period, the class member should have the opportunity to reconsider whether to opt out. The courts have taken varying approaches, with some allowing even substantial changes without new notice and opt-out rights, but with others requiring additional protections for all substantial amendments that may adversely affect class members' interests. This Section opts for the latter approach.

Illustrations:

1. Under a class settlement involving defective computer systems, class members would be paid $100 for each computer system purchased. Several class members exercise their right to opt out. Because the judge opines that the payment is too low, the parties agree to change the amount to $200. Before the settlement becomes final, notice should be sent to all opt-outs, permitting them to opt back into the class.

2. Same initial settlement as in Illustration 1, but the settlement is modified to defer payment of attorneys' fees by 30 days. No new notice is required.

3. Same initial settlement as in Illustration 1, but the settlement is modified so that class members are now offered only $1000 credit towards a new computer system instead of the original cash offer. New notice to the entire class, including opt-outs, is required.

f. Direct distribution of settlement proceeds. Courts should approve direct pro rata or per capita distributions of the settlement proceeds to class members when feasible, without requiring class members to submit claims. This is so even if the parties have proposed a traditional claims process. Direct distributions are usually feasible when the settling party has reasonably up-to-date and accurate records. This approach avoids the costs of administering a claims process and allows class members to receive the fullest practicable benefits of class actions prosecuted on their behalf.

REPORTERS' NOTES

Comment a. For examples of the wide variety of approaches to settlement, see, e.g., In re Am. Bank Note Holographics, Inc. Sec. Litig., 127 F.Supp.2d 418, 426–428 (S.D.N.Y. 2001) (addressing, inter alia, the difficulty of proving claims and damages, "litigation risks," the possible bankruptcy of one of the defendants, the threat of protracted litigation, the "arm's length" nature of negotiations between "skilled attorneys," the extent of discovery completed, and giving " 'great weight' " to the views of counsel); In re Austrian & German Bank Holocaust Litig., 80 F.Supp.2d 164, 174–178 (S.D.N.Y. 2000) (addressing, among other things, plaintiffs' "difficulty in establishing damages at a trial," the "arm's length" nature of negotiations, whether defendants could withstand a greater judgment, and the small number of objections); Wal–Mart Stores, Inc. v. Visa U.S.A., Inc., 396 F.3d 96, 117 (2d Cir. 2005) (considering nine factors);